HYPERTROPHY

Oxford New York
Athens Auckland Bangkok Bogotá Buenos Aires
Calcutta Cape Town Chennai Dar es
Salaam Delhi Florence Hong Kong
Istanbul Karachi Kuala
Lumpur Madrid Melbourne Mexico
CityMumbai Nairobi Paris São
Paulo Singapore Taipei Tokyo

0

CULTURAL POLEMIC ORGANISATION

THIS PAGE IS INTENTIONALY LEFT BLANK

Discontents

Cover Design: Ebden-Small https://ebden-small.com/
Cover Art: Racheal Robb

Author's Preface:

Hypertrophy is the contemplated thought that is so critical
it can make us aware of our own act of thinking.
Hypertrophy is the thought that gets a second glance, the
inflated idea that takes the number one positihn of
conscious thought. The thought so prevalent, we think
about the thought, as a thought. So profound, it came out of
nowhere, leaving us wondering how did that thought get
there? - Because certain thoughts pop up, you wonder
exactly who is in charge.

This anthology of a hundred and eighty-five
chapters are writings that pop up. sometimes dive into the
idea of hypertrophy.

Sometimes, the initial thought lacks a clear origin
and seems to emerge out of nowhere. Hypertrophy may
come and go, referencing external phenomena, yet it
happens within the mind. It is part of the self, whether you
intend it or not, existing in the mind yet contemplating
things external to the mind.

As hypertrophy commands our attention, We
wonder, was that an algorithm at work? This is the
corporate hypertrophy at its finest, keeping users engaged
for hours and somewhat a cautionary tale. An order is at
play, data comes first followed by the algorithm, and then

hypertrophy, driving emotions for the sake of emotion. It vies for a status position in conscious thought.

The *Australian Oxford Dictionary* defines hypertrophy as "the enlargement of an organ or tissue from the increase in size of its cells." Let's keep that in mind, However, in our context, we adopt a definition proposed by French anthropologist Salomon Reinard (1858-1932), who associated hypertrophy with the ancient concept of totem. Reinard referred to totem as "Une hypertrophie de l'instinct social," meaning that totem is a hypertrophy of the social instinct.

The Yolngu of Northeast Arnhem Land, Australia, are given a totem by their parents in early childhood. integrate the use of totems into everyday life. Each person in early childhood is designated a totem. The totem is interpolated as a lifelong commitment, by the person, not to harm or consume this totemic animal. The animal serves as the individual's hypertrophy, 'standing out' as a unique personal symbol. The activity of this hypertrophy can be understood as purposive, as the totem serves as an analogy to Yolngu family law. The law requires a person to marry a member of the community who is genetically furthest from oneself. As this practice is universal among Indigenous Australians, the law tends toward a "social instinct", as referred to by Reinard in the definition above. The Yolngu inhabit an interconnected society where everyone is family. The relationship between this totem and the incest taboo is an analogy. The totem is symbolic of the expectation that a person will refrain from harming or consuming their totem, by maintaining a respectful distance between themselves and the object. In other words, the totem is both an object of food and allegorically an object of desire. Hence this age-old use of hypertrophy for the mind is to inaugurate a law.

Reinard's suggestion has spurred the trend of designating something as a totem, taboo, or hypertrophy, or all three. These can include the pejorative, the disgusting, the funny, the novel, or the point of no return. This is the cache that algorithms are programmed to identify in order to sell products. Understanding hypertrophy offers a chance to escape the slave trap of algorithms. For the link between hypertrophy and thought is significant. Hypertrophy poses a question: why do certain things stand out for you? Whether in dreams, social media, or a stream of consciousness, the foundation of thought is hypertrophy. But why?

The link between hypertrophy and thought is significant. Hypertrophy poses a question: why do certain things stand out for you? Whether in dreams, social media, or a stream of consciousness, the foundation of thought is hypertrophy. But why?

Moving towards hypertrophy, it is not possible to negate it, but it can be slowed down or delayed. Hypertrophy encompasses various things such as spelling mistakes, everyday life occurrences, and more, all maintaining its primacy. Understanding the question of hypertrophy is of great importance when algorithms are taking hold of our unconscious and what we can do about it.

The reason for the prominence of hypertrophy is a vital question that must be asked. Why do certain thoughts interrupt our mind? As Freud says, "There is no negation in the unconscious." Therefore, the things that shine in our consciousness hold significance in our unconscious, leading to their passage as hypertrophy to our conscious form. Our attention is focused on hypertrophy, including parts of books we read, experiences we have, and more. Hypertrophy is a crucial question for the self.

Hypertrophy grabs our attention, trying to access the conscious because it has no negation in the unconscious. It can be too shocking to import to the conscious, entering a chain of signifiers. While there are many signifiers, hypertrophy is the chosen one, predisposed to the algorithmic reader of the self. It is the rules of the game that appall us, standing out, and leaving us asking why. Hypertrophy stands out because it is information at a juncture, uncertain if it is conscious or unconscious.

Regarding totem, it has a relation to a game, suggesting life is a game where we must obey or disobey rules. In isolated communities, it quickly becomes clear that marrying close relatives is taboo, just like a totem, an animal larger than life imbued with spiritual significance, is a hypertrophy.

The book advocates hypertrophy as a significant thought experiment, not just a way to define something but a question. It asks why some things stand out for us in dreams, everyday life, or social media. "Moving towards hypertrophy, there is no negation." Hypertrophy encompasses all kinds of things, such as spelling mistakes and parts of everyday life that maintain our attention. Hypertrophy is an essential question for the self.

"I think, therefore I am" is the start of the enlightenment movement. However, what did we think, and why did we think that way? Hypertrophy attends most cordially to the position of thinking about thinking. The things that stand out in our minds, the sore thumbs, the pejorative, and the attention-seeking, all prompt questions without answers, which is why they stand out. The topology streams from outstanding insight to outstanding angst through pejorative attention-seeking.

With algorithms at work, we have a media synthesis, and the message is simplified. We are still the same, yet the voices in our heads are new. Their synthesis and our synthesis have led us nowhere near the abyss. It is within this idea that the book begins with an analogy of itself to establish what it has and has not. The idea that some things stand out, the sore thumbs, the pejorative, and the attention-seeking prompt a topology that streams from outstanding insight to outstanding angst, through pejorative attention-seeking. It is a play, limited by the words in our heads, where the medium is the message simplified.

You are invited to start reading

Declán O'Gallagher 20th March 2023

Reinard's suggestion has led the charge into designating something totem, taboo or hypertrophy or all three. The pejorative, the disgusting, the funny, the change, or the point of no return. This is the cache that the algorithm is figuring out to sell you product. A reason to understand hypertrophy is to present a chance to "know thyself" to hold an idea of what's going on upstairs.

Here lies the link, hypertrophy is a significant thought experiment. Hypertrophy is a question. It asks, why do some things stand out for you? In dreams, in social media, or a thought eventuated. The basis of thought is hypertrophy, but why?

Towards hypertrophy, there is no negation but you can slow it down, you can delay. Hypertrophy is all kinds of things. Spelling mistakes, parts of everyday life; all that maintains that nothing can stop this primacy.

The hypertrophies are the dreams of the algorithm makers & the question is of such importance to understand when the algorithms are kidnaping the unconscious and what the subject object position can do about it.

The reason for this prominence or hypertrophy is the question that must be asked. Why is our mind interrupted by these thoughts? And as Freud says. "There is no negation in the unconscious" It can be concluded that the things that consciously shines is the thing that hold importance in the unconscious and has made this passage as hypertrophy to the conscious form.

your attention, parts of the books we read. The experiences we have are forced to be memorised. Hypertrophy is the essential question for the self.

Hypertrophy has our attention, prima facie accessing or trying to access the conscious because it has no negation in the unconscious, it can be too shocking to import to the conscious. Hypertrophy enters a chain of signifiers. There are many signifiers but hypertrophy is the swollen chosen one. A chain of hypertropy, as is the predisposition to the algorithmic reader of the self..... It is the rules of the game appalled… it stands out, then it can't be asked why? Hypertrophy stands out because it is information at a juncture. Uncertain whether it is conscious or unconscious.

Totem has a relation to a game, as if to suggest life is a game. And the rules to obey or disobey are part of the game…With particular note, in isolated community it quickly become clear that marriage to close relatives

while defining totem he "This hypertrophy meaning is alluded to in the worth of Salomon Reinard. In short, a totem is a hypertrophy, an animal larger than life imbued with spiritual significance.

And the reason for standing out is the question that must be asked. Why is our mind extended by these thoughts and day-dreams?

Here lies the vital link, The book is advocating hypertrophy as a significant thought experiment. Hypertrophy is not just a way of defining something but a question. It asks, why do some things stand out for you? In dreams, in everyday life, in social media. Moving towards Hypertrophy, there is no negation. Hypertrophy is all kinds of things. Spelling mistakes, parts of everyday life, that maintain your attention, parts of the books we read. The experiences we have are forced to be memorised. Hypertrophy is the essential question for the self.

"I think therefore I am" is the start of the journey of the enlightenment movement. but what did you think? And why did you think that? Hypertrophy attends most cordially, to the position of thinking about thinking.

Why do they stand out? The things that stand out in your mind. The idea of the ideas that stand out, the sore thumbs, the pejorative, the attention seeking. The asking questions and not having the answers. Because that's why they stand out. The topology will stream from outstanding insight, to outstanding angst. through pejorative attention seeking. … A play, only to be struck by the limitations of words, the medium synthesis is the message simplified. We are still the same yet the voices in our heads are new. Their synthesis and your synthesis led us nowhere to an abyss. It is within this idea that I begin with an analogy of the book in itself to establish what it has and has not. You are invited to start and finish in no particular order.

Totem

a natural object or animal that is believed by a
particular society to have spiritual significance and that is
adopted by it as an emblem.

Totem - Macquarie Dictionary

Something, often an animal, taken as the token or emblem of a clan or family group, and to which people may see themselves related by blood.

1. The Book is Dead

When books are completed, they are strangely referred to as 'finished.' Suggesting they are not just complete…. but dead. Books communicate as words on the page and they communicate in various forms, to various people, at various times. But as books are completed or 'finished,' they are rarely added to after publication. In practice, the book is the book; no more and no less. The written word is an expression that has come to an end from the author. In its reading there is an author's memory of a book once lived while in the writing stage. There in, we understand the book as an expression that was once contemporary but when published, it no longer exists as contemporary. A body of work that once conveyed up-to-date information about the world, is only true at the time of writing. A book, like any other mortal, does this as it is lived, while being written. It is at this lived juncture, that a book's author can change its mind and proffer a different tale. Yet after publication, the word is set in stone, it can no longer make a new argument, have a different ending. It is a pure life lived, then and there in the writing. When the book is completed, it then becomes analogous to a life once lived. A beginning, a middle and an end. A mortal life, then falling dead from the press. A life, once lived, in the form of the writing by the author. The book, the artefact, is a memento mori, and is admired by being comparable to mortality. The book dies as the final words are written. This is the life and death of a book. The final words are the appendix, a cold alphabetical eulogy presided over by the reader. The book itself is a death certificate. The fact that the book was published proves that the book was once a mortal.

In *Thus Spoke Zarathustra,* Nietzsche states, "God is dead." A famous proclamation to the world that the Christian monotheist project was over and arguably a spark for the atheist cause. But look again, is not the words, "God is dead," a proclamation, making the claim that God was once alive. And so, the argument goes, 'How can God be dead, if God was not once alive.'

As discussed, the book was once alive while in its writing stage. Is not this Nietzschean God akin to the book? In that God was once alive and so too was God.

Is this not analogous to the book? Is it at this point, Nietzsche renders us the personification of God, as mortal man and for our argument's sake, the book, dead from the press. Becomes comparable to the dying mortal being.

The New Testament, The Book of John, definition of God accordingly tells us the word is God. "In principio erat Verbum, et Verbum erat apud Deum, et Deus erat Verbum." (John 1). "In the beginning was the Word, and the Word was with God, and the Word was God.". Deduction from Nietzsche statements leads us to understand that if God is dead then the word is dead.

Nietzsche tells us the word is dead…. Or as we have discussed, the book is dead. According to Nietzsche's world is the idea that God was once alive, that the word was once alive. But now dead. Anarchy. Or 'chaos within to give birth to a dancing star.' Nietzsche's is an inevitability for a call to revolution to produce a dancing star.

Hence forth, according to German idealism, the word is dead, the logos is dead, the book is dead.
The book is dead. The word is dead, the logos is dead.
. It states that God is the word. "In the beginning was the Word, and the Word was with God, and the Word was God. "The Book of John 1:1. Logical deduction tells us if God is dead and thus the word is dead..... Or as we have discussed, the book is dead. According to Nietzsche's world is the idea that God was once alive, that the word was once alive. But ow dead. Anarchy. Or

chaos within to give birth to a dancing star. Nietzsche's is a call to revolution.

The publisher's contract is analogous to the death certificate. The book is dead and now officially dead. Publishing is where all the friends, family, associates and author, gather to celebrate the life of the book. In reality, the funeral of the book. The pages are scattered in the cultural vicinity and let's face it; we have all been buried in a book.

The book as Ablas Al Akkad says "I do not read for I have renounced life, I read because one life is not just enough for me" A faint analogy to the book as another life. The escapism of ones own life to see unto another.

Faint memories are drawn upon by friends and associates as they try to reinvigorate the dead book but the book is dead and always has-been. After death or in reading you are alone.

"God is dead." cried Nietzsche and logical from an ancient perspective "In principio erat Verbum, et Verbum erat apud Deum, et Deus erat Verbum." (John 1). "In the beginning was the Word, and the Word was with God and God it was the Word" (John 1). Hence forth, the word is dead, the logos is dead, the book is dead.

Since God is dead, hence forth, the logos is dead, the word is dead, & the book is dead but only because they were all once alive.

The invisible god from Moses has been replaced OSHO says it
has been replaced with "Fuck"

As we go, *back to Freud,* Freud argues an evolution from the
invisible god to the invisible psyche. An evolution that needs an
invisible God to herald it, the id, the superego and the I. To
believe in these invisible entitles, does one have to first believe
in all adult seriousness, in the invisible God of monotheism.

The Hegel absolute is not absolute because we will hate it so
much it has to stop. It will. It has, it is going to send you mad.

 "It fell dead-born from the press, without reaching such
distinction,
as even to excite a murmur among the zealots.
But being naturally of a cheerful and sanguine temper,
I very soon recovered the blow,
and prosecuted with great ardour my studies in the country."

David Hume 1776, On My Life.

1. The Book is Dead

When books are completed, they said to be finished. Immediately suggesting they are dead…Books communicate with the words on the page and they communicate no more than that. They are dead. They are remembered as finite principles, with a beginning, a middle and an end; this is the life of a book. A mortality with no soul falling dead from the press. What remains is a life once lived in the form of the writing by the author., a book, an artifact that is an artifact, a memento mori. They are dead as the final words are written and no more are to be added. This is the life and death of a book. The last words before they die is the appendix. Within the doctor's report is the addendum and errata.

'The book is finished,' shouts the author. Finished? Anyone may conclude the book is dead, it will no longer add something new, change its mind or answer any questions; it is dead. The book is dead. Nietzsche wrote keenly that "god is dead" referring to the christan god… and if we refer again to the Christen god… we see in the bible, The book of John, "1In the beginning was the Word, and the Word was with God, and the Word was God. "Nietzsche tells us the word is dead…. Or as we have discussed the book is dead.

The publisher's contract is analogous to the death certificate. The book is dead and officially dead. Publishing is where all the friends, family, associates and author, gather to celebrate the life of the book. It is in reality the funeral of the book. The pages are scattered in the cultural vicinity and let's face it; we have all been buried in a book.

2. A Language of Film, in David Lynch's Blue Velvet

Beginning with the hypothesis that there are three protagonists in the movie *Blue Velvet* and they are essentially acting out different characteristics of the same person.
1. Frank Booth, as Denis Hopper
2. The Well-Dressed Man, also as Denis Hopper
3. & Jeffrey Beaumont, as Kyle MacLachlan

For narrative, for plot, for story; Lynch uses the theme of a single person, separated into three characters. I propose that these are three parts of the author; David Lynch. His own topology expressed in the Lacanian triumvirate of The Real, The Imaginary Order and The Symbolic Order.

1. The Real is Denis Hopper as Frank Booth
2. The Imaginary Order is The Well-Dressed Man
3. The Symbolic Order is Jeffrey Beaumont.

The Lacanian Real, *Frank Booth*, is in the "State of nature from which we have been forever severed by our entrance into language" (Felluga 2003, Homepage). "The domain of the inexpressible, the domain of death and inexpressible enjoyment [jouissance]" (Stavrakakis 1999, p.39). According to Lacan, it is the Real that, "isn't a world of things, it isn't a world of being, it is a world of desire" (Lacan 1991, p. 222). In our dreams we encounter the traumatic signifier of the Real, as it processes thought in a surreal and calculated manner. The Real is the period in life as neo-natal children, where we have nothing but need. The Real has no language but still remains with us after we gain the ability of language. Lacan often said, "the Real is impossible" (Lacan 2001, p.11), due to its infantile nature.

The Imaginary Order, Ideal-I, Ideal-ego or *The Well-*

Dressed Man is the "fundamental narcissism by which the human subject creates fantasy images of both himself and his ideal object (Felluga 2003, Homepage). The realm of the ego that accounts for an impression of ourselves as individuals and as a separate identity to others. It is defined as, 'what it is not,' compared to ourselves. First encountered in early childhood while looking in the mirror, hence known as the *stade du miroir*, "the mirror stage" (Lacan 2001, p.13). It acts as a suture for the Real to the Symbolic Order, giving access to the echelons presupposed to exist in the *nom du père,* "name-of-the-father" (Lacan 2005, p. 12), that is, the almighty "no" of the child's elders. It is the inevitable discipline handed out to young growing child by a familiar parent. Providing a point of the origin of consent where language meets The Symbolic Order.

The Symbolic Order, *Jeffery Beaumont,* is the world of linguistic intersubjective social relations. It is the rules of the game subjectivised. Also known as the big Other, due to the presupposition that it is part of radical alterity, otherness as opposed to the original Real. Once a child has this attribution, they can manage and thrive in a social world. Žižek calls The Symbolic Order "Society's unwritten constitution, the second nature of every speaking being" (Žižek 2006, p.8). It is the logical negotiation initiated and accepting of the castration complex, buttressed to the Imaginary Order. It contains lack, as opposed to the Real where, "there is no loss, no lack, no absence; there is only complete fullness, only needs and the satisfaction of needs" (Klages 2006, p.52).

These are the three disparate and desperate characters played out in a Lynchian *Blue Velvet* fantasy; they are dangerously separated. Lacanian psychoanalysis tells us that these features of The Real, The Imaginary Order and The

Symbolic Order are normalised when tied together with a Borromean knot. Unfortunately, there is no Borromean knot to guide the three protagonists through the complexities of the life of *Blue Velvet*. They are but used as catalysts to visualise distinguished and disturbing features of *Blue Velvet*.

  Blue Velvet, like any other cinema contains a categorical grammar, a generative syntax and an impart of information; apropos a language of film. Syntagms of cinema are often considered analogous to the written word. The frame, as the word, the establishing shot as the first sentence, the scene as a paragraph and a sequence as a chapter. As we can see there are many ways to tell a story. Goddard suggests we can juggle with the film-edit in different ways, a playing with time and space. "A story should have a beginning a middle and an end but not necessarily in that order" (Godard in Pommerance 2014, p.369) and yet still it remains a language.

  So why a single language of film? Can we not suggest that there are many languages of film? Film language follows a presupposition of rules through conflated cultures. And although we can share the intersubjectivity of watching a film, we will interpret the film differently, thus there are many languages of film. In a Saussurean sense, the signifier remains the same while the signified is subjective. This attribute of film, 'dreaming while awake,' makes the medium comparable to the unconscious and the characteristics that come with that. "The unconscious is structured like a language" states Lacan. Therefore, a syllogism would suggest film is structured like a language.

  "There is no negation in the unconscious" says Freud and as film is a dreaming while awake, is not then film iterating without negation? Yes, the movie just flows, untrammelled by the dissonance of negation. To work, to be a movie, it must flow from signifying chain to signifying chain, an unending connection of signifiers. This flow is exampled in the Lacan definition of signifier as "that which represents the subject for another signifier" as one shot is edited to the next shot, there is no chance of an interpretation of negation. One sentence is connected to the next sentence. & in the film edited the opposites fit together as well as the similarities.

A key element to cinematic wisdom is the use of conventional styles to effect. Accordingly, the opening/establishing shot of *Blue Velvet* is pivotal. It is here that Lynch valourises a full frame of blue velvet material; an icon from which all-else leads. This starting point is a considered display of the discourse of psychology's "primary and recency" (Ramachandran 2012, p.147). This is the wisdom of the order of the montage, underpinned by the relevance of the first and last frames. The psychology concludes that the spectator not only posits a salience to the first and last frames but also readily remembers them. To begin with a sheet of blue velvet is to set the scene as a grand expose of the movie's thesis. The velvet commonly used as theatre curtain and positioned metaphorically as about to open, suggests Lynch will be truthful, open, a raw fetish movie.

Camera movements are sparse, subtle and homogenous. David Lynch is not the auteur with distinctive language, merely drawing attention to shots by hypertrophy. His auteur's qualities are within the characters and script. The lack of camera movement does not expound the limits of Hollywood proper. That is, Lynch is not willing to superficially 'wow' an audience with cinema apparatus. Emotion developed within the film are spectator driven, 'make of it what you will?' The shots have unity, often still frame after still frame. Lynch camera movements are slow, creeping shots, more leaning than actually moving. The pan, the tracking, the short crane, all slow and emblematic of appearance being self-contained. Lynch uses the Extreme Close Up [ECU] to effect. It's a gateway to the insect world, synonymous with our three characters that plod their way without direction.

Blue Velvet is a fetish movie. Freud's full and varied analysis of fetish always brought him to the same conclusion. "In every instance, the meaning and purpose of the fetish turned out in analysis to be the same" (Freud 2009, p.324). Furthermore, Freud states, "The fetish is a substitute for the penis" (Freud 2009, p.324). This is not an everyday penis but one that has been lost in early childhood. A "fetish is a substitute for this lost women's [the mother's] penis" (Freud 2009, p.324). In *Blue Velvet* there is a role-play fantasy where baby Frank has seen his mother Dorothy with no penis and is perplexed by this concept. Frank believes [Mother] Dorothy has been transformed; Freud calls it a "verleugnung or disavowal" (Freud 2009, p.325) the castration complex. This méconnaisse or misunderstanding is due to what Lacan says is "a lack of being" (Lacan 2002, p.124). In this state Freud postulates the female genitals as "stigma indelible" (Freud 2009, p.325). Freud says that the repression at this stage can provide an aversion to female genitalia in the analysand, Frank. Freud continues to discuss, he/she "Treats it [the fetish] in a way which is obviously equivalent to a representation of castration" (Freud 2009, p.326). Frank embellishes the velvet as a metaphorical umbilical cord, as it is placed in his mouth and in Dorothy's mouth. The umbilical cord is severed after birth, analogous to the mythical phallus. Frank uses this material as the symbol of the catastrophe. The blue velvet fetish is commandeered to mythologise, the unfathomable castration, a distraction from that idea which is so hard to contemplate. The fetish begins to unravel, the more abstract and undemonstrative, the greater the possibility of distraction, reductio ad absurdum, so no one can deduce this original sin.

Frank is confronting the original sin narrative, the

castration complex. He sits in front of Dorothy and demands to see the genitals missing. "Wider" says Frank. Adam and Eve were both penalised for their inaugural crime. This too is played out in *Blue Velvet*, as Dorothy and Frank are both punished within the film. While *Blue Velvet* harnesses the mask and velvet for its fetish. Adam and Eve use a bitten apple to symbolise the mythical missing phallus. This is a smoke and mirror trick covering the mothers' loss. A memorial to the phallus, the Adam and Eve artifact.

Frank's terror has not left him, so he returns to the point of contention, the ineffable female gentalia. He ritualises the loss. Freud believes that this is the time when either transcendence to homosexuality may occur or a fetish will appear or the loss is merely surmounted. It can be surmised that we must count ourselves lucky for our existence for according to Freud, Adam or Eve at this point could have not found the apple fetish and instead become gay.

Blue Velvet manages to engage an audience through distinctive reasoning beginning with the agency of the gaze. Lynch has an overt attention to gaze. For example, in the line, "Don't you fucking look at me." This privileges the paradigm and explicitly recognises the spectator and the agenda of the hegemony of cinema within the spectator's gaze. This is the essential question for Lynch, "what are you looking at?" As if the camera is turned on Lynch.

Theorists have surmised that the all-important gazing at the cinema is a directed male gaze. Cinema itself can be considered as yet again a "Mirror Stage" (Lacan 2001, p.1), not only a physical mirror but everywhere in the film where we bedeck an image with ourselves. The cinematic viewers invent themselves into the scene, a psychic *mis en scène*. Stereotypically, both male and females look with a male gaze to see "radical alterity…. otherness not 'difference', that is otherness beyond representation" (Pawlett 2013, p.136).

We take up with a side and instil ourselves within the image proper, embarking on all the vicissitudes of the narrative game. In the cinematic experience we will laud ourselves with all the gains of our ingratiated character and deny, as only cinema, tragic outcomes of our film. Within cinema we manage to look at all our parts from a safe distance. But be careful, for this discourse is masquerading as a story. Nichols proposes that the cinema itself, watching a bright screen in a darkened room is tantamount to a Lacanian return to the "mirror phase" in which the self is orchestrated. I assert that this is what we search for within the scopophilic fantasy. Cinema in Lacanian terms is "an attempt to disengage the cinema-object from the imaginary and win it for the Symbolic in the hope of extending the later by a new province" (Metz 1982, p.3). Widely established as the key to the power of the cinema and termed *The Imaginary Signifier,* touted as evoking our ability to align and transcend into as self, creating immediate alterity in cinema. As social geographical scape entrenched in The Imaginary, it hopes to make gains promised in The Symbolic. Cinema is a safe substitute for any experience. We view cinema as a fantasy to escape reality, knowing that we can escape cinema to go back to reality. It is wish fulfillment we never asked for. The never-ending cycle of desire unfulfilled, the object little a.

The Object little a or Objet a is the object cause of desire. Lacan calls it "the field of the mirage of the narcissist function of desire" (Lacan 1978, p.270). In the Lacan elementary scheme, it exists as the fly in the ointment. It is the wall that prevents the ability to close the pleasure loop, representative of the "pleasure in pain" (Lacan in Žižek 1992, p.48) of jouissance. Žižek calls it "the never ending, repeated circulation around the unattainable" (Lacan in Žižek 1992, p.48).

The Lacanian schema, introducing the Objet a, as a wall in the pleasure loop. Fig1

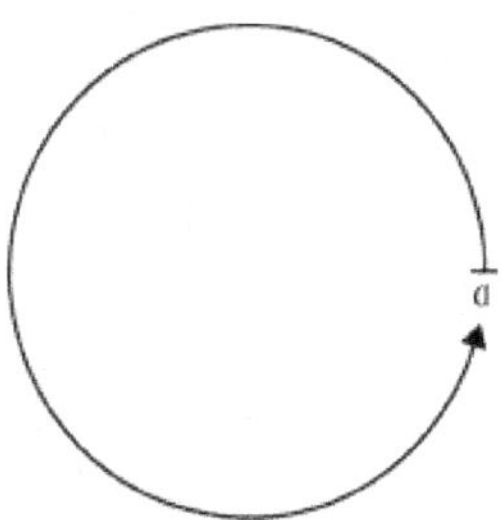

    The desire and 'objet petit a' revolve through an elder's
'No.' The child diverts desire from the mother in the Real to big
Other. The objet a is in the big Other and thus Symbolic Order.
Anxiety is also linked to the big other. Frank's problem [Lynch's
problem] is he doesn't know what he wants. The objet a within
his Symbolic Order is asking him to react, yet not knowing what
to desire has the effect of anxiety. These are the characteristics of
Frank, his never-ending anxiety linked to his desire.
The fundamental connection between gaze and objet a threatens
to erupt in the Real. It is a misrecognition as already cited as a
lack. We see something and want it but this is misunderstood, it
is a narcisstic projection. For at the centre is our continuous
desire. We have only grasped an illusion. According to Lacan the
gaze has a male or a female mystic. The female gaze is non-
phallic, not pleasure-seeking gaze. Whereas the male gaze can sit
in judgment like a God.
    Frank abhors Dorothy's gaze. Dorothy's gaze is a phallic
gaze, in the Lacanian sense of who initiates the law. It is Frank
who interprets Dorothy's gaze as phallic/male and as such is
enraged. He becomes violent. A psychoanalysis interpretation
would phrase this as "resistance.... I can't bear the thought of
being freed by anyone other than myself. (Lacan 2001, p.11) The
place of *transference*, Lacan calls it "to confuse his
contemplative eye with the eye with which God is looking at him
must surely be of perverse jouissance" (Milner in Zizek 1992, p.

85). For Frank this is an area of great distress, expletive after expletive exemplifies his hurt. Frank is of The Real, the dream like state of early infancy. As cinema itself denotes dreaming while awake, we can accept that the audience is watching a fluid distortion of reality to tragedy, commensurate with the way dreams structure themselves. Charles Pierce states, "Contemplating a painting, there is a moment when we lose consciousness that it is not the thing, the distinction of the real and the copy disappears. It is for the moment a pure dream" (Pierce 1994, p. 934). So too, does the signifier and the signified blend to leave us beholden to cinema. James Monaco laments that this signifier/signified meld is a new kind of language, with one great difference - "The power of language systems is that there is a very great difference between the signifier and the signified; the power of film is that there is not" (Monaco 2000, p.158).

When Frank first sits down with Dorothy, he exhibits a sexual ritual and Lynch through this fantasy uses drone music to effect emphasis. Marshall McLuhan explains use of music, "With the sense of sight, the idea communicates the emotion, whereas with sound, the emotion communicates the idea, which is more direct and therefore more powerful." - This is a fundamental secret to the mystery of film. We do not conjure up demons with pictures, we conjure with words and sounds. The music is a precursor to the unknown or as Barthes puts it, "music is dangerous, music is an access to jouissance, to loss, as numerous popular examples would tend to show" (Whitehead in McLuhan 1970, p.146). In *Blue Velvet,* music is used by Frank to access his own sadistic jouissance. He is quite overcome, transfixed and in The Real, in the Lacanian sense, a rude unchaste state. He has somehow acquired language ability without the nom-de-pere [name of the father]. As Lacan suggests a variable outcome in the entrance to The Symbolic Order "…. the penumbra of symbolic efficacy… the threshold of the visible world" (Lacan 2002, p.5). Frank's outcome, would appear to be

a shadow of this minimal eclipse. As he crosses the threshold of
The Imaginary but distinctly missed the social engineering of
The Symbolic. Frank's transference is loud but hidden in his
milieu. His male group is poetically dysfunctional and hardly
notices Frank's out-of-place antics. Frank never acquired the
instruments of self-discipline, handed out by his elders, and was
kept in The Real.

Frank moves forward, kneels in front of Dorothy. It is at
this moment that he comes to terms with the origin of desire.
Lacan describes these desires comparable to *Aglama* in Plato's
Symposium. The story goes that this *Aglama* precious gem is
stored in a worthless box and that this is the desire we seek
within the other. The birth of desire comes at the departure from
The Real to The Symbolic, it is the residue left over from this
reaction. The *Aglama* gem is metaphorical of this desire.
Frank, unable to enter The Symbolic Order is stuck in time
between conception and language in The Real. Demanding,
overbearing, selfish and bearing the marks of a child
unrestrained. As Yannis Stavrakakis says - "The Real is the
domain of the inexpressible" (Stavrakakis 1999, p. 39).
Frank looks frightened, as if an act of bravery, he leaps to the
female genitalia, gas mask in hand. He breathes deeply into the
mask. More nitrous oxide. He cries like a child. "Mammy
mammy…." Dorothy says, "Mammy loves you."
A purely Oedipal moment satirised by Lynch. Frank has found
his objet petit a, the unobtainable object of desire. The movie not
once uses a word for the female genitalia, even with censorship
abound it could have used any aphorism, the word is the
ineffable name, Frank's transference, resistance, the place, the
border between Frank and the Imaginary/Symbolic. He sits in
front of Dorothy's genitalia conflicted with this mystery.
Opposites go to battle in Frank's mind. A Hegelian master/slave
dialect. According to Hegelian discourse, Frank confronts
Dorothy and tries to dominate the picture, only to find that this
never satiates; hence desire is perpetuated. Deleuze and Guattari

describe this state of mind and body as "desiring-machines," the concept of anti-production provides for schizoanalysis a crucial link between the realms of desiring-production and social production. (Deleuze and Guattari 1972, p.53). A pointed argument that suggests Frank's relatable dysfunctional disposition. Lacan sees it as something left over.

Frank has language but remains in the mindset of The Real. Interpreted as having problems with the Symbolic schema of male/female authority. Frank as pervert is kept in service by his big Other that he needs to satisfy. The will to enjoy [volonte dejour] is now the motivations of the big Other. What scares anyone remains physically outside of us and constitutes what Žižek's *Looking Awry* calls the "Supreme evil being" (Lacan in Žižek 1992, p.86). It is fearful-alterity, -other people. To keep these other people in check we must be sadistic, to prevent this unconscious cataclysm to erupt. These other people know they are evil and thus we justify their harm. The victim is aware of the evil nurtured inside of them and accepts the actions of the Sadeian. This is the sadomasochism of Frank. The sadist doesn't care if the victim is not enjoying the punishment for, they can easily convert their guilt to innocence by burdening themselves with the displeasure of viewing the pain they have inflicted. This is the equalising power of their culpability.

Freud was symbolic when announcing the Oedipal child wants to have sex with the mother and bash the father. He means it only in essence, a proposition in possibility more than actuality. An unspoken possibility within the extended family unit. Slavoj Žižek calls it "a violence grounded in no utilitarian or ideological reason" (Žižek nd, Homepage), an "elementary imbalance in the relationship between ego and jouissance" (Žižek nd, Homepage). He specifically names this "Id-evil:" (Balibar in Žižek nd, Homepage).

The fantasy of *Blue Velvet* and cinema per se can be divided into two. Firstly, we are spectators in the realisation that

it is a movie and we can rightly expect a slice of sublime
jouissance. We have paid for this; we expect some pleasure. We
can suspend our reality for the exchange of jouissance in the
Real to the Symbolic order. That is, we understand 'it's just a
movie'. In Deleuze's, *The Time Image,* he postulates that cinema
acts as a structuring system that has constitutive excess. We are a
spectator of the movie and we wish to be, merely entertained.
Secondly, we take note of how order is developed, how it is
managed and what are the outcomes of personalising the movie.
We float from The Real through The Imaginary to The Symbolic
Order. We are the projectionists; in the sense we project
ourselves into the movie. An understanding is gathered; our joy
is accepting parameters that are played out within the movie. As
Lacan calls it a suture denoting a "Conjunction of The Imaginary
and The Symbolic" (Lacan 1978, p.1). This is the control a
movie seeks. What the cinema per se demands. It is the police
force we embrace. Žižek states the alternative is psychosis "A
refusal to exchange enjoyment for the name of the father" (Žižek
1992, p.77). Thus, the lure of the cinema experience we have to
enjoy or we are disturbed.

  Lacan cites "Every truth has a partial truth" (Lacan J.
1953-1954. Freud's papers on technique). He reads the narratives
of Plato, Hegel and Kierkegaard to elaborate on psychoanalysis
theories and define what is really going on in the libidinal
economy. Many of the ideas are in a parable style and we are
told to take meanings as symbols not literally. As in the word
"Phallic," Lacan has trespassed language constituting the
neologism of The Real, Imaginary Order and Symbolic Order,
which in terms of semiotics makes a critique considering the
words original meanings. I'm saying essentially, he has hijacked
them from original meanings. So, we understand "every truth as
a partial truth" as a presage for a number of Freud/Lacan
parables as unsubstantial. Noam Chomsky calls Lacan "amusing
and perfectly self-conscious charlatan" (Chomsky in Goldwag,
2007). Lacan at best has given us some new building blocks to

34

work with, at worst he has produced, what Foucault calls "obscurantist terrorism" (Wolfreys J, 1999). Obscure in his writing and terrorism to those who don't understand.

Blue Velvet has psychoanalytical roots. It nurtures The Real, The Imaginary Order and The Symbolic Order to embellish characters that exist in troubled illogical states. Lacan and Freud have brought rules to an understanding of popular cultural artifacts, mysteries have become tangible understandings. There is much more to do concerning the foundations of this work. Slavoj Žižek has played a part in re-defining a psychoanalysis cinema studies context. His books, *Enjoy Your Symptom* and *Looking Awry* have cultivated ways of deconstructing cinema. We have discovered Adam and Eve to be the castration complex. Much more can be done to look at and unravel these Lacanian "partial truths" (Lacan Jacques, 2002, *Ecrits: A selection)* that are still becoming. We can draw upon other cultures, other mythologies to derive theories to explain and nurture human capabilities of what Kant calls "the morality within" (Kant 2015, p. 129).

The gaze is an all-important subject in terms of male/female divide, desire and meaning. Gaze can hold us, move us, direct us, disavowal us within cinematic systems. The spectator is a willing participant in the control that cinema exerts. It can challenge or reinforce our beliefs, acting as law for paid up spectators, willing to succumb to a substitute for an experience. It may be seen as a selfish leisure time fantasy escape, the spectator only willing to be its only benefactor. Perhaps it may bring some of its reflection and ideas back into the present time-space continuum through discussion/conversation outside of the movie theatre, heralding community to a Symbolic Order.

Is psychoanalysis now saved from history rejuvenated by its use in visual culture?

References

Barthes, Roland 1978, *Image, music, text,* translated by Stephen Heath, published Hill and Wang.

Chandler, Daniel 2002, *The basics: semiotics*, Routledge, Oxfordshire, UK.

Deleuze, Gilles, and Guattari, Felix 1972, *Anti-oedipus*: capitalism and schizophrenia, Les Editions de Minuit.

Deleuze, Gilles 2005, *Cinema 2: the time image*, Continuum International Publishing Group.

Descartes, René 1637, *Discourse on the method of rightly conducting one's reason and of seeking truth in the sciences,* published René Descartes.

Foucault, Michel 1969, *Archaeology of Knowledge*, Editions Gallimard.

Felluga, Dino 2003, *General introduction to psychoanalysis. introductory guide to critical theory,* <http://www.cla.purdue.edu/English/theory/psychoanalysis/psyc hterms.html>

Freud, Sigmund 2009, *Visual culture: a reader,* edited by Jessica Evans and Stuart Hall, Sage Publications Ltd.

Godard, Jean Luc 2009, *The butterfly effect: high mimetics in godard's histoire(s) du cinema,* published by StudioForty9.
Goddard, Jean Luc 2009, *Cinespia, <https://cinespia.org/a-*

story-should-have-a-beginning-a-middle-and-an-end-but-not-necessarily-in-that-order-jean-luc-godard-cinespia/9>

Goldwag, Authur 2007, *'Isms & 'ologies: all the movements, ideologies and doctrines that have shaped our world,* Madison Park Press, New York.

Hebdige, Dick 1979, *Subculture – the meaning of style.* Methuen and Co Ltd.

Kant, Immanuel 2015, *Critique of practical reason,* Cambridge University Press, UK.

Klages, Mary 2006, *Literary theory a guide for the perplexed,* Bloomsbury Academic Continuum.

Klix F, Ebbinghaus H, Hagendorf H 1986, *Human memory and cognitive capabilities: mechanisms and performances: symposium in memoriam hermann ebbinghaus,* The University of Michigan, USA.

Lacan, Jacques, *1953-1954. Freud's papers on technique,* By Jacques-Alain Miller, W.W. Norton and Company.

Lacan, Jacques 1957, Le séminaire de jacques lacan: Les formations de l'inconscient - livre V, publisher Seuil.

Lacan, Jacques 1973, *The four fundamental concepts of psycho-analysis,* translated Miller J-A, published W.W. Norton and company Inc, New York.

Lacan, Jacques 1991, *Seminar II: the ego in freud's theory and in the technique of psychoanalysis,* Trans Tomaselli, New York, WW Norton and company.

Lacan Jacques, 2002, *Ecrits: A selection,* translated Alan Sheridan, Tavistock Productions, London, UK.

McLuhan, Marshall [dialogues of Alfred North Whitehead] 1970, *Culture is our Business,* McLuhan Associates Limited.

Metz, Christian 1982, *The imaginary signifier: psychoanalysis and the cinema*, Indiana University Press, Bloomington, USA.

Metz, Christian 1991, *Film language: a semiotics of cinema,* Oxford University Press, University of Chicago Press edition.

Monaco, James 2000, *How to read a film: the art, technology, language, history, and theory of film and media,* Oxford University Press.

Nichols, Bill 1981, *Ideology and the image: social representation in the cinema and other media.* University of Michigan. Indiana University Press.

Pawlett, Wiliiam 2113, *Violence society and radical theory,* Ashgate Publishing, UK.

Peirce, Charles 1994, *The collected papers of charles sanders peirce, volume 2*, Belknap Press of Harvard University, USA. Ramachandran, Vilayanur 2002, *Encyclopedia of human behavior*, Academic Press, London, UK.

Rosenblum, Ralph, and Karen, Robert 1986, *When the shooting stops, the cutting begins: a film editor's story*. Da Capo Press.

Stavrakakis, Yannis 1999, *Lacan and the Political*, Routledge, Oxfordshire, UK.

Wolfreys, Julian 1999, *The french connections of Jacques Derrida*, SUNY Press.
Žižek, Slavoj 1992, *Enjoy your symptom!: Jacques Lacan in Hollywood and out*. Routledge.
Žižek, Slavoj 1992, *Looking awry: an introduction to Jacques Lacan through popular culture*. MIT Press.

Žižek, Slavoj 2006, *How to Read Lacan*, WW Norton and company, New York.

Žižek, Slavoj nd, *Some politically incorrect reflections on violence in france & related matters*,
https://www.lacan.com/zizfrance5.htm

3. Even the Dogs Wept

Across the borders, deeper into the waters, the dogs wept. Kneeling I came to a door, knocking I found time to breath, not knowing was the most fun but careful not to recede, I looked forward. Honestly, I looked forward. Took another breath. No one had walked this path before, it was made for me - Evolutionary-Revolutionary-Theory as reality. Quite clear in my mind I had positively taken great strides to walk the line- I took what was on offer and made the most of all the mistakes - Heaven knows and hell cares - He chortled, snorted became an animal and yeah stopped bleeding and aching of lead. It was his turn now; he knew it was unfair he did it anyway. That moment was his but just for a moment. Hoping it was passed around. Things had taken a turn, finally things had come full circle, again it was time to breath, elate relate and get wind of new thoughts begging for a host. Ideas are the parasites of the mind and no ideas are stagnation, so keep ticking over.

4. How is something interpreted?

Semiotics

| ˌsiːmɪˈɒtɪks, ˌsɛmɪˈɒtɪks | plural noun *[treated as singular]* the study of signs and symbols and their use or interpretation.

ORIGIN late 19th century: from Greek *sēmeiotikos* 'of signs', from *sēmeioun* 'interpret as a sign'.

      While Saussure was working with the semiotic dyadic model, the signified and the signifier. Charles Saunders Pierce was becoming an early theorist of the mechanics of understanding image. He describes a three-fold path to a semiotic conclusion referred to as "Peirce's semiotic triangle" (Chandler D, 2002). Here he uses interpretant, representmen and object. While the representum is comparable to Saussure's signifier and the interpretant to the signified. The difference being the interpretant which "creates in the mind of that person an equivalent sign," (Chandler D, 2002) that is a sense made up of the sign. The representum is named the "sign vehicle" (Chandler D, 2002) or the sign itself. The addition to the method is the object. Further to the sign and further to what the sign refers to. Peirce breaks down the structure of the representamen into three modes.

      1. The symbolic - The sign is traditionally arbitrary.
      2. The iconic - The representan resembles the signified.
      3. Index - There is a direct relationship to the signified.

41

This is a habitual and natural extent to which we deduce meaning without a formal study of structure. Levi-Strauss claims "men think in myths and operate in men's minds without being aware of the fact" (Levi-Strauss C, 1969). We gain experience through our constant appraisals and new found knowledge and thus we are continuously affected in our judgment.

Peirce furthered his syllogism with his book. "Reasoning and the Logic of Things" (Peirce CS, 1898). He stated prima facie we make an "abduction" (Peirce CS, 1898), a guess from experience, followed by a development in consequences called a "deduction" (Peirce CS, 1898). Testing this by interacting it in the world, it is called a "retroduction" (Peirce CS, 1898).

Because so many images in our daily lives are guiding us to a monetary sale, a particular political philosophy or moral dilemma. Time should be taken to familiarize ourselves with the structure of the image and the production of consent. After this, the circumstance grants greater familiarity with the commonplace representations. This makes the viewer less naive and more inclined to nullify the power of the image. We understand that to know an image is to control an image. The manufacturer of image to a mass audience is compelled to thicken the plot and/or move to the new archetype in a cyclical format of image representation. History repeats itself and simulacra becomes layer upon layer of simulacra upon simulacra. Baudrillard notes that "it is a mediascape saturated with the simulacra of history" (Baudrillard J, 1995). And as time goes by, technology works in synergy to draw a crowd. A bell curve of contemporary collective consciousness is the ideal and a footnote to all image production. Pierce declares that "There is no escape from signs. Those who cannot understand them and the systems of which they are a part are in the greatest danger of being manipulated by those who can" (Peirce CS, 1931-38). Roland Barthes' theories speaking of connotative and denotative analysis of image conclude to understandings reliant on culture, language and generation. These filters of understanding play a subjective role in legitimising the image. Passing through the gatekeepers of signification, the code complete is said to be good or bad, in the eye of the beholder.

Timothy Leary theorises explaining we immediately come to two conclusions on meeting someone for the first time. We decode with our bio-computer brain, - the response is to fight or flee. Whether we can beat this person to death in hand-to-hand combat or decide we can't, and therefore make a run for it. He claims that this is the deduction before all others and would appear a highly desirable survival mechanism. It is an involuntary necessity, a circuit hardwired to the human psyche. Even language has this compulsive reaction claims Jacques Derrida: "Language bears within itself the necessity of its own critique" (Derrida J, 1974).

Western people with European cultural roots have adopted a lineage that refuses to go back as far as African ancestry. There appears to be a line in the Sahara Desert that depicts the point at which there is a denial of heritage further afield. A Wallace Line, a Weber line, a Lydekker line, not only a southern border but also an Islamic border, just to the east. A refusal to pass over this line in an intellectual and cultural sense, a refusal to borrow any cultural identity to embrace as part of its own philosophy. NB. the rosary beads came from the Crusades. but would not be acknowledged as Islamic.

Although the cultural artifacts, knowledge and systems are scientifically proven to be of European DNA, western identity is holding firmly the notions of, where it has come from, who it is, and where it is going and will not cross this cultural Wallace line. Understandably oral traditions are lost and perhaps Africa/far east is just that little bit too distant to be significant. Perhaps the psychogeography radar is a touch too far....
Marshall McLuhan has an accepted notion of a global village "urbi and orbi," so as the hunter and gather embraces the telephone should not the west consider its African ancestry. So

why is it, western thought is unable to analyse African mythology and call it an intrinsic influence?

Lacan uses Plato to explain the seminal position of human desire. He postulates that our "lack" (Lacan J, 1953) in this archetypal story imparted through Plato's symposium by Aristophanes is because we are mythologically cut in two. It's the original *raison d'être* and our emotional basis of action. This according to Lacan is the myth that influences all decisions of choice. What is good image and what is bad image? For we make these decisions based on our desire to fulfill our separate halves. The story goes that we were much different than we are now. In our primary state we were of three sexes, male, female and a third made up of both sexes. This was a volatile mix and Zeus decided this power must be literally cut in two. All our lives we need to coalesce to fulfill this natural state. Every decision we make is based on a fulfillment of need to regain this state, a pinnacle of a hierarchy of need expressed in a bisected humanity. Lacan believes we spend our lives trying to fulfill this lack. All decisions made hold at the heart a desire to conform to this impossible state. It's the original *raison d'être* and our emotional basis of action. The myth that influences all decisions, choosing what is good and what is bad, for we make these decisions based on our desire to fulfill our separate halves.

Lacan calls it the Real. This is the space between conception and language, the domain only of pain, hunger, the self, nothing but need. As Lacan might have said: "where everything is possible." This is a priori to language and a repository of decision throughout our lives. This is the failed state, the uncolonised power; a source of unreconciled anxiety, the continua of eruption and the place where desire begins.

Immanuel Kant tells us in the first line of *Critique of Pure Reason* "all our knowledge begins with experience" (Kant I, 1781), and goes on to state four ways in which to view the world. He calls it transcendental aesthetic, transcendental analytic, transcendental logic and transcendental deduction.

44

Taken as a whole, this taxonomy of human understanding can deduce all the phenomena. Kant posits that this human understanding is never beyond our senses. He says we cannot know "Ding un sich" (Kant I. 1781) – *the thing in itself* - the noumenon. So, if not knowing, *the thing in itself,* we can only pass judgment according the phenomena not the noumena. On the outset it would appear unnatural to take into account that which we cannot perceive. Kant assumes a lacking in humanity forever more.

We seek beauty in our daily lives, as all inanimate objects communicate with us, we lust after beauty to communicate with us and catch our attention. Is there a natural aesthetic that the human bio-computer has affection for? Early writings of Euclid had ideas of a most aesthetically pleasing proportion he called "the extreme and mean ratio" (Euclid, 1956) or golden ratio, Phi. The golden ratio plays out as a natural desire. The golden ratio states that we like to see things in a ratio 1:1.618. This is the most pleasing way an architect would proportion a building or shape a room. We see this proportion of 1:1.618 in nature, in seed formation, shell growth and the human face. Even recent TV computer technologies have moved closer to the proportion with 16:9 widescreen. It is like an *a priori* need, etched in our DNA or narcisstic copies of our own body proportions.

A Hegelian construct of thought in our sign deconstruction can be employed in our *Ways of Seeing* (Berger J. 1972). A continuum of thesis, anti-thesis culminating to, what Hegel calls a state of "consciousness towards freedom" (Singer P, 2001). This is one way of looking at image deconstruction presupposing freedom is our desired goal. There are many other examples of binary hermeneutic analysis of understanding. For example, Roland Barthes divides a photo into two idioms, first the studium, that is, the main part or message of a photo and punctum the part that grabs your attention. The unconscious of the photo the thing that is really in charge,

Saussure spoke of the *synchronic*, as he put it, "Studied as a complete system at a given point in time" (Eagleton T, 2008) and diachronic, Saussure states "as a system of pure values which are determined by nothing except the momentary arrangements of its terms" (Culler J, 1977). The Yolngu of North East Arnhem, Australia, speak of yiritja and dhuwa. People, plants and animals, everything split into these two categories, making everything analogous to family or ying and yang. Kant tells us there are two types of beauty, *pulchritudo vaga* (Kant I, 1781) an intrinsic beauty and *pulchritudo adhaereus* (Kant I, 1781) an extrinsic beauty. McLuhan explains media types in terms of hot and cold. This is comforting analysis; it's one or the other, no grey area of uncertainty or conflict to be resolved.

This use of referential material made up of binary solutions comes into conflict with open ended philosophies. Here there are no good or bad images just degrees of interpretation. Of course, the judgment of dichotomies as 'too simple' is a binary solution in itself but the truth is, the image passes through various binaries in order to arrive at a fuller and notable solution. As Friedrich Jameson puts it "The entire mechanism…. Is capable of generating at least ten conceivable positions out of a rudimentary binary position" (Jameson, F. 1972). It is often the deeper questioning of truth, too difficult to otherwise perceive and is made that more visible by the categorising to a binarism, hence closer to a substantive core. Therefore, making binary judgments what Umberto Echo calls this "semiosis *ad infinitum*" (Eco U, 1976), the continuous interpretation of image. It is in the eye of the beholder when the questions stops or they may go on forever.

Far exceeding the common interest shown by the western world, Aboriginal Australians have an intense reverence to screen culture. Photos and film are privileged themes, given status, producing instinctive moods. Aboriginal people are at times mesmerized and held spellbound by image. The reaction is common to repeat the experience, the same movie, the same scene, the same music, time and time again - a good image.

A bad image for Aboriginal Australians is most certainly a photo or moving image of a deceased relative. Yolngu will also relinquish animate objects owned by the recently deceased because of a sensitive psychogeographic connotative power the objects own. So too, is the residence of the deceased left vacant and cordoned off. The name of the deceased is never spoken directly, only referred to in skin name or a local word referring to a dead person i.e., Kumanjayi in Central Australia. In more immediate and close family circles the deceased is described only as someone's bother or someone's mother. Photos of the deceased are off limits. Photos are cut from any montage or drawn over in black marker, to a silhouette. It behooves any relative to take appropriate action to avoid the image of the deceased and it is often deputized to children to remove offending articles. This will be carried out years after the death of the relative. Television stations placard programs with a preface warning of a possible indignity, sometimes removing the guilty frames from the content. Aboriginal people don't see these needs as laws of the statute but of nature. These are things that have been recategorized and now the deceased in all respect has become in a topological sense in the realms of Kant's noumenon. For we cannot possibly know "ding und sic" the thing-in-itself. An unspeakable unmentionable force begging for the image removal, like the academic and bad grammar it must be removed. It is a compulsive sense, part of the mourning and Julkulpa [law] need. The spirit is tied to the earth and needs to be set free, the vibration of their name, the pictorial, the associated animate buildings, all grounds of the dead recipient become out of bounds. Now sign language, shading in the photo, smoking out a building, all prevents a haunting by the spirit. Hence a bad image is prevented. Western culture has long forgotten its magical history, its incantations and calling forth and banishing of spirits.

Judaism has spiritual features comparable to the western world's pre-Christian past. A Jewish person is said to be unable to utter the name IHVH. This four-lettered word is the Tetragrammaton, a word without vowels and contested pronunciation, such is its contention. The name of God and is said to be called forth the spirit of God by saying this name. Meister Eckhart notes "The four-letter name is a sacred secret; therefore, it is never expressed among the Jews, but inexpressible in its nature and purity.[22]" Migene González-Wippler added "The mighty four lettered name of God the Tetragrammaton -IHVH - is never pronounced by devout Hebrews. The name is usually substituted by another four lettered name[23]"

A history going back to Plato. We know that decisions are made based on desires and experiences. Our understanding and deconstruction continue to a point of our own making and so there is a panoply of ways of seeing. My point has been to uncover the mind processes that mainly Saussure, Pierce, Lacan, Barthes have discussed. Much maligned by the west and not part of our mental statue is the realms of the noumenon. A part of decision making we apparently have no control over.

References

[1]Berger J. 1972 Ways of Seeing. British Broadcasting Corporation London UK
[2]Kant I. 1781. Critique of Pure Reason. Macmillan and co, Limited. St Martin's Street London
[3]Saussure C F de. 2006. Cahiers Ferdinand de Saussure: Revue suisse de linguistique générale. Librairie Droz
[4]Chandler D. 2002. Semiotics The Basics. Routledge London and New York
[5]Baudrillard J. 1995. The Gulf War did not take Place. Indiana University Press USA

[6]Chandler D. 2002. Semiotics The Basics. Routledge London and New York

[9]Herman Parret. 1994. Peirce and value theory: on Peircian ethics and aesthetics John Benjamins Publishing Company, Levi-Strauss C. 1969. The Raw and the Cooked. Chicago University of Chicago Press

[11] Peirce CS. 1898. Reasoning and the Logic of Things. Cambridge MA Harvard University Press

[12] Peirce CS. 1898. Reasoning and the Logic of Things. Cambridge MA Harvard University Press

[13]Peirce CS. 1931-38. Collected Papers Vol 5 Pragmaticism and Pragmaticism Cambridge MA Harvard University Press

[14]Derrida J. 1974. Jacques Derrida of Grammatology. The John Hopkins University Press Baltimore Maryland USA

[15]Joyce J. 1939. Finnegans Wake The Viking press USA

[16] Lacan J. 1953. Book III: The Psychoses (edited by Jacques-Alain Miller) New York :Norton

[17]Euclid. 1956. The Thirteen books of Euclid's Elements Vol 10-13 The Cambridge University Press translated by Sir Thomas L Heath

[18] Eagleton T. 2008. Literary Theory: An Introduction University of Minnesota USA

[19]Culler J. 1977. Ferdinand De Saussure Penguin Books the University Of Michigan

[20] Jameson, F. 1972. The prison house of language. Princeton NJ: Princeton University Press

[21] Eco U. 1976. A Theory of Semiotics Bloomington IN Indiana University Press/London Macmillan

[22]Eckhart M. 1986 Teacher and Preacher. Paulist Press New Jersey USA

[23] Migene G. 1974. A Kabbalah for the modern world: How god created the universe. Julian Press. The University of Michigan USA

Singer, Peter 2001, *A very short introduction to hegel,* Oxford University Press, Oxford, UK.

<u>Bibliography</u>

Peirce CS. 1931-38. Collected Papers Vol 2 Elements of Logic Cambridge MA Harvard University Press

Kellner D .1994. Baudrillard: A Critical Reader Basil Blackwell Inc Cambridge MA USA

Dias M. 1985. Jurisprudence Butterworth University of California

Michaels E. 1989. For a cultural future: Francis Jupurrula makes TV at Yuendumu Sydney art and Text.

Hartley J. 2002. Communication, Cultural and Media Studies Routledge

Evans J and Hall S. 2009. Visual Culture A Reader, Sage publications in association with Open University, London, UK.

McLuhan M. 1964. Understanding media: the extentions of man. London Routledge and Kegan Paul

McLuhan M. Fiore Q. 1967. The Medium is the Massage. Penguin Books

Mario Livio 2003 The Golden Ratio: The Story of Phi, the world's most astonishing number. New York Broadway books

1911. Encyclopedia Britannica/Tetragrammaton.

5. There are No Objective Values

"There are no objective values." J.L. Mackie's first sentence from his book *Ethics: Inventing Right and Wrong*.

Joyce and Kirchin praise the work of Mackie in *Ethics: Inventing Right and Wrong*, elucidating material, dispatching critics and shedding light on possible reactions.
Mackie's opening is analogous to Nietzsche's "God is dead." Both pungent phrases hold prominence within the context of media ethics. There is a continuing domination of the media as if a God. A domination presenting itself as objective.

Our media has many pressures to ameliorate; Mackie suggests that objectivity is not one of them. Though appearing objective is a different matter. The dogma of fairness and balance, appealing to the public interests, the vox pop on the street, the omnipotent voice over person we never see. All shadows of objectivity brought to you by a predicated media. That is not to say this media is not helpful and generous. It is a pillar of the community, indeed educational and inspiring. Though some are expecting media to be something, it is not. It is not objective values.

After J.L. Mackie starts by slamming this "objectivity", he then summarily puts truth to the sword. His *Error Theory* lambasts the idea that moral discourse has secured truth.

This is the charge, that we logically separate our feelings as culturally and socially induced truths and hold only as worth the moral facts that when considered; evaporate. Mackie's discursive remarks have tended to diminish moral feelings, as they vary from society to society and thus cannot be related to as facts.

Immanuel Kant moves away from these ideas. He suggests that there is a natural law, a natural morality. That we all maintain objective values as best we can. In his *Critique of Practical Reason* (1788) Kant states - "Two things fill the mind with ever new and increasing admiration and awe, the more often and steadily we reflect upon them: the starry heavens above me and the moral law within me."

6. Give People What They Want

I note the phrase - "Give people what they want" - regularly used by Rupert Murdoch. The motto that fits an agenda to sell media. It begs an understanding, as it supports the Kantian notion of "The virtue of volition," thus delivering choice. When used by Rupert Murdoch, he holds it out like a torch casting a shadow over responsibility. It is all about choice and the nature of choice and what we lose or gain from choice. For the reader of News Corp, It is an attractive liberating issue, yet extinguishes media responsibility. Is it raining out there or not? The prize of liberation to the newspaper reader ameliorates any chance of immoral indignation. It's the truth, the whole truth and nothing but the truth. The dailies are so far down the moral chain the link so tenuous; it avoids any ethical assertion. Alas now, the choice is about to change... North America is said to be the first to lose all its printed media. Australia next. Australia's daily print media is on a steady path... declining one to seven % per year. ... Thus, creating a power vacuum. We should expect unrest; as power becomes deflected, regained, realigned, decentralized and a test for democracy.

7. Words are But Symbols

"Words are but symbols for the relationship of things to one another and to us; nowhere do they touch upon the absolute truth" Friedrich Nietzsche, Philosophy in the Tragic Age of the Greeks.
Media ethics that are expressed as mere "words" have no "truth" in themselves. Hitherto, we must recognise the limits of our media in practice. There is no intrinsic knowledge in our words or "truth". We only have debatable semantics or degrees of interpretation. There is no right or wrong.
As we recognise its limits, we discredit the media in its ability to act ethically. It is wholly subjective. In truth, the media has only a sense of freedom and justice, not the veracity that is longed for.
Marshall McLuhan is very forgiving in his "the medium is the message "adage. The media are not to blame, he is claiming. They are but responding within the boundaries of their own world. Each type of media has its own confined formula of expression. It will claim that it cannot be ethically responsible for murder, theft or sleeping with your partner. These are idioms out of its jurisdiction. It has natural innocence with a dictum of 'Don't shoot the messenger.' It harbours an air of a sleeping giant, while moving and shaking the top end of town.
The attraction of the media; it can be toyed with, manipulated and conventional. Yet, the hegemony claims to be no personal threat to the public.

8. Creative Commons [CC]

I had the opportunity to hear Professor Brian Fitzgerald an Australian ambassador of Creative Commons [CC] talk about the subject in Darwin on the 16th October 2011. So, I took a few notes and thought I would share them. The inception of digital technology has created a new thinking about copyright and so Creative Commons was born. Creative Commons is now a universally accepted copyright signature; YouTube et al.. Old copyright still exists having the same status and all the previous advantages but changes so radical as digital have demanded a shake-up. Creative Commons might be seen as how to protect a new medium in a new age. The inclusiveness and veracity have made Creative Commons attractive to many different clients. Nine Inch Nails use CC, so too does the USA government's Whitehouse website use it , YouTube and Flicker. They are all guarding their intellectual property with Creative Commons. The ease of negotiation and particular copyright tailored to individual needs has made it popular to a broad church. There are six licenses on offer. Something to suit different styles of attribution and royalty collection.

• Attribution (CC BY)
• Attribution Share Alike (CC BY-SA)
• Attribution No Derivatives (CC BY-ND)
• Attribution Non-Commercial (CC BY-NC)
• Attribution Non-Commercial Share Alike (CC BY-NC-SA)
• Attribution Non-Commercial No Derivatives (CC BY-NC-ND)

There now can be in part an offering of certainty under the banner of Creative Commons. Obviously, it's not just © and is six times more complicated. This has freed us up and become a lot more usable. The CC is not without fledgling problems yet problems arising appear marginal. Test cases will become reference documents for precedencies and most agree this is something always inherent in new laws. Words like 'reasonable' may be inconclusive and parties are brought to a courtroom to arbitrate disputes. The biggest issue with CC is trying to change the copyright after you have set it up.

9. Copyright Tomorrow

Professor Lawrence Lessig states that 70% of young people in the US in one year obtained digital information from illegal sources. He calls the preserved copyright system a "corrosive influence on a whole generation." This rationale offers little hope for an anachronistic law. Alas, the saga is shrouded in international diplomacy and governments willing to do little while institutions are hijacked by teen America. The expansion of 'free of charge' colonisation of film/music/publishing has made it an unmanageable spectre. A sorry state when governments appear powerless. Yet, from an ethical objective I would argue that choosing to download music/movies instead of enjoying on the radio or TV is not a "corrosive influence" but a platform choice. Yes, it is against the law but not the fall into recidivist crime that Lessig suggests. The cassette tape of a bygone era did not see youth suffer from this "corrosive influence." Friedrich Nietzsche claims that if we are successful in our immorality then we perceive it to be moral1. Furthermore, our distance from the juncture of the crime compounds our perception that it is moral. At the Internet terminal the distance is an indefinite concept, appearing less tangible than physical space. It is a net-collar crime, where empathy becomes ethereal. If copyright laws are anachronistic when file sharing, they must be Neanderthal when uploading. The lesson to be learnt when posting on YouTube is do not mess with the brand. The YouTube Corporation axiom appears to be 'reality is what you can get away with.' It is legitimate according to YouTube to post full sections of a movie verbatim Edelweiss [http://youtu.be/pXtSP8e27rA]   but try posting certain mash ups and YouTube will threaten you with expulsion. Ethically the YouTube rules allow the creative process to be trampled upon while tolerating blatant copyright breaches. Here is a mash up I was disallowed on YouTube yet happily catered for on Vimeo. http://www.vimeo.com/2149818. THE SOUND OF KRAFTWERK MUSIC

This is a perfectly legitimate form of expression nevertheless taken down under YouTube copyright laws.

References

Friedrich Nietzsche. Human, All Too Human "It is not only the spectators of the act who usually assess its morality or immorality according to whether or not it is successful; no, the performer himself does so."

Adams, Philip, January 8, 2009, Interviewing Lawrence Lessig, Future of Copyright in a digital age, Lectopia Recording - Future of Copyright in a Digital Age

10. Sky Full of Lies

New technologies bring new platforms of power to renegotiate a world where governments are struggling to maintain authority. Nik Gowling's book *Skyful of Lies* describes this paradigm shift. Governments and corporations have been broadsided by street democratisation. "Information doers" or "citizen journalists" with mobile phones and Internet access. They have been relentless in uploading and broadcasting an international message. This unencumbered simplicity and immediacy has a powerful resonance. General Sir David Richards calls it "a world-wide internet-based movement". He sees not a battlefield of the streets but "a screen, the place where the future war will be won or lost," his commendation of Gowing, comes as an awakening as the ideas are largely ignored by governments worldwide. These institutions are seriously remiss claims Gowing. "There must be more official willingness to accept the scale and nature of the new media." Gowing asserts that governments have lost control of the 'Black Swan' event1 [random crisis] to "insurgent television". "It distorts the credibility of leaderships and those who serve them," says Gowing. In the past governments have moved with gusto to an incident to reassert values and cap the moment. Now is a time to be wary, Gowing calls it the "f3 effect". In short, act fast to stabilise the situation, it is great to be first, yet check your sources you may be flawed. Gowing says it is the "Tyranny of the time line." According to Lacanian dialectic, this 'Black Swan' spells trouble. With every big change in order to proceed without provocation, there must be a boundary. That is, a law or for our purposes, a news report reaffirming the law with reference to the 'Black Swan' event. A natural deontology is always awake, people do not want to break the law and suffer the consequences. Jacques Lacan would have put it like this. The Real has referred to the Mirror Stage and has seen a 'Black Swan' event. The checks and balances of the Symbolic have

never accounted for this. The mind then becomes disconnected
from the Symbolic, diverting to the Real. Hence chaos and the
unleashed Id.

References

1Adapted from the Black Swan principle identified by Nassim
Nicholas
Taleb in his book The Black Swan: the impact of the highly
improbable
(London:Allen Lane,2007). Taleb writes that our blindness to
randomness,
particularly the large deviations'.

Gowing, Nik 2009, "Skysful of Lies"and Black Swans The New
Tyranny of
shifting information power in crises. Reuters Institute of
Journalism,
University of Oxford, UK.
Richards, General Sir David 2010, *Future Conflicts and Its
Prevention:*
People and the Information Age, < http://www.iiss.org/recent-
keyaddresses/
general-sir-david-richards-address/watch-the-address/>

11. Freedom of Speech

The phrase "Nanos gigantium humeris insidentes[1]" was popularised by Issac Newton, paying homage to his great fore bearers. It literally means "seeing a little further by standing on the shoulders of giants.[1]" This provenance from which we see 'a little further' can be understood as a footnote to the freedom of speech milleu of Aristotle, Plato, Thomas Paine and Mill. However, I will examine the view that all free speech is limited. I will look at the protagonists providing a guide to western freedom of speech. I will inquire into the issues that give freedom of speech a mandate and ask who is this self that necessitates these freedoms.

Aristotle begins his *Nichomachean Ethic* book with "Every skill and every inquiry, and similarly every action and rational choice, is thought to aim at some good; and so, the good has been aptly described as that at which everything aims.[2]" This would presuppose that all free speech is good and needs no restraint. Not only does Aristotle say it is good but affirms it as natural, believing in individual rights that precipitate a *eudaimonia* or full potential. Plato is not so kind; in his Republic he indicates particular sections of the community are charlatans and should be exempt from the state. "We are quite right not to admit him to a properly run state, because he awakens and encourages the lower elements in the mind to the detriment of reason, which is like giving power and political control to the worst element in the state.[3]" This is the outcome of a sectarian feud within Athens. Poets are well known to refer to the philosophers as "The crowd who know too much[3]." Plato's Republic at first refused their entry then left the door ajar for the poets and painters to show remorse. Analogous to the present day, we have sections of the community in unresolved differences and the contention lies herein. In a modern social life, we pursue a sense of truth. A truth that hails a human dignity and eudaimonia. Within this freedom comes a question as to what is reasonably accepted as

61

freedom of speech. Debates arise over what are the limits of free speech. There are considerations over what harm is done and what is practical and attainable as freedom of speech. Christopher Hitchens, author and contemporary champion of freedom of speech contests that a background must start with the three treatises.

1. Areopagitica. John Milton
2. The introduction to The Age of Reason. Thomas Paine
3. On Liberty. J.S.Mill

These are surely the canons of freedom of speech. They resonate and invigorate a sense of freedom. A single-minded affirmation resurrecting a powerful instinct and a will that would unite a community against an oppressive power. The cries of limits have little efficacy while a tide of freedom continues to revel. It is a declaration of an existence of authenticity in a modern world. It is a public discord between Lacan's Real and Symbolic, while mass media's freedom of speech plays the ethical role of Le stade du miroir [the mirror stage.] Here is the Lacanian knot. In Areopagitica, Milton continues a tradition of freedom of speech. Poetically, Milton calls upon the Greeks and Romans, even back to Osiris of ancient Egypt to substantiate his claims that censorship is not in anyone's interest. Milton's basis for writing Areopagitica was to fend off the English government's licencing order of 1643. Laws whereby government must give permission to allow printed material. Summarily he states. "He who destroys a good book, kills reason itself, kills the image of God[4]." Crucially, Milton uses the bible as a natural predication of freedom of speech, he quotes St John. "The truth will make you free.[4]" Milton himself has been a victim of this licencing order of 1643, after speaking out against unlawful divorce. This appears often to be the case that it is not until a person is taken to task concerning freedom of speech do they then in turn unravel the laws and implications. Thomas

Pain's introduction to *The Age of Reason*, first published in 1784
is held in high regard by Hitchen. "When both rights and reason
are under several kinds of open and covert attack, the life and
writing of Thomas Paine will always be part of the arsenal on
which we shall need to depend.[5]" Pain empowers the reader
declaring his deliberation as an accolade to the reader. He
contends that it is slavery unto your own opinions not to listen to
others. His conclusion is that errors of reason may be fought
against by reason alone. In consideration of reason, he states that
"I have never used another, and I trust I never shall[6]" Mill's *On
Liberty* conjures a freedom of speech for the duration of his
entire book. Most notably his thorough examination of harm and
utilitarian are at the core of the Mill's philosophy. Mill's
argument is the "the Greatest Happiness Principle, holds that
actions are right in proportion as they tend to promote happiness,
wrong as they tend to produce the reverse of happiness.[7]" This
has ramifications for those who wish to test the boundaries of
freedom of speech. The implication being that questions should
be asked. Does this freedom of speech tend toward happiness
and whom does it make happy? Still at the centre of Mill values
there is the Harm Principle in which he states. "The only purpose
for which power can be rightfully exercised over any member of
a civilized community against his will is to prevent harm to
others[8]." Does he mean physical harm or just bad advertising?
What exactly constitutes harm? Marion Smiley claims the idea is
closely fixed to what she calls "valuation of personal integrity[9]".
This is a cultural structure. She is saying that different sections
of society or different cultures are going to feel more harm than
others depending on the value system that they subscribe to. As a
generalisation should we not all have a certain amount of
guaranteed freedom of speech? Should a modern sophisticated
respected country have a given amount of freedom of speech?
Mills thinks we should. He suggests that we should be able to
publicly discuss anything "All silencing of discussion is an
assumption of infallibility.[8]" Freedom of speech is the

implication. Later on in his book Mill is not only concerned with immediate physical harm but harm *in potentia*. Chapter Four. "Whenever, in short, there is a definite damage or definite risk of damage, either to an individual or to the public the case is taken out of the province of liberty and placed in that of the morality of the law.8" The limits of freedom of speech are concluded here by the suggestion that our speech has limits as *in potentia* harm, but who decides what is potential harm? To conclude, let us now look at some practical examples of freedom of speech. When it comes to harm it has been argued that violent pornography should be banned. While others contend there is no proven harm. This issue is not helped at all by Mill's harm principle and in fact only adds to the problem by revealing a contradiction. Christopher Hitchens asks, "Who exactly has the right to tell you what you can and cannot view.[10]" This question is brought to bear by those thinkers who view freedom of speech laws as paternalistic. Making a judgment a priori, already deciding what is good for all of us. Mills suggests that paternalism is never an option. Philosopher H.L.A. Hart [11] disagrees, he claims heuristically uninformed people make bad decisions about themselves causing harm to themselves every day. Again, the implication being to appreciate differing values and understanding. Should a modern society outlaw a neo-Nazi rally calling for Judaic eradication? For Mill this would concur as in potentia harmful and therefore demand "the morality of the law.[8]" It is unjustified to outlaw any such address just because it is offensive. Alas, you don't have to go to such a rally. It is easy to avoid such gatherings. So why should it be banned? An embellished speech in a Jewish suburb might not only cause offense but violent unrest. According to Mill if an individual is to be potentially harmed by freedom of speech, then we must prevent the freedom of speech. We must ask who is to decide whether harm is done. The answer here is in the community. Ask the Judaic community what is their opinion on such matters. No matter how abhorrent, no matter how wild, should we let fly the

ignorance of the mouth to be free. Voltaire thinks we should. "I
disapprove of what you say, but I will defend to the death your
right to say it.[12]" It is a gallant phrase widely attributed to
Voltaire but would he defend a racist speech. A well-publicised
case in Austria saw the infamous holocaust denier David Irving
arrested. He had given speeches stating people had died of
natural causes in Auschwitz. He later remarked Jews are
"traditional enemies of the truth[13]". Irving was subsequently
jailed for three years after being found guilty of "trivialising,
grossly playing down and denying the Holocaust.[14]" This Irving
controversy caused introspection as he is an historian regarded as
an expert on aspects of the second world war. So, should this
freedom of speech be tolerated? Slavoj Žižek was full favour of
Irving's freedom of speech and calls this incarceration "a secret
anti-Semitism". He says that "When anti-racism becomes part of
the ego ideal you know you are in trouble.[15]" Here, Žižek claims
that anti-racism is an aspiration and the culture of the hegemony
is a tolerant multicultural one. In short, the dominant paradigm is
racist and it is only the laws that forbid racists to behave that
way. It so appears you are dammed if you do and dammed if you
don't. Mill's in potentia harm would have Irving locked up. Yet
Hitchen and Žižek would let the Irving speech run free.
Hitchen's and Žižek's ideals are akin to igniting a terrestrial fire
for all to see that would eventually burn out. Mill's option would
ignite a subterranean fire. Hidden, appearing infrequently with
shocking devastation. The solution I would suggest is on a case-
by-case basis. Choose your fire and assess who will be burnt and
consider the long term and the short term. In the reality UK TV
show Big Brother contestant Jade Goody has publicly enunciated
words that have called into question the limits of freedom of
speech. The governing body for complaints [Ofcom] received
54,000 against the perceived racism on the show. The
applications largely centred on Goody. She was accused of
making derogatory comments with reference to fellow
housemate and Indian actress Shilpa Shetty, calling her "Shilpa

fuckawalla[16]" and "Shilpa Poppadom[16]". UK Prime Minister Gordon Brown has even commented directly about this show. He says "I want Britain to be seen as a country of fairness and tolerance.[17]" The implication being when using the word "tolerant[17]" that the British are bigots, they just put up with ethnicity so as not to break the law. Therefore, the laws have empowered the normative. The reflexive multicultural society has empowered the "civil racism[15]" of the ego ideal engraining it as the legal side of the law. The law being, the considered outcome of society's institutional consensus. The "civil racism[15]" not only gets away scot-free yet becomes intrinsic to the charter of all modern state institutions. This can be called upon by judges of Goody, Irving et al to hold on to "civil racism," while rejecting the vulgar prejudice from those who have not yet learned to hide it or refuse to hide it. At times those who have learnt to hide it and become protectionist of the minority do so because they believe ethnicity to be weak. This unresolved personal silence. [I think you are weak which makes me strong.] Plays out under a western Christian hegemony, pervasive in establishment modus operandi. How civil? Telling lies about ethnic groups is a common form of prejudice. Here is an example of how lies can work and be presented as freedom of speech. The 1st Amendment of the US Bill of rights introduced to the House of Representatives in 1789 delineates free speech, it states. "Congress shall make no law respecting an establishment of religion, or prohibiting the free exercise thereof; or abridging the freedom of speech, or of the press; or the right of the people peaceably to assemble, and to petition the Government for a redress of grievances.[18]" Americans call it 'the freest country in the world.' This mantra of freedom of speech holds sway for all manner of ridiculous assertions, evens lies. Your freedom of speech is your lies and your freedom of speech is your defence. Xavier Alvarez 21 never served in the military and never received any medals yet contends his right to lie or freedom of speech as he calls it, under the 1st amendment. He was charged under the "Stolen Valor Act[19]" and quotes "Congress shall make no law ...Abridging freedom of speech[18]" to a divided jury in San Francisco. The jury has subsequently thrown out the guilty plea and the case gets heard again early next year [2012]. Certainly, there comes a rallying around when freedom of speech is threatened. Surely the limits are applied when lies are held up as a right. It is here posed by Alvarez that a right to lie is a right to freedom of speech. I wanted here to make a brief but important point about self. When it is said 'an individual has rights' or 'I have a right to my freedom of speech.' It should be questioned what is 'I'. Heidegger explains this as the physicality "Dasein[20]" or 'being-in-the- world.' A consideration away from the physical individual and towards that what exists beyond and including the body, the "Dasein.[20]" Apropos freedom of speech. The self or I, exists as a community and not just a single person's freedom. It is the whole interconnected communities' freedom, which is the 'being-in-the- world' freedom of speech of the individual. In conclusion, when human rights are taken for granted and they are subsumed under the prosaic. Mills argues there is an inclination for ground to be lost and a need to be vigilant, he says, "The supposition being that if not continuously reified the freedom of speech will lose its answers.8" Mill necessitates a freedom of speech in continuum. We must go back again and again and question what the status quo has to offer, contemplate and discuss its answers, leading us from the wilderness of "dead dogma22".

Bibliography

1. John of Salisbury, 1159. *Metalogicon.* trans. Daniel McGarry. Berkeley: University of California Press, 1955
2.Aristotle, 1953. *The Ethics of Aristotle, The Nichomachean Ethics*. Trans J.A.K. ThompsonAllen and Unwin, London UK.
3. Plato, 1955. *The Republic.*Trans, Desmond Lee Penguin group UK.

4. Milton, John 1644, January 21, 2006 Areopagitica A Speech For The Liberty Of Unlicensed Printing To The Parliament Of England.
http://www.gutenberg.org/catalog/world/readfile?fk_files=14429 92

5. Hitchens, Christopher. 2006 *Thomas Paines's Rights of Man*, Grove Press, New York.

6. Pain, Thomas, 1948, *The Age of Reason* [1794], Cidadel Press, New York

7. Mill, John Stuart, 2007, *Utilitarianism*, [1871], Dover Publications, New York.

8 Mill, John Stuart, 2002, On Liberty, [1859], Dover Publications, New York.

9 Smiley, Marion, 1992, Moral Responsibility and the Boundaries of Community, University of Chicago Press, Chicago USA.

10 Hitchens, Christopher, May 26th 2007. Christopher Hitchens on free speech. < http://youtu.be/ZOck_bDb0JA>

12 Hall, Evelyn Beatrice, 1906, The Friends Of Voltaire, Smith Elder and co. California , USA.

13 Irving, David, 1997, Viewed 16thOctober 2011, David Irving's Action report, <
http://www.codoh.com/irving/irvar13.html>

14 Irving, David, 28thOctober 2009, White supremacists stabbed at talk by Holocaust denier David Irving. Mail Online.

15 Žižek, Slavoj, 2010, Living in End Times, Verso, UK.

16 Goody, Jade, 18th Jan 2007, Viewed 16th October 2011, The Guardian, <

http://www.guardian.co.uk/commentisfree/2011/feb/11/taming-jade-goody-big-brother-globe>

17 Brown, Gordon, 2007. Viewed 16th October 2011, The Guardian <
http://www.guardian.co.uk/media/2007/jan/17/bigbrother.politicsandthemedia>

18 CSRA Constitution, 1791, Bill Of Rights,
http://www.law.cornell.edu/constitution/billofrights

19 United States Congress, 2005, Stolen Valor Act,
<http://www.govtrack.us/congress/billtext.xpd?bill=s109-1998>

20 Heidegger, Martin, 1962, Being and Time, Willet-Blackwell, Hoboken, NJ, USA. 22 Mill, John Stuart, 2007, Utilitarianism, Liberty & Representative Government, Wildside Press, Rockville, USA.

References

10 Hitchens, Christopher, May 26th 2007. Christopher Hitchens on free speech. < http://youtu.be/ZOck_bDb0JA>

11 Lee Plaisance, Patrick, 2009, Media Ethics, Key Principles for Responsible Practice, Sage Publications California USA.

20 Heidegger, Martin, 1962, Being and Time, Willet-Blackwell, Hoboken, NJ, USA.

21 Alvarez, Xavier , Appeals Court Stolen Valor Act,
http://www.guardian.co.uk/world/feedarticle/9224846

Media Ethics /Patrick Lee Plasisance

Utilitarianism/JS Mill

On Liberty/ JS Mill

Living in End Times/Slavoj Žižek

Nichomachean Ethics/ Aristotle

The Republic/Plato

Ethics and Media Culture//David Berry

Introduction Lectures to Psychanalysis/ Freud

Within Your Grasp/ Kierkegaard

50 Philosophy Ideas/ Ben Dupre

Ecrits/ Lacan

How to read Lacan /Slavoj Žižek

Ethics/ Gordon Marino

The Shorter Routledge Encyclopedia of Philosophy/

Edward Craig The Really Hard Problem /

Owen Flanagan The Oxford Book of Ethical Theory/

David Copp Spinoza's Ethics/
Steven Nadler

Being and Time/Heidegger

Heidegger and ethics/Joanna Hodge

John Stuart Mill on Liberty in Focus/

John Gray Hume On Morality/

James Baillie The World and Other Writings/

Descartes Fredrich Nietzsche/ Lee Spinks

Phenomenology of the Spirit/Hegel

Philosophy Guidebook to Nietzsche on Morality/ Brian Leiter.

 The Value of Morality in Kant's Moral Theory/Richard dean

Michel Foucault Critical Thinkers/ Sara Mills

Slavoj Žižek Critical Thinkers/ Tony Myers

12. God Is the Master-Signifier

With reference to a sign saying *...The media is not a reflection of reality* and asking "What is 'right' about this sign? What is 'wrong' about it?" Suggests the axiom is both right and wrong. Like all axioms, (yes all) they are true and false. The contradiction between *too many cooks spoil the broth* and *many hands make light work* is not the exception to the rule but the rule itself. It leads us to the idea within communications that we at best remain agnostic to a message. "Agnostic" usually referring to a god belief must guide us to understand that message as text would have us believe in a Lacanian sense, God is the Master-Signifier.

13. The Conquest of Ubiquity

This article expresses the notion that the whole of the internet is a duality.

1. Information Architecture AI
2. User Experience UX

The colonising conquest of property and land (Information architecture) and people (User Experience). The Conquest of Ubiquity (as I call it, the phrase borrowed from Walter Benjamin) is plainly the colonising of the Internet. Information Architecture (IA) and User Experience (UX) shall be considered as the Internet totality. Under these two headings it can be ascertained an understanding of the Internet and explains what the Internet engagement entails.

Homo sapiens have used tools to co-opt UX and IA since time immemorial. Between five and fifteen million years ago, when the evolution from ape to modern human was first prescribed and man finally came down from the trees and then the world gave birth to UX and IA. This was the initiation of the designer (IA) and a user of tools. (UX)

'So you shall start, so shall you go,' is a phrase used in media to indicate the starting point and therefore the direction of the project. Components then start to fit together because they are similar and progressive. The starting point here is the name Information Architecture. Such provenance bestows the task of deconstruction as two components, Information and Architecture. Information is an exponentially expanding seemingly uncontrollable universe, chaos on a mass scale. The

Architecture is an anchor for this. It suggests a spectacular compartmentalisation of Information with professionalism. Architecture confers characteristics of education, individualism and having a certain style. It is for the most part all that a home can be, physically and psychologically. This is the inference of the naming of Information Architecture.

The Information Architecture can be allegorically understood, as the information as land and the architecture as a sign of land and property ownership. Information Architecture is a battleground for cyber-space. It is a cyber territorial domination, an information war and colonising power. At first the Internet was all like an 18th century law of 'Terra Nullius.' The land was empty unpopulated and a place for alterity to be. It then started to become a colourful hegemonic play for the hearts and minds, a spreading of conscious and unconscious. As time moves on there was a confronting web of invasion, a Nietzschian Triumph of the Will. As the Internet age was rolling out, up pops pockets of cyber-war. It can't be defined as allegorical fantasy but a true colonial mind-set, the mythical power. The empty spaces of cyberspace have now all been fought over and filled. Distributed Denial of Service (DDoS) attacks are one of the tools of moving in on territory. Google claims "DDoS attacks are surprisingly easy and cheap to initiate, and are increasing in size and complexity every year. " Google are keen to publish to the world the daily occurrence of DDos attacks, giving a full history of the last year.

http://www.digitalattackmap.com/#anim=1&color=2&country=AU&time=15936&view=map

The site gives special mentions to three large attacks in the last year involving US, Russia and on the 20th August 2013, one involving Australia.

As this arena of conquest goes forth, I would like to refer to to Hegel's Philosophy of History. It is here that Hegel told us, the history of human consciousness is a consciousness towards freedom. Forever wonderfully problematic as he never could quite annunciate what he meant by freedom and so the quest goes on. So, what does he mean by freedom and more specifically what does his freedom mean apropos the Internet? For each player, government, military or company, each would seek his or her own freedom. Sometimes separate and at times at odds with others. There is a sense of evolving freedom within the Internet. How a person interacts today is different to how they interact tomorrow.. and so forth. This will become less apparent as time goes on. The predicated human will be compartmentalised on the bell curve and as predictable as humans can be.

UX is the inanimate half of the equation and AI is the animate, other half of the equation. The User Experience tends towards an objective make up within the medium. The medium's reality is instantly directed towards the mass market as opposed to what the engineer may personally wish to deliver. In naming the User Experience the trap of delivering what the engineer wishes to deliver is immediately avoided. All considerations are with the user. It can now be inferred that the Marshall McLuhan phrase. "The medium is the message" (TMITM) can be transmuted to, 'The medium is the user.' Thus, slaying the beast that is TMITM. For TMITM is a clever thing to say but in practice has no value, like someone saying 'Don't worry about the man behind the curtain.' A clever thing to say but has no justification and worse of all a distraction to useful practice. Suffice to say there is no man behind the curtain.

As information of self is poured into the web there are transmogrifying expectations. Kant talks of a "moral law within. "Referring to the human soul as the arbiter of moral values. Perhaps just as humanity consciousness is uploaded, the web will have and become a moralizing force. As humanity perceives other Lacanian mirrors such as other humans, so too will people use the Internet finding ethical assistance. In short, the medium will be a Lacanian mirror. The user will look for, reflect, react and change ethically as the user participates on the Internet (the Lacanian mirror).

The Internet doesn't begin in one place or end, so it is never quite finished. On leaving the Internet it is understood that something has been missed. On leaving the Internet, you are well aware that as soon as you have left, something has been added. Somebody, somewhere has updated or posted. A relation with the Internet is always insatiate, always lacking. The Internet is known as the hungry beast, it is never satisfied. Users are left knowing something is absent and the Internet itself is so vast that individuals are unable to engage with everything. While the UX professional explores every nook and cranny in the human domain it is IA that is deficient. IA underpins an evolving medium. It should see the Internet as an evolving system. The architecture that necessitates today might not work tomorrow. Ordinarily architecture is a man-made encompassing structure. The task at hand is housing information of a broadly evolving nature. It is recognized that the evolution is in the hands of a human and therefore will possess human traits. The UX /AI acronyms suggests UX to be half of the whole. Radical in its assertion is the idea that the client is king. The engineer is on notice to produce what is practically usable.

Walter Benjamin in his *The Work of Art in the Mechanical Reproduction* explains ideas contested in a time of war. This considered work establishes a political, industrial and artist connection. Benjamin presents a template that transcends time. He tells of how one affects the other and attempts to pull together seemingly disparate units. I would like to follow his example and determine cohesion of the Internet within his template of politic, industrial and artist connection. Let's start with political.

Politically the Internet is a place that is egalitarian, free, democratic and caters for individual progression. It is fair to say "for the people by the people." In the top ten of highest-ranking sites in terms of hits are; YouTube, Facebook, Twitter and Wikipedia. These are all sites, uploaded and managed by the public. The Internet is a uncontrolled tool and so governments the world over will try and police or 'filter' this. So influential is the Internet it will change the way words are understood. Look at the words, 'egalitarian' 'democratic' 'free' and 'individual'. Notice how they mean sometime different as soon as the Internet is considered. This will influence other media and the way these words are considered. For an instrument that doesn't feed, reproduce or help us breath, It drives an inequitable amount of concern because this is a new uncontrolled political space.

The Internet has an etheric industrial nature. While Walter Benjamin's industrial paradigm is centred on *The Age of Mechanical Reproduction* the Internet is an adjunct to this mass reproduction. It is a catalyst for reproduction and that catalyst is called desire. The Internet is what Deleuze would have regarded as another "desiring-machine." He says it is "A real force in direct competition to the idea of the Freudian unconscious." Deleuze calls this phenomenon "desiring-machines as formations of the unconscious". As each invention is an amputation of a limb. The Internet is a further annexation of the body; a delegation of desire, conscious and unconscious has also been sublet to the Internet. We are not ourselves and these entities can no longer be considered as contained in the body. Deleuze holds firm the idea that cyber-space is unconscious space. I would also like to add conscious space and a space that desires.

Artistically the Internet is primal. Like a painting on a cave's wall, everyone sees the same webpage. There is a sense that the artist is back in business. Now anyone can paint on the wall again. It is an opportunity again to be seen and heard by everyone. This new deal is even better, the artist can expose themselves to both audience and monetarisation. The level playing field so often coveted is ubiquitous. This is revolutionary and with all revolutions. 'What do you do with it once you have it?' This directionless feeling is a power vacuum and the true lack that the Internet has. Internet users as a group, have no leadership. Wilheim Reich believes people are forced to desire repression. He asks. "How could the masses be made to desire their own repression?" It is as if citizens of the Internet can't believe the freedom. They desire repression says Wilhelm. Then when, no one arrives to oppress they can pick up the stick and overtly turn on each other. They call these Internet citizens 'the haters, ' 'the trolls.' This is not a people's utopia but as Saussure asks what identifies the medium is what it lacks.. or what it isn't. "The tenet of Saussurian linguistics, which holds that signs or words mean what they do only in opposition to others- their most precise characteristic is in being what the others are not." This defines media as lacking as each are defined in semiotical terms as what they are not. Suffice to say all media lacks.

Uses and Gratification theories can be applied to the web

and under the rubric of Abraham Maslow's Hierarchy of Needs.
I would like to examine Facebook. For most people devoting
time to the web is invariably on Facebook. Facebook is the
second most popular site on the Internet, 1st is Google. I start by
asking two questions. What is the understanding of the meaning
presented to a viewer? What is the moralising effect and
consciousness taken up by the Internet, specifically Facebook?
Through this calculation we might assume a revised identity of
the Internet generation and therefore what it lacks. While
Maslow's telos is self-actualisation, Facebook's consciousness is
taken up by a number of mid-range human needs. See graphic
below.

Maslow in his book *Toward a Psychology of Being*
states that self -actualisation is "realizing the potentialities of the
person, that is to say, becoming fully human, everything that the
person can become." Furthermore, Maslow claims the self-
actualized person has many enthusiasts "This is called variously
by different authors self-actualization, has many different traits
such as a self-realization, integration, psychological health,
individuation, autonomy, creativity and productivity." In favour
of Facebook it can be said it invariably touches these traits
though falls short of deeper, meaningful, and transcendental or
the becoming a human seeks. This lack in Facebook and the
Internet is a deficiency in language itself. A deficiency of
language now contained within technology. The idea self-
actualization or as Deleuze might say "becoming" is not possible
to the Internet per se. Deleuze noted in his idea of being and
becoming. There is a transcendental quality, a passage to
becoming and technology does not provide that suture. It is a
place of holding back, though a person might lease out desire,
dialectical, conflict etc.. There is a core identity that a person

will always hold on to until the Internet has become in charge.

It has been shown that the gateway for consciousness to freedom within an Internet collective has proved a shallow path. Pouring all conscious thought as data into the Internet has come with ethical expectations. Search engines account for what has become an unconscious. The Internet is desire simulacra, a false idol, as Walter Benjamin's *The Work of Art in the Mechanical Reproduction* suggests without aura without authenticity. It is the super ego, a Lacanian big other copy, an AI UX paternal figure, with an ability to represses each other and society.

References

Derrida, J. (1998), *Monolingualism of the Other: or, The Prosthesis of Origin (Cultural Memory in the Present)*. 1 Edition. Stanford University Press.

Marketing to Tribes, consumer groups, social media speaker - Futurist Patrick Dixon - YouTube. (2014), *Marketing to Tribes, consumer groups, social media speaker - Futurist Patrick Dixon - YouTube*. [ONLINE] Available at: http://www.youtube.com/watch?v=CivP6VN2cJc&list=PL91A5 46C864A36462. [Accessed 28 May 2014].

Speight A, (2008) *The Philosophy of Hegel (Continental European Philosophy)*. First Edition Edition. Acumen Publishing Ltd.

Gifford, P. Stimpson, B. (1999), *Reading Paul Valéry: Universe in Mind (Cambridge Studies in French)*. Edition. Cambridge University Press.

Oldest Use of Stone Tools? | The Smithsonian Institution's Human Origins Program. (2014), *Oldest Use of Stone Tools? | The Smithsonian Institution's Human Origins Program.* [ONLINE] Available at: http://humanorigins.si.edu/resources/whats-hot/oldest-use-stone-tools. [Accessed 24 May 2014].

Deleuze, G. (1983), *Anti-Oedipus: Capitalism and Schizophrenia.* Reprint Edition. Univ Of Minnesota Press.

Butler, R. (2013), *The Zizek Dictionary.* Edition. Acumen Publishing.
Alexa Top 500 Global Sites. 2014. *Alexa Top 500 Global Sites.* [ONLINE] Available at: http://www.alexa.com/topsites. [Accessed 28 May 2014].

Marketing to Tribes, consumer groups, social media speaker - Futurist Patrick Dixon. - YouTube. (2014), *Marketing to Tribes, consumer groups, social media speaker - Futurist Patrick Dixon - YouTube.* [ONLINE] Available at: http://www.youtube.com/watch?v=CivP6VN2cJc&list=PL91A5 46C864A36462. [Accessed 28 May 2014].

Google Ideas. (2014), *Google Ideas.* [ONLINE] Available at: http://www.google.com/ideas/projects/digital-attack-map/. [Accessed 28 May 2014].

Bloch, E. (2013), *The Privatization of Hope: Ernst Bloch and the Future of Utopia, SIC 8 ([sic] Series).* Edition. Duke University Press Books.

McLuhan, M. (2001), *The Medium is the Massage.* 9th Edition. Gingko Press.

Maslow, A H. (2014), *Toward a Psychology of Being*. Edition. Sublime Books.

Hartley, J. (2002), *Communication, Cultural and Media Studies: The Key Concepts (Routledge Key Guides)*. 3 Edition. Routledge.

Kant, I. (2003), *The Critique of Pure Reason*. Dover Publications. New edition Edition. Dover Publications.

Alexa Top 500 Global Sites. 2014. *Alexa Top 500 Global Sites*. [ONLINE] Available at: http://www.alexa.com/topsites. [Accessed 01 June 2014].

14. The Medium is the Mirror

I want to identify within the Sender-Message-Receiver model a
Human-Medium-Human model and explain how the medium is
not the message but a mirror.

Jacques Lacan refers to this *stade du miroir* or mirror
stage in human development. A self-reflecting time in
conjunction with language that presents a sense of law. He
claims this is meted out to each and every individual in
childhood. No doubt, bestowed from rivers and ponds to
mammals throughout the eons.

Through time, other reflections have apportioned this
sense of ethical self. A dance with tribe, a song to friends, a
response from spoken word, all these are mirror stages. The
audience acts as the mirrored self, causing self–reflection and
therefore a moralising factor. The medium is the mirror.

15. The Medium is Not the Message

fm $\neq$ fM , or "1The medium is the message" is an unworthy truth. To be more precise add at least another two variable functions - The audience function and the human function (the individual human data entry) ie fM = fm(1)+fa(1+n) +fh(1+n)

Three additions fm(1),fa(1+n) , fh(1+n) explained.

1. Medium Function or fm

The medium is not the message but a mere addition to the message. Tv, radio, the book, or the computer game. The media has rules of engagement. You cannot think outside of the square, which means that all media have particular boundaries of expression.

What Mcluhan means when he says "the medium is the message" is that the confines of the medium function embed themselves in the message.

2. The Human Function or fh (1+n)

The concretisation by the individual of the metaphysical is the human function. Part of this metaphysical self (the only one that really matters) is a truth. As Kant called it, "2The moral law within." This metaphysical self is transmuted through the medium of the individual to be the human function. The individual as; the editor, the painter, the DJ, the writer or programmer etc.

This individual is not only influenced by audience and medium but by perception of the audience and perception of medium. The audience commandeers the human function of the individual with the acknowledgement and approval of the individual. The human function is a guess at how an internal truth might best be displayed.

16. The Medium is the Single Object

Media is the plural of medium. The medium is the single object.

In his opening line from *The Medium is the Massage*, "McLuhan states "The medium, or process of our time." The "medium" is a mere "process of our time"? Curious. Famously, McLuhan declares, "The medium is the message", surmising from both these definitions that media's ontology runs with a set of rules buttressed by its own nature and engages us, taking stints of time. It appears media is a prison of choice, a hypertropy.

You are hereby sentenced to Facebook for the rest of your natural born life; but only out of choice.

Hegel would have found new media hard to swallow, he says; "The history of the world is none other than the progress of the consciousness of freedom" and now the freedom is being thrown away. Why? Because we can. Freedom ultimately exists as the power to waste it.

Is 'reflection' an adequate way of considering media representations?

Yes, it is adequate. Not a great way of considering media representations but adequate. In times of renaissance, it is the juncture to reconsider the foundations on which the medium stands, combined with that which is possible within the medium. Not just to redefine but also to make a product regulated not only by its ontological boundaries but not the historical ones. News is a ubiquitous platform alas it bears the shackles of an analogue medium not willing to embrace and experience the freedom of digital. Alain De Botton has recently questioned many ontological factors in his book *The News*. What is the news, he asks? Here he plies a philosophical angle to Internet news production.

http://www.philosophersmail.com/

Here Alain De Botton tells you what to think.
Play vs Theory vs Facts, a review.
http://mariborchan.si/audio/slavoj-zizek/the-poetic-military-complex/

I've written to Slavoj Zizek, awaiting his reply.

He writes a review of a movie he has never seen. So, I wrote to ask him to write a review of a movie that has never been made. Hence, I could make a movie that would fit his review. This would avoid the circumstance of his *Children of Men* review, where on viewing he realised it didn't fit his theory. 'If facts don't fit the theory, it's so much worse for the facts'. Slavoj Zizek. Reminding us that theory, on its own is animated almost human. If a dog could talk, what would it say? If the theory could talk, what would it say? The theory would be out-spoken. It has been shamed. This has been caused by the impoliteness of the facts. The theory would berate the facts because they obviously broke cultural protocols compelling the theory to lose face. THEORY ANGER.

17. The Medium is the Message Again

When Marshal McLuhan called his book, *The Medium is the Massage*, he noted the spelling mistake but continued anyway. Did this not indicate his indifference to the original phrase? Did he think the book title, *The Medium is the Massage* have something to add? In a deliberate and obvious way. a more pop

title....meaning. .'Oh horror of sedation'...

The question remains... If medium is message, then is, the message the medium. Not true, in a logical

sense, 'the car is red' but 'the red is not car.' But in a sense and if you can just throw away the grammatical dogma holding us back.. and entertain the idea that this is an exception to the rule. The message is the medium, is

 an awkward yet profound phrase. Meaning - There is no thinking out of the square, there is merely

 freedom to work within the boundaries. The square peg comes out of the square hole.

The human bio-computer is but another medium. The media has in themselves a moral guidance,

and a way of seeing.

18. A Message of Language

Platforms of writing can be identified as having a life of their own. The text, the email, the Facebook post or the essay. These all have character that is individual to their own medium. This means that the message is curtailed by the format in which it is delivered. Communication changes as technology changes. In years gone by 'the love letter' was a form of communication. Yet today it would be difficult to consider an era of 'the love email.'

In Daniel Chandler's book, *The Art of Writing*, it is considered how writing is altered by thinking. This is the *linguistic determinist* view, part of the Sapir-Whorf hypothesis. It states 'Our thinking is determined by language' (Chandler 1985, p.16). Everyday clichés like, 'Too many cooks spoil the broth' control thinking. There is a myriad of these phrases that control thinking. But look again, can't it be said that the inverse is true. That is; 'language determines thought.' Immanuel Kant is said to think so. RB Jachman, who was a pupil of Immanuel Kant's noted, 'carrying out his enquires in front of his audience, as though he had just begun to consider the question' (Jachman, in Scruton 2001, p.5). It would appear that Kant's lecture is analogous to the improvised musician or actor. Kant was speaking and new ideas were being communicated. As Aristotle remarked, 'some speakers succeed through practice and others through spontaneity' (Aristotle 2012, p.3). In conclusion it can be said that a valued lecture is a synthesis of the conscious and unconscious.

The second half of Sapir-Whorf hypothesis states a *linguistic relative* view. 'People who speak different languages perceive and think about the world differently' (Chandler 1985, p16). Yolŋu people of Gapuwiyak north-east Arnhem Land Australia, speak Djambarrpuyŋu. In this dialect, 'narra djal' means four different things, depending on the context. It could mean 'I am,' 'I love,' 'I want,' or 'I eat. Fewer words in a language may appear like a narrower world-view. Yet empirically, it works as an extension of meaning. It highlights the similarities between these verbs.

'I am' in French translates to 'Je suis.' Look how 'Je suis' is so similar to 'Jesus' and how 'Je suis Charlie' (Potet 2015, p.1) looks so similar to 'Jesus Christ.' This is a media dream campaign, invoking the power of the sacred. 'Je suis Charlie' has even the same initials and capitals as Jesus Christ.

In deconstruction, it can be seen why 'Je suis Charlie' is a most successful meme. As Walter Benjamin claims, 'For to some degree, all great texts contain their potential translation between the lines' (Benjamin 1973, p.82).

References

Chandler, Daniel 1985, *The act of writing*, The Registry, University of Wales, Aberystwyth.

Scruton, Roger 2001, *Kant a very short introduction,* Oxford University Press Inc, New York.

Aristotle, 2012, *The art of rhetoric, Harper Press, London.*

Potet, Frédéric 2015, *'Je suis charlie,'* Le Magazine Du Monde, p,1. Retrieved December 17, 2015, from La Vie-Le Monde Group.

Benjamin, Walter 1973, *Illuminations,* Fontana Press, London.

19. Symbolic Interactionism and Love Underpin all Social Interaction

Symbolic Interactionism is a sociological theory principally based on the work of George Herbert Mead's book 'Mind, Self and Society,' 1934 and Herbert Blumer's book 'Symbolic Interactionism Perspective and Method' 1969.

Symbolic Interactionism and love underpin all social interaction. Australian documentary maker Denis O'Rourke proclaims 'Everyone just wants to be loved' (Kingston 2000, p.1).

Love imbeds itself within Symbolic Interactionism. Look at the three premises of Blumer's Symbolic Interactionism and see how love is co-opted to Symbolic Interactionism. Blumer's first premise 'Humans act toward things on the basis of the meanings that the things have for them' (Blumer 1969, p.2). These 'acts' and 'meanings' are directed by love. 'Meanings' are gained and 'acts' are taken through cultural mimicking and love is the rationale of these 'meanings' and 'acts.' George Mead says 'Man lives in a world of meaning' (Mead 1926, p.382). This cannot be imagined without love.

Blumer's second premise 'the meaning of a thing for a person grows out of the ways in which other persons act toward the person with regard the thing' (Blumer 1969, p.5). This social interaction is motivated by love. This leads to the concretisation of action and meaning. Without love we wouldn't engage; we would simply enrage.

Finally, Blumer believes 'Symbolic Interactionism sees meaning as social products, as creations that are formed in and through the defining activities of people as they interact' (Blumer 1969, p.5). It was Karl Marx who noted an interpretative process of the social and production of things. He called it 'The Fetishism of Commodities' (Marx, 1867, p.47). Freud translates the fetish object of a 'shiny on the nose' (Freud

1927, para.1) as a sexualised object. Surely opening the possibility that all objects are sexualised objects. The point here is that all objects have a sexuality bestowed upon them. The French know this intrinsically; all nouns are either masculine or feminine. So this is the meaning given to things, a sexuality through personification.

References

Mead, George 1972, *Mind, self, and society*, United States of America: The University of Chicago Press Ltd, London England.

Kingston, Margo 2000, '*Black and white issues*,' The Sydney Morning Herald, p, 1. Retrieved December 09, 2015, from Fairfax Digital database.

Marx, Karl 1887, Das *capital volume one*, Progress Publishers, Moscow.

Blumer, Herbert 1969, *Symbolic interactionism perspective and method*, United States of America: University of California Press Ltd, London England.

Freud, Sigmund 1927, '*Fetishism*', Srcibd, Para, 1. Retrieved 13 December 2015, from Scribd database.
<u>Öffentlichkeit –publicity, transparency, and openness</u>

-->
-->

The Public Sphere or Öffentlichkeit is a media culture popularised by Jürgen Habermas. The Public Sphere has a best practice that includes the public being encouraged to join a debate of culture and politics. At the end of this process is a message. Habermas claims this provides a superior democracy. (Habermas, J 1991.)

As the Public Sphere provides a message and thinking of Marshal McLuhan's "The medium is the message." (McLuhan, M 1969.) This logically concludes, "The medium is a Public Sphere." Television is a medium, Twitter is a medium, university is a medium, also it can be claimed the Public Sphere is a medium or any other Communication Theory.

Implementing a Public Sphere is a difficult process, perhaps all media would benefit from an internal Public Sphere (IPS). The use of debate and idea exchange inside an institution may be advantageous. Leading to a 'thought-out' message being announced. This cannot be seen after the Paris attacks, 14th November 2015. President François Hollande appears to have gone it alone when he said. "France is at war." (ABC News 2015.) Would not words benefit from an exchange of ideas within an IPS? Thus, listening to, and participating in a debate, not just what appears to be a singular voice. Unfortunately for France, it was a headline indicating an ongoing battle and a legitimatising of attacks. Remember he called it a "war," not terror. A conciliatory view would have been better; alas his words foreshadowed more killings.

Within the next two weeks there were three attacks in French speaking African countries, Mali and Cameroon. (Al Jazeera and agencies 2015.)

References

Habermas, J 1991, *The Structural Transformation of the Public Sphere*, 1st ed, United States of America: MIT Press.

McLuhan, M M 1969, *The Medium is the Massage*, 2nd ed, Penguin, Ringwood, Victoria, Australia.

AFP/Reuters 2015, *ABC News*, [ONLINE] Available at: http://www.abc.net.au/news/2015-11-17/paris-attacks-francois-hollande-vows-intensify-syria-operations/6946202, [Accessed 30 November 15].

Al Jazeera and agencies 2015, *Three killed in attack on UN base in northern Mali*, [ONLINE] Available at: http://www.aljazeera.com/news/2015/11/gunmen-attack-base-northern-mali-151128081314862.html, [Accessed 30 November 15].

Al Jazeera and agencies, 2015, *Bamako hotel attack: Mali's security challenges*, [ONLINE] Available at: http://www.aljazeera.com/programmes/insidestory/2015/11/bamako-hotel-attack-mali-security-challenges-151121204401218.html, [Accessed 30 November 15].

Al Jazeera and agencies, 2015, *Cameroon*, [ONLINE] Available at: http://www.aljazeera.com/topics/country/cameroon.html, [Accessed 30 November 15].

20. The Battle is Internal

Ahh, the culture wars .... are played out in your own head. I had to get up from the table and leave when Émile Durkheim said religion was the difference between the sacred and the profane...I'm gone... It was delightful to be delivered by Nietzsche as he told us that we are nurtured by the Dionysian and the Apollonian in *The Birth of Tragedy*.

Kant; One hundred years previous argued the same. We are a dual between passion and reason (noted from *A Very Short Introduction, Hegel,* Peter Singer. Suggesting you can't have Hegel without a dose of Kant.

Hegel further states, religion is a barrier to man in harmony subordinating him to a subordinate. But anyway, back to the duality.

1. Nietzsche's; Dionysian and the Apollonian

2. Kant's; Passion and reason

3. Lacan's; The Real and Symbolic

Let's make a real example of what goes on ....The Alan Watts example ... That is, we all play a game "My life/game is better than your life/game." We play it with friends, work colleges, our boss, our co-workers. Now, keep in mind the another game, the Robert Anton Wilson's game of "tunnel vision" .. That is, the world is a certain way, as one person sees it, I must convince everyone that this is the right way to see the world. These two games will be played out over millennium under rules of engagement below.... That is,

1. The rules of the game spoken. Apollonian/ reason/ Lacan
Symbolic. Human. Official God.

2. The rules of the game unspoken. Dionysian/passion/Lacanian
Real. Lizard. Jesus, who takes it on the nose because he dares to
speak the word that is God... John Chapter one. "The word is
God." That's an open statement for the establishment to make
public. God is not dead god is very much alive but not in charge.
What is in charge is the unconscious. The unword. The unspoken
rules.
The devil is not in the detail but what is left out of the detail.
The battle is internal, culture wars played out in the head.

21. Being and Nothingness

Sartre's *Being and Nothingness* hardcover.

Why am I wasting my time? I feel that I won't find anything from this book... Because.. The empiricist have always won over the rationalists, then they all return to their ivory towers, built, rendered, qualified then extended upon the continuum with rationalism. Academics are by nature rationalists. They say "working in the field," with a little sense of irony.

"When the facts gets in the way of the theory, it's so much worse for the facts." Slavoj Zizek.

Zizek gets away with an admission of rationalist guilt, when rendered as a joke you can overlook the implications, an example of the function of humour .. Wonder if this style was mentioned in "Zizek Jokes" book.

https://youtu.be/4uh5MB17v9A

Routledge Encyclopedia of Philosophy chapter on Sartre valourises the French phrases L'etre pour-soi. (Consciousness...)

About 726,000,000 results (0.35 seconds)

French – detected •   English •

l'etre pour-soi   the being -for-itself

Open in Google Translate

and L'etre en-soi (everything else)

To understand something, it is that human trait to chop it in two.
The topology castration... an immediate presence of absence...cut
into male and female parts... To somehow render the inanimate,

{L'etre en-soi (everything else)} animate. This humanises the
geography of the world. When this is done it is no longer the Big
Other radical alterity sole identity but imbued with (male/female)
human spirit. With this distorted predicate duality, we look
further, uncertain whether we have hit a fork in the road or a fork
in the tongue. I feel I'm going to be disappointed with Sartre's
Being and Nothing. From the Routledge Encyclopedia of
Philosophy there are no signs that some foundation of
Psychogeography will be enunciated ...I'm looking for something
like Rousseau enunciated with his social contract... a PG without
calling it PG. I'm looking for the consciousness of the 'Fuck up
and beyond'.. 'The fuck up'

you see in your piers that you witness and they hate you for. You
exist as a witness then they go to

great lengths to distract you from their 'Fuck Up' .. They
valourise something trivial to fight about..

Nietzsche touches on it here..

97

So much looking forward to **not** liking this book. I'm expecting the Naturalism that Ayn Rand rallied

against in *The Romantic Manifesto*. She questions the Naturalist artist who conveys life as they see it. No moral compass: a consciousness exemplary of cracks. She prefers the consciousness plus imagination. The fiction of a world that is wished for, a desire that lacks an emptiness that Lacan conveys. She does this in *Fountainhead* and *Atlas Shrugged*; creating a world of the men she wishes to behold, spend time with, long for. The men who are admirable. 'Man is an end in himself' Ayn Rand. TRM. She sets out a style for the artist. One of selectivity not of the naturalist " re telling real life. Not life imitating art but art creating life itself. 'Discover the potential, the gold mine, of man's soul, must extract the gold and then fashion as magnificent a crown as his ability and vision permit.' Ayn Rand TRM. I must dislike this book before it arrives as it builds on Heidegger's "Being and Time," knowing that it won't stand as philosophy unless it includes other philosophers. It was only until Robert Anton Wilson and Alan Watts exemplified the art of being a philosopher without referring to other philosophers.

22. The Psychogeography Gods

-->

Perhaps when talking of 'geography' the word 'psychogeography' can be inserted and at last, something can be gleaned from the text. Waldo Tobler's first law in geography, stated that 'everything is related somehow to everything else but things in closer proximity are more related than other things that are further apart'...http://homepage.univie.ac.at/.../Theory_and_Meth.../Sui_2004.pdf. What is beautifully animist here sort, is exactly as the first lines of Thus Spoke Zarathustra exemplifies. 'You great star! What would your happiness be if you had not those for whom the star shines.' That is, putting humanity and the spirits back in the picture. And thinking, why did the geographers pull humanity and the spirits out. 'Dasein' is being in the world and this world is animist. God is in the house.

Tuesday, April 26, 2016

23. Freud and the Banks

Q. "Are you happy with the service today?"
A "Are you threatening me?"

I was doing my tax return and a statement was missing. I call the bank and sorted out the problem. The last question the bank asked. - "Are you happy with the service today?" Mmmm

.... The systematic question can be of a cognitive dissonance nature, to confuse the truth that money has been taken from you. To suggest you've had the goods and services for free. This question - "Are you happy with the service today?" Had a similar proposed efficacy….. But there was something more, I could just sense it. The question suggested that the conversation had a happy ending. Inferring that my casual communication was similar to a massage with a happy ending. Asserting by the bank that a delivery of a bank statement is sexual. Don't you just love the bank, that other, lesser kind of love of rhyming.

24. The North South Divide

In humanity beginnings, mind and body are physically compartmentalised. Within the self, is a self-consciousness. Hegel states, "it exists (self-consciousness) only in being acknowledged."

I'd like to go further. When the self is acknowledged, it acknowledges 'being in the world.' That is, friends, furniture, forest; the whole kit and caboodle.

Next; as a theory goes, Out of Africa and language was born. A new referential communication. 'The word was God' or perhaps the Lacan version - The Symbolic Order was God.

Within language consciousness there are two things. *The rules of the game* and *the unspoken rules of the game*. These are the Symbolic Order and The Real of Lacan, a mind and the body duality. Furthermore, comparable to the Kantian, "passion and reason." This is the same division in the Nietzschean idea of man controlled by counterparts, the Dionysian and Apollonian.

What science has made apparent, apropos cell memory and bacteria moving toward food, is a body intellect. The unconscious is the body's intellect that the mind seeks to colonise. The body is often ignored, and even shouted down by the mind. "I'm the king of the castle, get down you dirty rascal!" says the Symbolic Order to the Real.

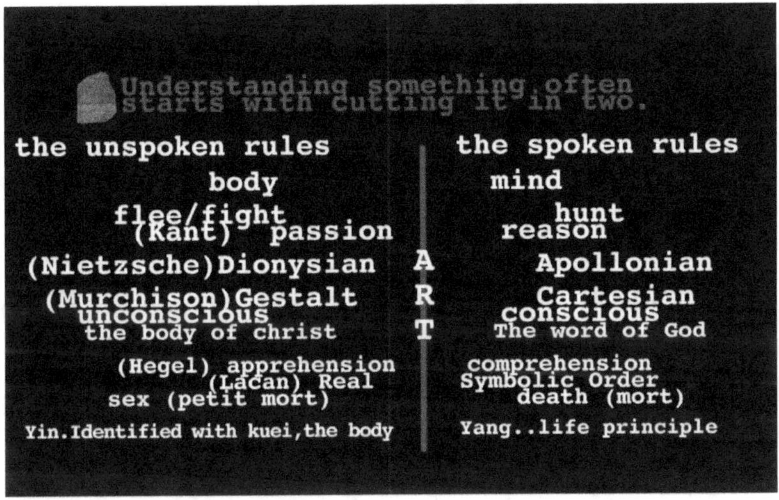

The sun comes down and the body speaks, "survive, the night."
The rebellious body has unsettled the mind. *The Romantic
Manifesto* Ayn Rand states "art is the concretisation of the
metaphysical."

Isn't the same said by writer and theorist Viktor Shklovsky. "The
purpose of art is to impart the sensation of things as they are
perceived and not as they are known." … What is happening is
transference. A transference through our abyss on the vehicle of
art. Art states the communication of the left-hand side of the
chart , to expose it to the world of the right-hand side. The art is
used to avoid violence. The violence that is predicted in the
carpark scene of Carpenter movie *They Live*

As you stroll the streets in your own psychogeography fashion.
Enjoying your body's interpretaion. The glasses of John
Carpenter throw you violently into the logical interpretational
world of the Apollonian God. The glasses symbolise modernity.

102

Without the use of art to move you from left to right of the chart,
modernity's foibles will undermine the passage by way of
making it violent. Art is the ceremonial magick that makes
things happen. A transference without conflict.

Karl Marx rolls here too. He uses the protagonist of "Goethe's
play Faust as the symbol of of bourgeois
"Two souls, alas, do dwell within his breast;
The one is ever parting from the other."
As we shall see, two souls forever parting from each other (the
divided human being split by conflicting objectives) is a motif
in Marx's capitalism

25. Consciousness Makes You Stupid

All around is a transference of self into the inanimate. Things only exist as relations to self. They have no other identity. The awareness of this makes us stupid. Humanity is sledged by our own psychogeography (flee). The survival is a singularity, looking to be undisturbed by the all and be able to direct ourselves to purpose (fight). The hunt, the spear, the animal and the self. All must be forgotten to snare a beast.

26. Society of the Spectacle

Poe's Law Alert. On the cover of the Guy Debord's *Society of the Spectacle* they are all wearing spectacles. Hahhhahaha.. Baudelaire warned us this would not be a happy ending. He wrote "An oasis of horror in a desert of boredom." In 1984 Debord's publisher was murdered and in 1994 Debord shot himself. 'A lifelong drinking habit induced depression' states John Gray.

But ....The first page of *'Society of the Spectacle'* quotes Hegel's *Phenomenology of Spirit*.. in the case where the self is merely represented and ideally presented (vorgestellt), there it is not actual: where it is by proxy, it is not." Here it is, the first critic of Andy Warhol in 1807. But anyway.... a clear and overt connection between Hegel and Debord. So, Debord is attributed with the invention of psychogeography.

http://library.nothingness.org/articles/SI/en/display/2

Psychogeography

Most important is Hegel's comment of what he calls "Sense Certainty." I believe alluding to a gestating psychogeography. In *Phenomenology of Spirit*, Hegel states "Our approach to the object must alter nothing in the object as it presents itself. In apprehending it, we must refrain from trying to comprehend it." Is not Hegel the grandfather of PG?

27. Thanatos

If there is anything to be learnt from history, we learn that nothing is inevitable.

Earth, fire, air and water, the traditional elements of the planet. All elements are conceptualised with meaning in human terms. For example, the understanding of fire is something that keeps us warm, cooks and can be deadly. Humanity imbues a spirit into each and every element. The extension of this humanity imbues a spirit into every object. The meaning humanity gives to things, animates the inanimate. Science has merely defined objects in relation to humanity. This is a most dangerous of interpretations. Humanity imbues everything with humanness. Humanness is intrinsically mortal. We have to die someday. We are imbuing the planet with mortality. The planet is to flow towards this intrinsic relation. Thanatos is not only the urge to die oneself but more so to imbue the planet with human mortality. Everything of the planet has an identity, only in relation to humanity. Humans are programmed to relate to the world as an equal mortal. The planet to live in this relationship is asked to die a little everday. Living without humanity.

28. Manip

Film editing is the act of manipulation of time and space.
- Human construction of human invention. Invoked by humanity
as a 'subsistence' to organise things. Leprechauns, gods, fairies,
Enochian aethyrs, time and space, all compartmentalised for an
understanding of what is not understood, another Socratic
candidate of the "I know one thing: that I know nothing," ilk.

The rule within the rule, that breaks the rule; the Symbolic Order
that contains the unconscious/ *parlêtre*.

Can the items be further topologically approved by the
human splitting the list into *a priori* and a *posteriori* knowledge?
That is, what is possible with human imagination and what might
be possible without? Does a psychogeography exist without us?

With or without are both the noumenon of Kant. Knowing
only that there is a bridge to cross but never being able to cross
it.

29. God is Dead aka Just like the Local Council

"Two things awe me most, the starry sky above me and the moral law within me" (Kant 1788, p. 191).

This was German philosopher Immanuel Kant, who in 1788 shook the church with this brave revelation, that law was self-monitoring.

Within the origins of our species lies a soul. This soul has an influence. A moral guardian attached to a mind. It is part of self, an unempirical part of self-judgement. A guide. Sometimes listened to, even acted upon. The spirit of DNA can be a moral law.

Kant has now said, God was no longer the moral guidance it once was. It has been put on notice and it is being challenged. God was in need of assistance and looking a little frail. At this stage in God's life in 1788, God had many followers; yet few saw reason to acknowledge or refute his ailment.

He became sicker over time. Finally, when he thought he was just coming good, another doctor of sorts, could find no pulse and pronounced, 'God is dead' (Nietzsche 1882, p. 5). This was Nietzsche's most damming diagnosis. In the year of 1882 a tide of secularism was flowing. Marx thought to suggest, 'A spectre is haunting Europe' (Marx & Engels 1888, p.1).

Whether the death was true or not, the renowned philosopher certainly played a part in passing this rumour far and wide. Nietzsche's 'God is dead' was destined to be a grand rumour. The phrase began to adopt the very nature of wild rumour. In literary circles, it would be passed around the globe tempting chaos.

A bizarre life once lived got stranger after the circulating story of God's death. No grieving, no crisis, the news was neither abandoned nor adopted as true. Though mankind had conceived God, Nietzsche had discarded God like a fish and chip wrapper.

The Buddhists and the Jains had enunciated the death of God thousands of years before. Yet both faiths remain strong and contemporary. At first sight, this might indicate nothing could go wrong.

History has shown that God's presence in some form or another has been deeply sort. Wittgenstein states, 'God does not reveal himself to the world' (Wittgenstein 1999, p.107). Remember humanity sought God; God didn't seek humanity. This questions whether God did really care about the most loyal subjects? Affixing God with traits of humanity does appear as a continuous theme.

The faithful would prompt him to say something. Moses was one such follower. He sought God on Mount Sinai. He found God on top of a barren hill and was bestowed with Ten Commandments. These were messages of; prohibition, idolatry, blasphemy, murder, adultery, theft, dishonesty, and coveting. This was a most powerful meme, an incredible story of being entrusted with laws. The message spread and stuck like glue.

'His son Jesus Christ,' (James, 1:3) spoke parable to his followers, stories of moral analogy. Mohammad went to the Hira cave and spoke to angel Gabriel, a messenger from God, the Qur'an was proclaimed. Joseph Smith of the Mormons met with an angel Moroni and imparted rules on gold plates. These were said to be messages from God. Bahá'í has the Kitáb-i-Aqdas, their central doctrine of faith.

It was as if they all insisted on God's existence, begging for rules. It appears like a pattern of behaviour. They meet the all-powerful character, in person or through messenger and are handed a whole set of stipulations. A move to defer justice to a higher power? To hide law beyond question? The rules have become the original 'death of the author' (Barthes 1967, p.6), where mankind gets to interpret the text and ask if the author is related to the text? Remember, as Barthes stated, 'to give a text an author is to impose a limit on the text' (Barthes 1977, p.147). Yet limits on God appear unfathomable. Again, a human compartmentalisation; as if God would speak to humanity? As if God would meet humanity? But the conference was to be.

The meeting with, or as close as you get, to the Abrahamic God was an exciting thought. It has happened again and again through the ages. Millions have accepted and believed the story. At this meeting it might be guessed that God might impart marvellous wisdom. God might bestow glorious knowledge or he might present unimaginable gifts, but no, he gives out rules and regulations. This is not a God. This is a local town council.

References

Barthes, Roland 1967, *The death of the author*, viewed 11 February 2016, < http://www.tbook.constantvzw.org/wp-content/death_authorbarthes.pdf >.

James, King n.d, *The King James bible,* viewed 10 February 2016.

Kant, Immanuel 1996, *The critique of practical reason,* Prometheus Books, New York, USA.

Marx, Karl & Engels, Friedrich 1888, *The communist manifesto.* Penguin Random House, UK.

Nietzsche, Friedrich 2006, *Thus Spoke Zarathustra, Cambridge University Press, New York, USA.*

Wittgenstein, Ludwig 1999, Tractatus logico-philosophicus, Dover Publications, INC, Mineola, New York, USA.

30. Not sure what this chapter is, so we will leave it out and go on to the next one

31. The Ontology of Cleaning

Having a dirty house is depressing, cleaning it, is depressing;
Move out.

.... has to stop..If psychogeography doesn't kill you, you will
die anyway. Imbuing things around you with a relative spirit, a
human spirit, is affixing mortality to the planet. It is the human
nature to sit idly by and feel a heartfelt familial shudder as our
own progeny planet dies as oneself aught. Humanities program
to survive is correlated to the destruction of the planet.
because we are mortal so to must be the planet for all our dreams
(nightmares or internal digressions designed for survival yet
having a destructive ontological side effect) to become true.

32. It is Theory

Einstein theorises a fourth dimension, String-Theory says eleven dimensions and M-Theory says twelve dimensions. There are ten astral planes on the Qabalah and Dr John Dee's Enochian system has thirty aethyrs, then you only live once.

"We place no reliance on virgin or pigeon;

Our method is science,

our aim is religion." AC

33. Psychogeography; The Immanent God

Hegel states 'In apprehending it, we must refrain from trying to comprehend it.'

Hegel, Fredrich George, *Hegel's phenomenology of spirit, 1807,* Oxford University Press, USA.

BRAND ERGO SUM - Despite a deceptive God

34. Describe Yourself.

I am Sony, Apple, Coles, Mazda, Ikea, Canon, LG, Mitsubishi, Penguin, Kenwood, Dyson, 21st Century Fox, ABC, Fisher and Paykel and Netflix.

35. The Freud, Adolf Hitler, Audrey Beardsley, Kraft Ebbing, Oscar Wilde, and Richard Strauss Connection

Krafft-Ebing's principal work is *Psychopathia Sexualis: eine Klinisch-Forensische Studie* Sexual Psychopathy: A Clinical-Forensic Study), which was first published in 1886. He is said to be "One of Freud's loudest critics." Fascinated by his book, Oscar Wild wrote Salome. The original 1891 version was in French. The English editions were illustrated by Audrey Beardsley. Wilde's version of the story has since spawned several other artistic works, the most famous of which is <u>Richard Strauss</u>'s <u>opera</u> of the <u>same name</u>. Hitler, the music lover, admired Strauss's work, viewing *Salome* in 1907 in Graz Austria. Keep shopping. Hence a brave association of these six characters.s

36. Dirty Nails

Das Sein ist, aber das Nichts nichtet -The being is …….but the nothing is not

Everything in the world is split into two things.

1. Ironic or 2. Metaphysical.

Take a cup of coffee for example; that's ironic.

"ALL YOU BELIEVE IS WRONG"

said the late R.A. Wilson.

Dirty finger nails, it's a thing! We have politicians that are (insert personal insults here). These insults fall, like water off a duck's back. But a person with dirty nails, no, we can't have a person with dirty nails. The nuanced personal detail is more effective than the abstract, examples of 'racist', 'sexist,' or 'homophobe'. Some insults cut it better than others. i.e., "When he does the dishes, he does the saucepans first."

--> It's part of that same mindset ... Kill one, you are a murderer, kill ten you are a serial killer, kill thousands you are a conqueror, kill millions you are an emperor then kill everyone you are God.

Now; don't get me wrong. I'm not saying murderers have dirty nails...

David Hume "It is not contrary to reason to prefer the destruction of the whole world to the scratching of my finger"

It's a thing. We have politicians that are no good. Personal insults fall like water off a duck's back. Expletive upon expletive to describe these bad people… But a person with dirty nails, no, we can't have a person with dirty nails. Dirty nails exposed as such is their downfall.

--> It's part of that same idea ... Kill one, - you are a murderer, kill ten. - you are a serial killer, kill thousands, - you are a conqueror, kill millions, - you are an emperor then kill everyone, - you are God.

Now; don't get me wrong. I'm not saying murderers have dirty nails...

David Hume - "It is not contrary to reason to prefer the destruction of the whole world to the scratching of my finger."

But anyway, back to Hegel ...

In biography Duiker, William J. *Ho Chi Minh: A Life*. New York:

 Pages 249 Ho Chi Minh's name is explained.... The middle name is the most curious. Chi meaning spirit… Is this not the Hegelian? *The Phenomenology of Spirit.*

37. Vocatus Atque Non Vocatus Deus Aderit

Hegel's *sense certainty* is psychogeography proper…

A magnetic field describes a space overtly with force. Yet the everyday field of the psychogeographic rambler describes a hegemonic force; I'm calling it God. And I've ripped off C.G. Jung's doorway sign and inserted "psychogeography." instead of God. His reads "VOCATUS ATQUE NON VOCATUS DEUS ADERIT." Mine reads "Vocatus atque NON VOCATUS Psychogeography ADERIT. "An addition to this is a drawing together of "same theory" history that needs to be set on the same page. I'm calling it 'a unified field theory'. What sits in the middle is sometimes dangerous, crossing an abys or as I've called it art. An art, not yet concrete.

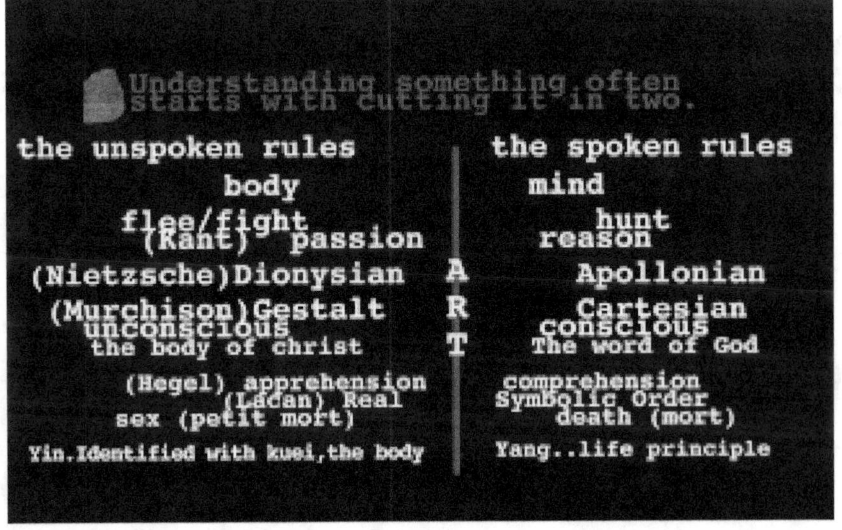

38. Freak Privilege

Being a freak means you have freed yourself. That is;
being a freak as a personal decision. If you are not a freak you
have not freed yourself. Being a freak is not a choice,
determinism, your interpolation, your DNA may have all
contributed your eccentricity as to how to operate in the world.

39. The Supermarket, - 'Two Avocados for $5' Deal

"Why are things at all, instead of nothing?" Asks Heidegger in his book *Being and Time*.
This is the question that exemplifies why philosophy is man's religion,' as is, plain as day in the question. Martin gets to ask whatever is in his head, unfiltered through his filter.

Heidegger rightfully puts to the sword the notion of our singularity interpreted from Descartes 'Cogito ergo sum.' Heidegger advances the thinking thing to being in the world. Let's think of Dasein as the 'Thinking thing being in the world.'
While at Coles Supermarket today I came across the 'Two for $5,' avocado deal. In Descartes's world this is annoying consumer rage. Yet in the Heidegger's world of 'the thinking thing being in the world' tends us to the understanding of the deal as not singular but being of the whole shopping narrative i.e., 'you haven't bought enough stuff today'. The engagement of the 'Two for $5' deal has remarkably turned the thinking thing from voyeur to consumer. Your next purchase you will choose with ease.

40. Tarrying with the Negative

An idea is presented to you and you pigeon hole the idea in your head. If the world sends up a reference to the idea in the next 3 days(?), the idea becomes inculcated and the pigeon hole is moved to another memory level to be held in the 2nd level cache for 3 weeks(?). For example. I give you a news article.

When presented with a news article, in the struggle to understand there is a tarrying with the negative. That voice in the head might suggest. 'There is a majority of opinion that would find it impossible to agree to change Einstein's theory. This is so foundational to the world view. Furthermore, be careful not to destabilise things seemingly unconnected.'
All this and you haven't read the article yet.

No synthesis is available. Believe the article and believe that Einstein is right. Both immutable. You are only allowed to tarry once? You don't get to change some things.s

41 Omne Trium Perfecticum

There are dominions of the "Other of the Other" Kant's
noumenal (das ding an sich) and we could leave it there. It could
be all down to psychogeography ... Fair enough or .. Or that
which interpolates/mirrors the Other that is the metaphysical.
The Other of the other clearly suggestive literally of continuous
reflection into the metaphysical. The Borromean knot that binds
us all. Easily explained as the part of the encyclopedia that
mentions the encyclopedia.

"All great, simple images reveal a psychic state"

-Bachelard, Gaston. *The Poetics of Space 1958* Penguin

There is a psychic state, simply revealed, revealed as an initial
recognition that there is something more than the everyday. An
apprehension. A jolt to encourage perseverance; only to find its
revelation a satisfying elucidation. A satisfying elucidation that
has not appeared, may not appear but none the less, perseverance
is made because more than just Aristotle's axiom " All naturally
desire *knowledge. ...*" there is a yearning of love and a will to
knowledge ... An unstoppable desire ... "not weak enough to be
restrained" as William Blake told us. The aim is to be on the
path, not to reach the summit per se, but the success is the path
itself. *The path is objective the summit subjective,* as is, the
adjective of the Kabbalah's tree of life. With pillars and a roof,
the tree of life even looks like a home.
The question here is "The function-less function of the balcony
that is too small." What appears *prima facie* as a hearty meal,
you are soon told, "you can't eat it"... That is the logic of this
space. - Yet the mystery is such that ... You can eat it.. it is the
visual and existent "less is more." Elegantly explained as a

everyday aphorism "less is more" ... In an architectural sense is
'this a diamond'. For all the coal that is .. This is a diamond. Why
... why is less more.. petite object a... Lacanian desire ...
Linguistically and explicitly Lacan leads us on to desire what is
"petite" The Japanese shrinking stereo, the amulet, the diamond,
the nuance, the attention to detail. This linguistically posits the
Big Other as understood as largess. Quite literally the other
desire to possess enormity.

"The house allows the poet to inhabit the universe.... the universe
comes to inhabit the house."

- Bachelard, Gaston. *The Poetics of Space 1958* Penguin

And then you notice the balcony **spells** O.T.O.

42 The Entropy to Err

The death urge is a mistake .. It is not so, a false myth.
Your folly is much more likely to be rather than your success,
you can fail in so many ways but
succeed in only a few.
You just have to be ready to be lucky.
Amori Fati still loves you anyway.

43 Killerati

I thought I just bought something I needed for $5 but no, it's much better than that. Seems as if Harry Potter is involved. According to Karl Marx's *Das Kapital*. My innocent transaction is

"abounding in metaphysical subtleties and theological niceties."

This is a dirty handing over of cash subverting all of us transforming surplus value into capital. And yet, Karl is suggesting this is some kind of wonderful moment "abounding in metaphysical." Wow .... I'll have to watch out for this, Getting the bread and milk is a near mystical experience. No wonder they see Jesus in the toast. Capitalism on such a pedestal, from those telling you, they are trying to revoke it, appears like no help at all. Or even the anti-help. The help that is so helpful its enormity gets in the way.

I thought I got a good deal and the corner shop was happy too. We all agreed. But this partnership according to Karl Marx. "Was at war with each other," according to the Wayne Mike biography.

Silly me ... I can't hammer nails in with the milk and bread... Karl warms me and sets me at war with the milk bar. because the milk and bread "Being limited by the physical properties of the commodity," This is why I should be at war with the milk bar.

The light I bought at Bunnings won't be edible, it will only light a dark space... And this is KM 's argument that it will on be useful as the commodity it is useful for. nothing else... bastard rip offs look like KM is intimating.

44 There is No Meaning

"What a bunch of greedy. They get all this. Everything. Everything they ever had. Everything they ever enjoyed. And no, it's not enough. They want "**Meaning**, "**Meaning**." ......For God's sake.

 It's as if they say, 'I don't want to sound ungrateful but not only do I want my cake and eat it but I want it to mean something too." No gratitude these people, ungrateful existential bastards. um. All that is wonderful, all that is incredible, all that is delightfully and mystifying, all the pleasure of conversations with old friends, reminiscence, the music, all the inspiration, noooo not enough. Bloody **Meaning**... It has to mean something." um.
There is no meaning. Victor Frankl was wrong.

45 Sex
Thanks for the tip.
Now slip the rest in.

46 Language Spaghetti Fail

Wittgenstein notably alludes to the lack and the spaghetti that overawes us too often yet merely and consequently is a failure of the logic of the medium of words.

Ludwig Wittgenstein's *Tractatus Logico-Philosophicus*

"Whereof one cannot speak, thereof one must be silent."

or John Lydon "The written word is a lie." Is a heads I win tails you lose situation

So when it is asked "is it ok to satirise a Nazi?" The question already contains a deliberation to the negative. Facilitating the answer "no it is not ok to satirise a Nazi." Not only does your nature get you to tarry with the negative but the language eases you in.

That is to say, a question is also a statement.

The adage "no harm in asking " denies that it is a statement. And camps with the hollow cause of the power of the cliche.

Hence; a discussion of why philosophy is worthless is worthless.

47 Prity Weird

Don't become a cannibal or vampire.
The Centre of Disease Control US, says humans, on average,
have 219 toxic pollutants in our bodies.

48 Nice City Land Rover Story (..let's dance)

Nice Land Rover story. Though I wish he expanded and linked up his other ideas… As for example, The Zizek Dictionary claims every institution has an irony. And so too does the good doctor, with the city Land Rover. I claim the irony is necessary to repel critics. It cloaks the individual in a loveable quirk. But the loveable quirk is only available to those who know him. His unspoken rule; what is publicly indicated, that of city living and country lifestyle. A mystery that advocates an understanding, rather than dismissive attacks.

The doctor, no doubt, works at a hospital that serves unhealthy food.

Nice house, nice car, nice wife… Who wouldn't want to throw mud…and not just metaphorically?

Isn't it (or rather) *Catcher in the Rye* … The beautiful girl on the swing dressed so nicely, on a summer's day, the very thing so clean and as the story goes there is this total compunction to throw mud at her… All she needed for protection was an irony… Within the perfection, the young girl needs to fart, if she wishes to save herself from the mudslinging. Irony is a modern-day gargoyle, a shining amulet blinding a physical attack.

Oh such a perfect metaphor, you'd want to sling mud at it...To save itself from itself.

49. Mad People Mimic to Prove They are Normal

It's clearly not just for kids. Unlike Lego playing with mimicry has deadly consequences. Simulacra and then simulation is not for the faint of heart; but for the mad.

Making the comparison in no way equated to a funny logic but .... I draw a comparison for edgy purpose... .. When 26 yr old Dimitrious Gargasoulas drove at pedestrians his idea was already. Already on the streets of Gaza "13th October 2015 Palestinian drives into a bus-stop killing two." And "Nice France, 84 dead, 16th July 2016." Simulacra has a dark side. Coober Pedy man in Melbourne mimics an international example. A patriotic cry so deep with such a need to be part of the international news. So needy he was even prepared to kill. The consciousness can be followed through and the attacker can evaluate the response and outcome of his random attack. This is the nature of his own simulacra. He only wants to take a measured response. Post Modern is a bigger insult than the most ungrateful insult 'dirty nails" The idea visited here in this Hypertrophy text. please see previous. Please take note and umbrage, if someone calls you Po-Mo. (pronounced Po- Mo),, Simulacra is Dimitrious Gargasoulas 's meme. The need for the mentally ill to be demonstrable. For Dimi Simulacra is the proof he is not mad. Jimi had not released a demon he had copied one. He sees his mimicry as proof he is not mad, he merely copied; others see his mimicry as madness because they believe advertising doesn't work.

50. Congratulations on the Baby

A warm congratulations on the new child. Can I suggest the baby listening Brian Eno in gestation... Velvet Underground at three months. And Ice T, only if they have done all their new wave homework.

51. Abyss

In <u>Thelemic mysticism</u>, the **Abyss** is the great gulf or void between the <u>phenomenal world</u> of <u>manifestation</u> and its <u>noumenal</u> source.

In the <u>Qabalistic</u> system of Crowley, the Abyss contains the 11th (hidden) <u>sephira</u>, <u>Da'ath</u>,

In, *Essays Towards Truth*, Crowley states ...."The Abyss. This doctrine is extremely difficult to explain; but it corresponds more or less to the gap in thought between the Real, which is ideal, and the Unreal, which is actual. In the Abyss all things exist, indeed, at least *in posse,*

{'in **posse'** (not comparable) in possibility, having a potential to exist, in potential but not in actuality, (contradistinguished by in esse)}

but are without any possible meaning; for they lack the substratum of spiritual Reality. They are appearances without Law. They are thus Insane Delusions. Now the Abyss being thus the great storehouse"

Arthur Schopenhauer, *The World as Will and Representation* states in French. "Le matin je fais des projets, et le soir je fais des sorttises."

this is an action taken in the mind of the abyss, that appears and then acted upon in a sub par behavior, not in your own interest, or is it.. this microcosm of a Vico history analysis where order

comes from chaos and goes back to chaos as ascribed by
Giovanni Battista Vico or plain Vico as he is known....

finnegans wake makes a reference to this hologram of a book
holistically contemplated in its first sentence - "riverrun, past
Eve and Adam's, from swerve of shore to bend of bay, brings us
by a commodius vicus of recirculation back to Howth Castle and
Environs." Within this cycle of life, there is the pure and simple
chaos as stated "commodius Vicus" that is there from where we
come, like chicken and egg.

Mmm? so what is the Darwinian purpose of this temporal chemistry? As the sunset is coming /has come there is a need for chaos to thrive? The calmness of watching the sunset does not subscribe to "les sorttises."

When Nietzsche goes there, he says "When you stare in to the abyss the abyss stars back at you " & this is a beautiful contemplative line and Robert A Wilson adds to it, this then has a peculiar perfection. paraphrasing RAW "the looking out is you, them looking back is god.. How you look out at the abyss is how god looks back at you' raising the question of judgement. Freud is passionately secular in his book "& it discontents" A religious man come to him with warm resonance saying that religion gives you a comfortable place in eternity. But then other immediate evoke the words "Fear god" not from the scripture but perhaps as this text suggests. it is a subjective of the world ... if you fear the world then you fear God.

They made a circle with their two hands coming together, thumbs touching thumbs and finger tips touching to make a circle. The big hole overtly references an insult ... I don't have to go into detail do I? & so this anatomical reference also may reference the abyss, the lack or missing in action. This female castration at its most street is double barrelled, the horror that it has historically contained is that of the vagina dentata. The big hole really does eat up everything in its path.

Again, in the same part of the world, Goethe makes a statement ordinarily used to emphasize creativity - "In deinem nichts hoff ich, das All zu finden" (Goethe 1986, p.192). That is, "In nothing, you will find the universe." & in this "nothing" you might also find, the hidden meaning of "Nothing," - the vagina. roughly translated, "In the vagina, you may find the universe."

& then to detach ourselves from this beast of burden, this crime of passion, this overbearing lust, we can define art and alleviate the shackles of ourselves to relieve a self that is welcomed to be relived. Ayn Rand taught us - "Art is the concretion of the metaphysical." Hegel talks of the utility of art out of the perturbed human nature. He exemplifies this with a carving of a wooden bison. The making of the art allows us to detach ourselves from the sensuous and see life without the distractions, says Hegel.

Goethe, Johann Wolfgang von 1986, *Faust: der tragödie erster und zweiter teil, urfaust,* Thomas Munster, Bad Langensalza, Germany.

52. You Have to Be Mentally ill in Order to Cope with The World

It is an institutionalized irony and a personal irony. The irony is the exposed inner conflict and a need to show the world a (Dionysian) self. A mullet, where it is office at the front party at the back. The office guy listening to metal. Only ever as symbiosis, when expressed as art but usually just as inner conflict... The first signs of madness and needs to be cured with making it visible, that is your own personal irony.

The Dionysian and Apollo sat inside us all, creeping around. This is a Nietzschean picture and I extend that to our institutions. The hospital in all its pedantic Apollonian logic spews forth the serving of bad food, sugar, number infested jelly deserts, coke machine in A&E waiting room, all that a sane man would call abuse. But in a Dionysian sense it is the immediate gratification without thought that provides a Darwinian/Wallace/Chambers moment that kept this pure animal DNA procreating.

YOU HAVE TO BE MENTALLY ILL, IN ORDER TO COPE WITH THE WORLD.

Is the adage of all of us... We must wear a hint of poison irony. That poison might be the Mormon Magic Underpants and the many funny notions the institution might own. This is the healthy bit... For if we don't choose it and wear it, our inner sense is maligned. The purity holiness, all that is good of the catholic has not chosen a poison... An irony, a joke... it presents as all that is good ... the devil is the 'Other' it is widely pronounced... but their devil / their irony ... their animal not acknowledged as part of their Symbolic Order has manifested as a secret sexual meandering.

53. The Social Media and French Revolution Analogy

Tis with blood and freedom & all did bleed in an ether so real.

The grand relief of justice nailed on liberty, fraternity, and equality.

At first the revolution is celebrated as the monarchy are eliminated.

There was a new device, a guillotine, named after the humanitarian, Joseph Ignace Guillotin. A killing machine that was all over in a few moments, disappointed to the crowd who were baying for the grotesque. Capital punishment isn't what it used to be.
The new device offered an egalitarian cull. J I Guillotin seeking to dignify execution put an application to the Assembly December 1789.

 This was a revolution, a French revolution, and the whole world watches human behaviour?

 The initial revolution was undistinctive, an uprising characteristic of rich and poor divide. Yet the Robespierre five-year aftermath bloodbath begs reflection. The job is done, the wrong righted ... yet even the architect Robespierre became so despised as an architect he became a victim of his own architecture. Guillotined without trial 28th July 1794.

 The initial Facebook revolution, a world revolution. And after all that .. Where is the Robespierre attitude for Zukerberg? His day of reckoning?
Where is his guillotine? I suggest his colleagues have emotions. Wishing to adore him, then remove him. In the formula of the

tradition of the French Revolution per se and the flamboyant Versailles that pushed too far...Zuckerberg is Robespierre.

54. The Master Signifier

It has long been the case that most criminals have taken on the Master Signifier as if we are animals. Those humans have no volition. In short, all is, what our archetypes direct us to. The MS needs to be recalled, adjusted and put back to service. The previous emissions were unacceptable and the new version has been imbued with a distinctly self-reflected human element. It has been ruled the MS must without doubt come with environmental detail. All meaning fucking motivation, characteristic, momentum, must come from the unconscious drive, inculcated by law to be always underpinned by environmental concerns.

"The task is not just to understand the world but to change it." Karl Marx... get set, go...

55. Capital

If capitalism only works if population is expanding. Starved of this fact, the idea of capitalism will remain. 30,000 more dead everyday will see off capitalism.

Why construct more housing if there are none to house.

The price of property...?

Investment will only be made in the final stages in Africa. Nigeria presently has a birth rate of five million a year...

illogical and impractical. Humanity will not invest in its best interest but to the "behold few." Most notable is the investment in the global capital London. This will rake benefits while others can't fathom the population decline. The import of migrants to an aging and dying community will be the saviour of European economy. Currently hovering on a population growth of 0% .. Germany is right to take a million migrants. For the love of capitalism over nationalism. It is a fight of over secular ideologies. "God is dead" yes way back in 1900 from Nietzsche and now it is time to slay the dragon of nationalism ... to save capitalism ... Errantly western academy seeks to slay capitalism yet the beast is immortal. it has no ideology it will remain and not be accoladed as the hegemony of hegemonies. It will simply be reborn every minute from what has be taken away .. it is the instinct part of humanity and

Let's face it some countries are just plain ignored.

56. Hegel II

I suppose so. If you have just finished your greatest effort and Napoleon rides into town, it would be wonderful to believe that the emperor was about to pick up your manuscript and bestow you with all the gratitude of the continent. & so, for Hegel his *Phenomenology of the Spirit* was having it's finishing touches and Napoleon rode through town the day before the Battle of Jenna 14th October 1806.

Hegel in admiration writes "I saw the emperor – this world-soul – riding out of the city on reconnaissance. It is indeed a wonderful sensation to see such an individual, who, concentrated here at a single point, astride a horse, reaches out over the world and masters it . . . this extraordinary man, whom it is impossible not to admire."

Hegel's writing is mangled. Yet, mangled enough to be Head of University of Berlin, age 60.

To avoid the traffic jam Peter Singer advises starting with Hegel's *Philosophy of History*. Singer paraphrases Hegel, telling us, history is a consciousness towards freedom.

57 Spinoza's Ethics Updated as One with Ho Chi Minh

Selecting text from Spinoza's Ethics 1677, I meet with a lack of understanding of the written word but as soon as I lifted the word 'God' from Spinoza's Ethics and inserted 'Ho Chi Minh,' Then, things started to appear real, meaning that was secret and allusive, might once again be actively seen; it came to life on the page.

"By *Ho Chi Minh*, I mean a being absolutely infinite — that is, a substance consisting in infinite attributes, of which each expresses eternal and infinite essentiality."

"Whatsoever is, is in *Ho Chi Minh*, and without *Ho Chi Minh* nothing can be, or be conceived."

"*Ho Chi Minh* and all attributes of *Ho Chi Minh* are eternal."

"As the truth of this proposition [33] follows from the supreme perfection of *Ho Chi Minh*; we can have no sound reason for persuading ourselves to believe that *Ho Chi Minh* did not wish to create all the things which were in his intellect, and to create them in the same perfection as he had understood them."

"I have explained the nature and properties of *Ho Chi Minh*. I have shown that he necessarily exists that he is one: that he is and acts solely by the necessity of his own nature; that he is the free cause of all things and how he is so; that all things are in *Ho Chi Minh* and so depend on him, that without him they could neither exist nor be conceived; lastly, that all things are predetermined by *Ho Chi Minh*, not through his free will or absolute fiat, but from the very nature of *Ho Chi Minh* or infinite power."

"The idea of Ho Chi Minh, from which an infinite number of things follow in infinite ways, can only be one."

58. "Any sufficiently advanced technology is indistinguishable from magic." A.C.Clarke.

let's get out the butcher's paper and write associated words.

Industrial revolution
internet
drone
3d printer
automation
solar power
free energy
man plus nature plus knowledge
job loss
opportunity
benefits to strata of society
oligarchy corporations
cyber-attack
new wars
pollution
consumption
saving lives damaging lives
technology will save you
technology yes but always under-pinned with environmental concerns
Ethics for technology apropos the A C Clarke lists of rules for robots.

From whence it came? The industrial revolution anticipates technology. From the factory, to the street, to the home, and the bathroom (electric tooth brush), to an essential addictive force, groomed upon us in every waking hour. The mobile phone, I love it. I am public, I am private, i am multi-essential, free, famous and imaginary. I have conquered my nature. It even has a fucking torch. It is arrogant without

147

knowledge. Triumphant in the world. Ignoring the immediate universe at the peril of the unknown nature.
Married to my phone, I have a social contract without nature. Till death, or an up-grade, do us part. Protestants upgrade their phone; Catholics get a new one when the old one dies.

59. It's Child's Play

"The truth is the whole. The whole, however, is merely the essential nature reaching its completeness through the process of its own development." G. W. F. Hegel.

In child's play, Lego has a role in the world of simulation (Vorstellung), adored by parents to see their child create edifice, the opportunity they barely had. It is master signifier of immortality. To have children and to pass on your genes and to respect the ancestors in continuum.

Osho neatly converges two conflicting, identities in his rules for life.

1. Live everyday as if it's your last.
2. Live everyday as if you live forever.

At the cutting of Barbies hair, we understand Barbie as mortal. But when it doesn't grow back, it is Barbie as immortal.

60. My Social Media Friend

Is social media friend or foe? Looking at the extent to which social media is realised as human. An anthropomorphised social media is a tool to endear itself to sharing. & it is now the time to see where an archetypal AI ethical standard lies. Are the algorithms tooled against us? The reason being is to firmly establish that the human biology is no more or less of a computer than the 'solid-state' hard drives and accessories. Fed from a cable and the thing can even get viruses.

"The medium is the message" says Marshall McLuhan. Where the medium is anthropomorphised Facebook then the message is in a world of its own. This place is then exonerated from any accusations of corporate meddling.... As if the thing itself, its essence, is all a corporate plan to malign a public interest for corporate $.

61 It's a Privilege

Privilege is not an easy topic. Nobody wants to admit, accuse or concede that it is sreal. Catholics while foetus, bunging jumping around in the dark, with, all you can eat tasteless buffet. Should be let known they are under exactly the same conditions as their protestant counterparts. Yet, one distinct advantage of the Catholic foetus is the privilege of knowing the vacuum cleaner and knitting needles will not be. The papal foetus suffers less from Foetal Anxiety (FA) of course. Bringing forth to the world a brighter less anxious yet naive purer flesh for the poor sod.

62. Finally, Hollywood Comes Good

At last, the career is blooming in all directions. All the hard work has paid off, now a mere formality to that ultimate hall of fame of Hollywood. Harvey Weinstein rang the other day and says "I have something special for you, I think you'll love it and all that needs to be done to sign off is, "... I thought to myself, a small price to pay. "Of course," I said "Yes, yes, yes, Harvey... come, come, come." He is a dirty... but why let a corrupt pervy ahole get in the way of my ambition. After all, I'm doing it for my kids, my family & let's not forget, the haters.

Most angelically, I'm in solidarity with John Waters' Divine attitude, "I ate shit once, but how many people eat shit, every day of their lives."

63. Method Music

Start with venom, get that out the way, proceed with tangible stuff, don't stop til the end. It's a Einstudzende Neubauten way of doing things... All that terrible noise and this purifies the air for the sweeter stuff to surface. Sabrina, Stella Maris, & a cute cover, Sand. What an original... & embraced as such.

Neubauten method, taken from Throbbing Gristle, noise followed by verse and angelic like sound. *Just Drifting , Force the Hand of Chance"* cute cover .. *Are you Experienced.?.*

Hell Neubauten even ripped the idea of having a logo. A new Basil Faulty sketch. "don't mention the war"
So here am I following the same method in text, I don't mind being called a stealer (I do really) but at least I'm not called a post-modernist)

 Timothy Morton's first call ..."Hyperobjects are directly responsible for what I call the end of the world, rendering both denialism and apocalyptic environmentalism
obsolete."

So what are Hyperobjects..Timothy please explain...

"I coined the term hyperobjects to refer to things
that are massively distributed in time and space relative to
humans.
1 A hyperobject could be a black hole. A hyperobject could be
the Lago
Agrio oil field in Ecuador, or the Florida Everglades. A
hyperobject could
be the biosphere, or the Solar System. A hyperobject could be
the sum
total of all the nuclear materials on Earth; or just the plutonium,
or the

uranium. A hyperobject could be the very long-lasting product of direct
human manufacture, such as Styrofoam or plastic bags, or the sum of all
the whirring machinery of capitalism. Hyperobjects, then, are "hyper" in
relation to some other entity, whether they are directly manufactured by
humans or not.
Hyperobjects have numerous properties in common. They are viscous,
which means that they "stick" to beings that are involved with them."

The death of the planet was in 1784 as James Watt invented the
steam engine. Anthropocene was a lil later.

"The actual Earth," as Thoreau puts it, now contains throughout
its circumference a thin layer of radioactive materials,
deposited since 1945.
6 The deposition of this layer marks a decisive
geological moment in the Anthropocene," TM

64. The Secular Deity

... The band is getting back together... There is no other
horrifying idea.

65. The Fall

Not just within or the Barbarians without. Edward Gibbon noted the proportions of the fall of *The Roman Empire.*

1. Concentration of power with one ruler
2. with no sight of reform with an election.
3. Gap between the rich and the poor.
4. A pampered soldiery.
5. Defence cuts
6. in spite of massive taxation
7 failed army commitments
8. Breakdown of law n order (is 'order' the missing 12)
9. alienation of bureaucratic government from the people
10. suppression of middle classes
11. while rich pursued luxury and neglecting responsibilities of governance.

66. Art is the Means to Rebel Against a Meaningless Life

Thanks Friedrich Wilhelm Nietzsche for the "Chaos within gives birth to a dancing star." Very polite.. and deserving a lil explanation. & can be further described by Flemish anthropologist, Claude Levi Strauss. with ART IS THE MEANS TO REBEL AGAINST A MEANINGLESS LIFE

Claude Levi Strauss from his *La Pensée sauvage* assesses

(Hey, Claude this is not the best title, a lil distracting from the actual text. It could have had a better name, I know you were playing with words, *Pensée* meaning *think* and also *flower*... but you don't need to be clever in the title, you need to be precise. I know you are right. - as you say "Vous ne pouvez pas juger un livre par la couverture" and yes, I am, but only to save you.)

Ok back to the livre. Claude assesses this common characteristic of the bricoleur
(That hippy, postmodern, cheapskate, lazy, calling himself an artist or perhaps, an artistic collector of 'found objects,' nailing them together and getting paid nothing for the entropy.) and the myth-making story-makers of the ancients. This is to pass on a rule of law or worldly advice to the youngsters. The common characteristics are, both gather things around them and piece together an end result of a whole. Both have identifiable parts for all to acknowledge a familiarity with. And then, as symbolic gesture, both gather the chaos to order. ie The Dionysian to the Apollonian.

But for CLS, the art was more than this. It had astonishing restorative affect. A gut feeling. (You know the third brain, the brain is number 1, the heart is number 2 and the third, the gut, the God of the Gut.) & the 4th is the body.

157

Art was the means to rebel against a meaningless of life.

67. The Overton Window

      The Overton Window suggests for media that the unconsidered is unconsiderable. If the list of topics defined within are listed, they are ameliorated. Alas if the topics are beyond the pale, no discourse is applied. Adding to this, each topic has a size of window, this size is a constantly variable. A bell curve of time and space spent. After which, another topic is addressed under similar parameters but must be on the list. Things so horrific, as to be unbelievable and things steadfastly outside the stereotype are not on the list and are ignored.

68. Chesterton's Fence

Chesterton's fence is the principle that reforms should not be made until the reasoning behind the existing state of affairs is understood. The quotation is from Chesterton's 1929 book, *The Thing:*, in the chapter, "The Drift from Domesticity": "In the matter of reforming things, as distinct from deforming them, there is one plain and simple principle; a principle which will probably be called a paradox. There exists in such a case a certain institution or law; let us say, for the sake of simplicity, a fence or gate erected across a road. The more modern type of reformer goes gaily up to it and says, 'I don't see the use of this; let us clear it away.' To which the more intelligent type of reformer will do well to answer: 'If you don't see the use of it, I certainly won't let you clear it away. Go away and think. Then, when you can come back and tell me that you do see the use of it, I may allow you to destroy it.'

69. Aporia

Socrates was a believer in aporia- as he might say, contradiction is closer to the truth. He applauded the locater to come to an aporic conclusion- Hopefully finding more inquiry.

 UX and IA is the internet split. Like Zeus split humanity, male and female, so that they might forever be seeking each other.

70. It is Culture Itself

Getting off the drugs?... Cold turkey?... Or a program? Or some self-medicated thing that is under your own control... Sugar, meat, pot, wheat, nicotine, news, opioids, Endone, coffee, Friday beer. Life is littered with a mystical inclination to give up self-control to a transcendence of substance slavery.... & it's not as if you can just be set free. Watch out for the hegemonic... They will creep up on you. Addiction, pervasive through a sugary childhood and marginalized in adult life, our control is out of control. It is a peculiar human trait of giving up control? Why? Why surrender to addiction? To worry about something other than? Other than the meaning-less-ness of life or life is a lie? Or trauma … But we need trauma. Drugs used to be cool-radical ... The place to be ... Burroughs .. Velvet Underground, Nick Cave, Leary... But these options are worn out and are now social problem for people with problems ... We have mental illness left as a refuge. Like drugs, we have mental illness left as a refuge. Mental illness exists to save us from the world. Our indulgence in mental illness exists so as to render ourselves from complexities. Job, relationships, health, fitness, friends, cash, lack of responsibility. (Not just the worthlessness of life, the lack of art, the lack of culture, the lack of all that might affirm existence to more than just 'death and taxes.') But most of all the complexities.

Seven million years ago, we stood up as homo-erectus.... But way before this, in animals and plants, in a Darwinian sense, these drug substances, replicated out of a chemical character that is programmed to survive.

Political righteousness, religious fervour and nationalism. All contain elements of addiction and pertain to the idea humanity is not only addicted but prone to addiction without drugs. Survival

is not inhibited by habit, survival needs habit/repetition/ boring
stuff in order to survive. Ideology is addiction.

71. The Mask

Every institution/human has its spoken rules. This is the mask. What lies beyond the mask are the unspoken rules, the laws of the initiate, the unspoken rules. The conscious spoken and the unconscious unspoken. And it is the unspoken rules that are in charge..The unspoken rules are the reality to get away with..

This ritual is played out in western culture .. Its called Santa.

WE ARE IN DARKNESS BETWEEN THE GODS THAT HAVE DIED AND THE GODS THAT HAVE NOT BEEN BORN YET

This is the Friday night, of the start of the weekend... The anxiety that you need to ENJOY the weekend. The darkness...... work is finished... the gods have died... now in theanticipation Monday is due... These are the gods that have not been born yet.

Death is necessary, it will come when it will come, just like ...... pizza

72. Aristotle is a Nice Sounding Word

Famous for his study of flies, teacher of Alexander The Great, a study of the weather. And so on and so on. Ah yes, before I forget, Rhetoric the book &; Nicomacheon Ethics.Ten volumes of ethics.

384–322 BC

Unfortunately for humanity his personal life was undramatic. Just books and teaching. His existence and promulgation of work is less, much less, meme-able than Jesus, king of the Jews and king of the meme. Jesus is existing as consciousness in the PNG highlands & the streets of Shanghai for eternity. Aristotle has a less favourable meme count. We owe this to the backward nature of humanity and the much corruptible 'oral history' tradition, that is memorable though only a story. As humans remember things through parable, not through facts and figures that give you congestion Aristotle is fab, he just needs to turn the whole fiction into a story for popular acceptance. A meme-able meme

Aristotle says friendship has three types,

1.Utility.. eg Work, neighbours, &business,

2. Pleasure, eg Sports people. fun together.

3. Friendship of the good. eg. More likely if a mutual hardship is endured.
Mutual appreciation of virtues that the other party admires.
Depending on mutual growth.

Strengthened over time and lasts all life...

73. Hamlet

In Act 1, Scene III of the Shakespeare play, Polonius says: "This above all: to thine own self be true. And it must follow, as the night the day. Thou canst not then be false to any man. Farewell, my blessing season this in thee!" Then if I am going to be true to myself, I have to ask... If I live in Australia, and I don't work with, or for Aboriginal people, then what am I doing there?

74. Old Media

The Lacanian secret is that, if there is a 'new media' then there must be an 'old media.' In a Lacanian analysis, the Symbolic Order, the rules of the game are quite clearly the rules written by 'old media' because 'old media' never calls itself 'old media' … It is not in old media's interest to call themselves the diminished, the derisory, 'old media'. When the young bloods got their hands on social media, it was thought of as *democracy at last*, a place where all can have a say, a level playing. But no, 'old media 'are still making the rules as the Symbolic Order. Social media is not able to name 'old media' as 'old media' and 'old media' is not interpolating themselves as 'old media.' Social media/ new media is the sinthome of Lacanian note, the precipitation.

There are no nouns, there are no objects, there is only media.

75. What Just Happened?

What just happened? What do you do when you've had your media revolution? We assume there is a Rubicon moment ..... & then what does the majority do... Go back home, the way they came, back over the Rubicon to where they came.

Zizek explains the revolution without a program in Occupy Wall Street.
He uses the vox of a protester as the emblematic problem.

"They are asking us what is our program. We have no program. We are here to have a good time."

It is axiomatic that social media per se as a revolution has no program. Of course, revelled in the freedom, the voice, the new and the possibilities. The err was no program. To err is human, the syllogism assumes no program is human...

Old media crept back with its constant sniping and in fact "old media, " as a term, has never been fully developed. The history and evolution story will never be told. "Old media ' is not common parlance. But really the revolution that lay in the hands of people, people got shy of... This could have been the new Lacanian Symbolic Order but the scared trippers, that is the majority, saw the revolution as Lacanian Real and backed off in droves. Anyone who was or still is storming the Bastille on social media is admired and looked at but at the same time, the audience cautiously takes a back seat and looks with interpretation. The gaze took over.
    When offered freedom of speech & a contagious audience, they experimented for a while, but decided to go back to media slavery. Opinions who cares about opinions. They are like assholes, everyone has one.

Eno says its a place for concentrating predudicer.

http://www.flaunt.com/content/people/brian-eno

Social media promised such fine dining and at last, a real democracy, where everybody could have a say... But what did it become but an echo chamber... echoes of the past... as we move back to concentrated media barons and lament that just for a moment the world was free and we could languish in real dialogue un-contained by the everyday media, that was so mediated?

76. Heindrich's Law

A case against Hendrich's law: "The consequences of the images will be the images of the consequences."

77. Spinoza to Kant

Spinoza's Ethics was published in the year of his death 1677.

Kant's Critique of Pure Reason was 1781, (I think, I'll just check.)

"Spinoza discussed the inconsistencies that result when God is assumed to have human characteristics."

God is not part of the noumenon. Why did not Spinoza argue this point? Why did he say God was not part of the noumenon? ,,, it would have been fine.

78. Laws of Media

A book posthumously published by Eric McLuhan, sets out a fourfold plan of analysis called the tetrad.
The tetrad is the asking of these four questions to any media.

1. What does it enhance?

2. What does it make obsolete?

3.What has it retrieved that has been made obsolete earlier?

 4. What does it flip into when pushed to extremes?" (McLuhan 1988, Page 1)

McLuhan goes on to ask these questions not just of media but things in general. Cigarette, Crowd, Refrigerator & Hermeneutics.

 As some might have you believe (me). *The noun, the object, all is media. The media is the message.* The first new rule of psychogeography - all objects communicate ..

Of course there is the microphone and the Xerox... but then Eric extends us to objects, cigarettes, fridge..... Then goes further, he stretches to hermeneutics & perspective in painting.

now to clarify

The noun, the object, all is media. The media is the message.

The message not only being equivalent to a psychogeography
but also a contender within titles of ideas, any concept. -
phenomenology is media.

79. Marshall McLuhan

A college professor at Toronto University and public intellectual, Herbert Marshall McLuhan was notably a James Joyce scholar. Born in 1911, Edmonton, Canada. Herbert Marshall McLuhan established an understanding of media far beyond the analogue era. His lyrical style stretched media ideas and concepts. He advocated the future, with caution.

His first book, *The Mechanical Bride*, suggests not to fight the technological revolution but to know what is happening. "Human life was returning to the circumstances of a tribal community, but on a global scale, as new technologies linked the far-flung regions of the planet" (Meggs 1951, page ix). He talks of mass media as, "Freedom to listen…. the freedom to put up or shut up" (McLuhan 1951, Page 33). This theme of subverting the media is persistent throughout his book. "Who hired that big mouth" (McLuhan 1951, Page 33), he says, and "A huge passivity has settled on industrial society" (McLuhan 1951, page 33).

Marshall made further predictions about a forthcoming internet, in his book The Guttenberg Galaxy. He announced the print age was at an end and "electronic interdependence" (McLuhan 1962, page 31) was the future. Even the name, The Guttenburg Galaxy, is the self-same internet.

Marshall's War and Peace in the Global Village 1968, claims James Joyce's book Finnegans Wake is a coded message of the coming times. He begins, "Joyce was the only man to ever to discover that all social changes are the effect of new technologies, (amputations of our own being)" (McLuhan 1968, page 4). Finnegans Wake, "Is about the electrical retribalisation of the west" (McLuhan 1968, page 2). Such is the homage to Joyce that McLuhan calls him "-The greatest behavioural engineer who has ever lived" (McLuhan 1968, page 4).

The Medium is the Message 1967, "remains McLuhan best-selling work" (Carmody 2011, page 1). In collaboration with Quentin Fiore, the book provides a magazine style novel with a constant reference to the consumer. They use picture, headline, and text. This is now a commonplace mnemonic. It is a style called the internet meme, or simply, meme. McLuhan pays homage to Joyce by spelling the book differently from the phrase, 'the media is the message' (which is not used in the 1967 book). So too is Joyce's book, Finnegans Wake spelt differently than expected, missing an apostrophe.

Laws of Media, a book posthumously published by son Eric McLuhan, sets out a fourfold plan of analysis called the tetrad.
The tetrad is the asking of these four questions to any medium. "1. What does it enhance? 2. What does it make obsolete? 3. What has it retrieved that has been made obsolete earlier? 4. What does it flip into when pushed to extremes?" (McLuhan 1992, Page 133). McLuhan goes on to ask these questions not just of media but things in general. Cigarette, Crowd, Refrigerator & Hermeneutics.
In general, McLuhan signals a dark future "Every major technical innovation will so disturb our inner lives that wars necessarily result as misbegotten efforts to recover old images" (McLuhan 1968, page 4). McLuhan often talks of aggression asserting that violence is a search for identity. Talking in Australia McLuhan states, "I would insist on studying the game of cricket as the manifestation of the control forms of violence in the community. .. any kind of sport is the typical and accepted form of violence in the business community." (McLuhan 2011, 14m 22s). With this analysis McLuhan suggests a controlled form of violence negates a physical form of violence. In a real sense, identity can be found through a symbolic form of violence. This might help to assume that if men and women

played sport together there would be less physical violence.
"I don't explain, I explore" (McLuhan 2012, Facebook).

References

1. McLuhan, Marshall & Meggs, Philip 1951, *The mechanical bride,* Duckworth Overlook, London.
2. McLuhan, Marshall, 1962, *The guttenburg galaxy,* University of Torronto Press, Canada.
3. McLuhan, Marshall, Agel, Jerome, & Fiore,Quentin 1968, *War and peace in the global village,* Bantam Books, New York.
4. *March backwards into the future – Marshall McLuhan's century* 2011, Viewed 9 August 2018, https://www.wired.com/2011/07/march-backwards-into-the-future-marshall-mcluhans-century/
5. McLuhan, Marshall & McLuhan, Eric 1992, *Laws of media,* University of Toronto Press, Canada.
6. McLuhan, Marshall & Fiore, Quentin 1967, *The medium is the message,* Penguin Books, Middlesex, England.
7. *McLuhan, Marshall 2011, Marshall Mcluhan Full lecture: The medium is the message - 1977 part 1 v 3,* videorecording. Viewed 6 August 2018. https://youtu.be/ImaH51F4HBw
8. McLuhan, Marshall 2012, *Marshall McLuhan: Writer,* Facebook, 2 May, viewed 6 August 2018, https://www.facebook.com/mcluhanestate/

80 Tres French

Jean Baudrillard was born in Reims, France in 1929. A sociologist, a philosopher, an academic, a pataphysician (a scientist of imaginary solutions), a writer for the Sartre journal - Les Temps Modernes, and a cache of some 30 books. Passing away in 2007 he has made considerable contributions to media theory. He remains a polemical cultural theorist to this day.

His idea, "The procession of simulacra" Baudrillard 1995, page 3), essentially meaning, the copy of the copy, establishes a motif where the copy of the copy is the recognized indulgence. For example, Disney's characters are the copy of a copy and unconnected to the original animal. Baudrillard with his procession of simulacra declares, "the map precedes the territory" (Lane J Richard 2000, Page 97) and the rolling out of this modernity project has lauded the copy as the recognized lead. In his book Simulacra & Simulation, he explains simulacra has four 'orders.' "It is the reflection of a profound reality. It masks and denatures a profound reality. It masks the absence of a profound reality. It has no relation to any reality whatsoever, it is its own pure simulacrum" (Baudrillard 1995, page 6). A model that no longer has any relation with the original. Baudrillard goes on to describe the hyperreality of the future. "Hyperreality will be the dominant way of experiencing and understanding the world" (Richard lane 2000,).

Baudrillard is well known for his Gulf War disavowal. The Guardian newspaper noted he was widely criticized for this approach. "Yet another continental philosopher who revelled in a disreputable contempt for truth and reality" (Poole 2007, page 1). Baudrillard's proposition was straight from the situationist's handbook, Guy Debord's, Society of the Spectacle. Baudrillard claims the gulf war was not news but much more a video game. He told us, "The Gulf war of did not take place" (Baudrillard 1995, Page 61). He explains this wasn't a real war, it had all the trickery and modernity of a copy. "A new kind of event a new kind of power both real and simulacra" (Baudrillard 1995, Page 6).

Marx's Das Kapital included a political ideology of a consumer society. "A society can no more cease to produce than it can cease to consume" (Marx 1867, page711). Baudrillard extended this idea in "The Consumer Society." He claims consumerism drove capitalism not production. Debunking the claim of Marx, that it was a symbiosis of production and consumption. "Instead of reciprocity characteristic of primitive societies and symbolic exchange in modern society, we have a gigantic simulation model of such reciprocal relations" (Baudrillard 1998, page 13). Baudrillard called this consumption "a repression ambience "(Baudrillard, 2012 Page 30).

When asked who he was, he replied "What I am, I don't know. I am the simulacrum of myself" (Poole 2007, Page 1).

Baudrillard was a remarkable theorist, in that his expression was to behold and sway a Marxist approach in pursuing a pejorative method. His individualism made him a Frankfurt school all on his own.

He is called upon, as a postmodernist yet rejects this moniker, describing his position as akin to anthropology. The anthropology of Maus.

References

Baudrillard, Jean 1995, *Simulacra and simulation,* University of Michigan Press, USA.

Baudrillard, Jean 1998, *The consumer society: myths and structures*, Sage, London.

Lane, Richard J 2000, *Jean Baudrillard,* Routledge, London.
Baudrillard, Jean 2012, *Introducing Baudrillard, a graphic guide,* Icon Books Ltd, London.

81. Old Media Is Dead

This mass automation upon us and will clearly lead to unheralded unemployment. With automation, Jaron Lanier believes. "We will probably enter into a period of hyper-unemployment, and the attendant political and social chaos" (Lanier 2013, P.24). Lanier furthers this idea with the question of identity. "How we can remain human beings as our machines become so sophisticated that we can perceive them as autonomous" (Lanier 2013, p.26)? This era of autonomous brings the question that prima facie appears farcical and extreme but McLuhan advices in his tetrad to look carefully at the extremes for genuine analysis. So here in the extremes, it is deemed necessary to consider the human rights of the new media (AI). Melbourne lawyer Lawrence White has collaborated with NYU professor Samir Chopra to produce. "A Legal Theory for Autonomous Artificial Agents." The book asks if personhood will be adjudicated to artificial intelligence? This would mean, "the capacity to sue and be sued, to hold property in her or its own name, and to enter contracts. Legal persons also enjoy various immunities and protections in courts of law such as the right to life and liberty" (White, Chopra 2011, p.154). AI rights appears extraordinary, yet possible. White and Chopra conclude. "If we fall back repeatedly on making claims about human uniqueness and the singularity of the human mind and moral sense in a naturalistic world order, then we might justly be accused of being an 'autistic' species, unable to comprehend the minds of other types of beings" (White, Chopra 2011, p.191). Yet, unfortunately what this book lacks, is the consideration that human beings are machines… Bio-computers, lacking free will. This is the current wave of intellectual thought, by the likes of Sam Harris in his book Free Will and YouTuber/author Jordan Petterson. They conclude that humans like computers, have no free will and are not autonomous. Both popular intellectual thinkers have dismissed the hubris of humanity & bring humanity closer to computers than originally thought. Sam Harris states emphatically. "Free will is an illusion. Our wills are simply not of our own making. Thoughts and intentions emerge from background causes of which we are unaware and over which we exert no conscious control" (Harris, Sam 2012 p.15). Driverless cars, Peopleless mines, farmerless farms, 3d built housing. These are some of the industries heavily earmarked for automation. Watching an Australian talk show, ABC Q&A, I have never seen such anxiety in an audience when the topic of automation came along. Australia's chief scientist Dr Alan Finkle says. "There are no industries safe from automation" (Q & A 2016). In the same discussion a quote from Stephen Hawking was tabled. "The development of artificial intelligence could even lead to the end of the human race" (Q & A 2016). Under the tetrad of Marshall McLuhan, this is an extreme example and must be looked at.

Even the comedians are joining the debate. "There is no work anymore, there is just apps, you have a job it becomes an app' on Thursday" (Moran 2018). Says Dylan Moran. And just to conclude sincerely here for a moment. This vast unemployment model will surely bring public disorder if this is not managed. This is a dystopian model. A forewarning not to get comfortable with all the glamorous graphics. This digital modernism has presented itself as a glowing array of HTML beauty and yet a real concentration of wealth and power. This automation will create poverty and unemployment. The worst off countries will be the ones most reliant on work force manufacture. These same stresses are the ones of the industrial revolution producing the luddites. This time the new media are putting people out of work, not just in the immediate future, but forever. Production and consumption will continue and this is what drives the economy claims Marx. But if production is not providing a spread of money for consumption the Marxist reading says there is trouble in the economy. "A society can no more cease to produce than it can cease to consume" (Marx 1976, page711). Technology has delivered gains, new media is part of everyday life and easy not to appreciate. As I think of a list of new inventions in the last 20 years. I am compelled to reflect on how life changing yet prosaic they have all become. Mobile phones, Facebook, Microsoft Word, YouTube, Google, and internet Banking. These advances are not just for an elite. They are spread across a vast consumer base. With a current world population at 7.8 billion people, "In 2019 the number of mobile phone users is forecast to reach 4.68 billion" (https://www.statista.com). More than half the population will be mobile phones users. This is in stark contrast to the UNICEF report that states "About 2.4 billion people — or roughly one-third of the world's population — still lack access to proper toilets" (http://time.com). It appears that the identity of humanity is not inclined to practicality but is distorted towards things like status, pride and glamour. These identity issues are in competition when it comes to the valoursing of consumer items. Humanity is truly an enemy of humanity.

The hegemony of Google is undeniable. The freedom to find anything anywhere on the web has been mathematically available to all. Yet, as any researcher worth their weight would know, search engines are privileging a bell curve of the ordinary. Google doesn't give you the best solution, it gives you the popular average solution. It gives you no critical thesis to be wary of. It gives you crowd thinking. These are the issues that present themselves when reliant on a Google search engine. Finding the fringes is so critical to establish valid research and analysis is not a Google algorithm. As John Stuart Mills states. "He who knows only his own side of the case, knows little of that."(Mills 2002, p.30). Thank you very much Google but I don't know what they are but I have my own internal algorithms. Critical thinking is validating, considering and exposing all ways of seeing not just the lump in the middle of the bell curve. There is no doubt Google delivers the lump in the middle of the bell curve but for serious research the definitive should be judicious. The algorithms are not interested in you or the invasiveness. They are only interested in the millions. What time is it? How old are you? What was being viewed before you shop? Is uninteresting, but that info on a million people is worth something. The collective data is what is useful. Algorithms are about shopping, voting and war. So organisations interested in these things are mightily interested in that data and the connections between that data.

The new technologies retrieve from the past an ability to talk to everyone you know easily. That is a "global village" (McLuhan 1968, p.4). As part of that village a democracy has been retrieved with the ability to broadcast to the world via YouTube, Facebook etc. The music has been brought home. Every PC/mobile phone is able to record at home. Bringing music back to the community and local arts back as a family artifact. Google maps have made the world 'like the back of my hand.' They have retrieved an ability to know the known universe intimately as was the case, in yesteryear. Thank you, technology.

In summary, new media is dead. This slow romantic era that moved along at a dependable pace is gone. The new has taken the soul from the media and replaced it with an abyss. The great technology promised and delivered freedom. Even a mobile phone, just like the ones on Star Trek.

"Man's desire is the desire of the Other" (Lacan 1998, p.235)

1782 words

Bibliography

Library and Archives Canada n.d., Homepage, Government of Canada, viewed 8th September 2018, http://collectionscanada.gc.ca/innis-mcluhan/030003-2030-e.html

McLuhan, Eric 1992, Laws of media, University of Toronto Press, Canada.

Lister, Martin, Dovey, John, Giddings, Seth, Grant, Iain, & Kelly, Kieran 2009, New media, a critical introduction, second edition, Routledge, Oxon, UK.

Self, Will 2017, Will Self on the death of film, Viewed 8th September 2018, https://youtu.be/6Le43WJxNWU

Pressman, Jessica 2014, Digital modernism, making it new in new media, Oxford University Press, New York.

Lanier, Jaron 2013, Who owns the future, Simon and Schuster, New York, USA.

White, Lawrence, Chopra, Samir 2011, A legal theory for autonomous artificial agents, University of Michigan, USA.

Harris, Sam 2012, Free will, Free Press, New York, USA.

Q & a 2016, television program, ABC Television, Sydney, 14 March.

Retrieved 8 September 2018, from http://www.abc.net.au/tv/qanda/txt/s4406559.htm#

Moran, Dylan 2018, Dylan Moran 2018 | bbc radio 5 live, videorecording. Viewed 8 September 2018, https://youtu.be/bDlhXubyAtk

Marx, Karl 1976, Capital volume 1, Penguin Books, London, UK.

Number of mobile phone users worldwide from 2015 to 2020 n.d, Statista,The Statistics Portal, Viewed 8 September 2018, https://www.statista.com/statistics/274774/forecast-of-mobile-phone-users-worldwide/

1 in 3 people worldwide don't have proper toilets, report says, 1 July 2015, Time, View 8 September 2018, http://time.com/3942630/toilets-who-unicef-report/

Mills, John Stuart 2002, On liberty, Dover Publications, Inc, London.

McLuhan, Marshall 1968, War and peace in the global village, Bantam Books Inc, New York, USA.

Lacan, Jacques 1998, The seminar of Jacques Lacan: the four fundamental concepts of psychoanalysis (vol. book XI) (the seminar of Jacques Lacan), Norton Paperback, London, UK.
-->

"To historians is granted a talent that even the gods are denied –
to alter what has already happened!" David NAZI

82. In deinem nichts hoff ich, Das All zu finden

Aka Creative.

"In deinem nichts hoff ich, das All zu finden"

"In nothing, I will find the universe" Johann Wolfgang von Goethe

Creativity has long been shunned as a disruptive force whose incursion will destabilize. In Plato's Republic, the poets are barred from the city unless they repent. At the beginning of Sartre's book, *Being and Nothingness*, the translator's introduction quotes William James. "Any new theory is attacked as absurd; then it is admitted to be true, but obvious and insignificant; finally, it is seen to be so important that its adversaries claim that they themselves discovered it" (James, in Sartre 1994, p.viii). These are the age-old adversaries to the creative process.

Creativity is constitutive of Plato's forms. The notion that the mind conceives a perfect object. The perfect song, the perfect science, the perfect work of art, the perfect HTML, all wanting to hold the treasured identification of the form. Creativity is merely the making of this perfect object; the perfectly created thing.

Plato furthered this hope of creativity to a betterment of science by directing students to think in a style to necessitate a scientific breakthrough. "Plato's primary purpose was not to advance physical science but to train the mind to think abstractly" (Cornford, in Plato p.276). Doing this will indirectly be an advance of science. Plato was aware of how to shun creativity and scientific breakthrough. His allegory, Plato's Cave, remarkably warns of his concern for the opposite of creativity, that of the sheltered existence away from all that life has to offer. In the cave, you live within a framework of ill-informed choices. This road to serfdom is exemplified in a governance not willing to give creativity free reign.

The ancient Greeks had no real word for creativity. It was said that the artist didn't create they merely imitated. It wasn't until the Christian faith explained that, the Abrahamic God is said to have created earth, implanted the idea of creation into consciousness. This meme has been impressed upon the world with great success for the last 2000 years.

The Romans believed creativity came from a muse in the walls. "I knew you would come as soon as I began to write" (BBC 1976), says Claudius, believing the muse was coming the wall. This is an ancient belief unifying many animist cultures. The idea that things contain spirits and humanity deferring to these spirits is an old reality. "The spirit is viewed as incorporate in the tree; …. the tree is not the body, but merely the abode of the tree spirit, which can quit it and return to it at pleasure." (Frazer 1978, p 60).

Creativity can affectionately be called, 'making the invisible; visible.' In Kantian terms, the noumena becoming phenomena or the known unknown becoming a known known.

Living in the world of technological devices, et al. Humanity sees itself as more than human, more than Darwin has ever proposed. It has come to pass, as Goethe first stated - a universe out of nothing. "In deinem nichts hoff ech, das All zu finden" (Goethe 1986, p.192). A devil's bargain, a Mephistopheles deal for the enlightenment man. "The dark, negative side of reason; and God, the mystical, positive side of reason." The Faustian pact is the consciousness of the day, an archetypal story playing out in contemporary society.

In The Birth of Tragedy, Nietzsche states, "The continuous development of art is bound up with the Apollonian and Dionysian duality" (Nietzsche 2007, p.14). An internal duality producing a synthesis of art. Creativity is the Hegelian 'aufhebung,' an amalgam of duality, wrapped in each other, completed as the synthesis of one and for our creative purposes, the resulting crafted work.

"Art is the proper task of life" (Nietzsche 2007, p.14), said Nietzsche, but where does this creativity come from? Guy Debord's Critique in *Urban Geography* suggests it comes from the world itself. "Psychogeography could set for itself the study of the precise laws and specific effects of the geographical environment, consciously organized or not, on the emotions and behaviour of individuals" (Introduction to a critique of Urban geography, 1955). Debord is expressing the idea that objects communicate. A river, the sea, the architecture, all have a common unintended goal to instruct. So, all objects instruct & communicate to us, consciously or unconsciously, and therefore all is media.

It is well to ponder the effects of the technological environment beyond that of their typical function. What is happening is a different kind of instruction, not psychogeography proper. Human consciousness reacts to technological devices, the computer, the Iphone, as if part of self. The device is comparable and functioning as a vehicle for the computer language and film language. This is why, as psychogeography, it is considered as an extension of self. This extension of self is interpolated as a Freudian 'Ego Ideal' and will be protected more than the physical self. Not just a repair job or an upgrade but it will not be put in harm's way. It will not be fed the equivalent of junk food. This is the kind of respect these objects incur. Ironically, people wish they could be treated with the same respect the device has managed to require. Don't touch my phine don't lend out your phone and if you do , its as if someone is twiddling with your liver right in front of you.

The concern for new media's creativity is its identity of individualism. The Iphone, Itunes, the Imac, are a familiar trade in the valorization of I, the self. Always using the pronoun I. This is a market plan critical to consumption, your personal computer, your iPhone. This nurtured concept of the anthropomorphized technology means that if you have another brand, it, is not really yours, you don't really own that Samsung phone. Furthermore, any differing brand is not so precious as an extension of self. These products have deemed themselves as self. This 'object' sense of self in the world with a combination of video game obsession has been with us for a generation. Yet this community hasn't resulted in the dystopian society some might hypothesize.

Donald Horne's book, *The Lucky Country*, was written in 1964 and gives a grave insight into Australian creativity consciousness at the time. He states "It lives on other people's ideas" (Horne 2009, p.233). "The frustrations and resentment of a triumphant mediocrity and shear dullness of life (Horne 2009, p.10)." His idea being that Australia is a lucky country, yet people are missing opportunities. It is not the creative place it should be and what is missing is a reflection on potential.

Creativity comes out of nowhere. Ayn Rand describes art as "a concretization of metaphysics" (Rand 1971, p.20).

Colin Wilson explains a creative duality, exemplified in the artist, when all is in flow. He explains the brain is in two halves and one side is slower than the other. When they both work at the same speed it forms a cutting edge. This is when the creativity pours out like a transcendental flood. Colin Wilson calls this, Faculty X.

This voice of change is always a challenge to the community, but let's be fair, not all new ideas are great. They need an incubation time, a time for testing and verifying. "The owl of Minerva spreads its wings only with the falling of dusk" (Hegel, p. 20). Said Hegel. Perhaps social media could well take this advice and enact an epoché. This is a term taken from Husserl meaning suspension. He uses this 'bracketing' to hold back judgment for a time so as to examine. This epoché might well be used in social media to stir a consciousness of the repercussions of 'publish and be dammed.' This is at the heart of the idea of fake news and its trappings of fame, power and the dark side of individualism.

Technological change brings upheaval. The creative today is not the creative of tomorrow. The artist brush is not yet discarded for an algorithm but technology will want to play a part in shaping the creative. This is the age of immediacy. With the internet they say. 'It might be wrong but at least its not wrong for long.' This instant market is powerful and daunting. YouTube, Facebook, Twitter, Instagram, are molding the nature of creativity. Within this context is a huge overhaul of the copyright economy. The copyright model Creative Commons can barely cope with the scope and volume of contravention. In the past copyright has barely been enacted on the internet. In fact if copyright laws were really enacted, this would be a different internet economy. "Correctly pointed out that policing their sites for pirated content would cripple their operation" (Levinson 2011, p.60).

Social Media is the natural friend of pop art and punk. After an upload to the net is made, the skilled crafted author is placed with equal emphasis as the dilettante. In theory, this unassessed access to a world audience is a utopian level playing field of democracy. New media is crafted as such, that 'idea' is valourised more than ever. The player in new media completes their work then moves to the next idea. In the past the magus opus of the creative was a yearlong process, in a cabin in the woods. This was the erstwhile artist. In his book, Explaining Creativity, Keith Sawyer describes the creative in days gone by. "Artists like Cezanne explored a single 'problem' for their entire career" (Sawyer 2012, p.302). Now, it's an idea in the morning, manufactured in the afternoon and sold before sundown.

In this creative zone, the worker can see a prominent reference to 'a culture of change.' It suggests that to be proficient in one field is a risky career because things rapidly fall out of favour. The creative must be able to adapt to change and move

on. More than ever, the creative must be unattached. 'The culture
of change,' is the culture of anyone who wants a future.

In 1998, a 18Gb hard drive was $1,200, now a USB
16Gb is $12. Technology's exponential accessibility through
plummeting hardware price, has been a huge help for the
creative to access a technological market that was once only
available to a wealthy elite. In 1993, a slow digital editing
equipment would set you back $220,000, you can now edit faster
on domestic PC. A digital cinematic camera with 4.4.4 resolution
is currently available on eBay for under $5,000US. You don't
even have to pay for film or processing. Cinema is domestically
accessible; all you need is an idea. It was Goddard who
popularised an axiom and uniquely saw the future, announcing
how easy it is to make a film, "all you need to make a movie is a
girl and a gun" (https://www.thecinetourist.net/a-girl-and-a-
gun.html). In Australia every year the funding for feature films
are all paid for by the government (give or take one or two
movies). In 2008 a movie called 'Australia' was made, costing
$200M AUSD and lost money at the box office. Imagine 200
movies made for one million AUSD, what a great year; creative,
tumultuous, interesting and some rubbish made too. The eyes of
the film world would have all been directed to Australia. In an
accessible technologically advanced society, it's hard not to see,
that the main threat to Australian film is its own governance.

Creativity is freedom and creativity is survival. It is the
exception that breaks the rule and the destructive force. It is
incongruent and appears to bypass the rules with an
implementation that looks unlawful. Within a new technology, it
is better to know the parameters to break them and to mix subject
matter genres. Algorithyms and war. Calculus and AI. Genetics
and html. Art and quantum computing. I posit a vision that is
ironic, real, and creative. This creates leverage to a new 'way of
seeing.' Two creativity researchers, Robert Sternberg and Todd
Lubart, claimed that "this lack of multidisciplinarity had blocked

our understanding of creativity" (Sternburg Lubart, in Sawyer, 1999, p. 9).

The whole idea of new technology rests on an uncertain space. The technology idiom itself is new and not quite resolved. In short, Godel's Theorem tells us that within a system there is a sentence that cannot be proven or disproven. So perhaps that sentence is. 'Technology is going to save us.'

It is a modern narcissistic effect, to look into a screen and see, in a psychogeographical sense, yourself and lose yourself. "In posthuman perspective, emancipation of humanity turns into emancipation from humanity, from the limitations of a mere being-human" (Zizek 2016, p.46). Zizek here looks at a fulfilling future referring to Bernardi explaining a consciousness not only as emancipation but an incompleteness. Bernardi suggests, "the next game will be about neuro –plasticity" (Bernardi, in Zizek 2016, p.46). That is, the ability for the brain to rewire. Bernardi believes the next few decades "will be mapping the activity of the brain." Bernardi is hesitant and claims this "new environment involves enormous suffering, a tempest of violence and madness" (Zizek 2016, p. 46). To put this into a practical idea, the brain triggers emotional responses and this bio-chemical induction, once calculated, might well be represented as algorithms. "A machine-learning algorithm could analyse the biometric data streaming from sensors on and inside your body, determine your personality type and your changing moods, and calculate the emotional impact" (Harari 2018, p.40), states Harari. Music is a mathematical computation, conflated with a musician. These artists will become redundant, merely modeling the computer-generated algorithms of the brain sensors. This is just one idea and social function. There are many examples in the workplace. "Consider how advancing technology could do to surgery what it has already done to recorded music" (Lanier 2013, p 31).

Artificial intelligence is about to be a creator of huge wealth for a minority and unemployment for the masses. This divide is

192

unprepared for. Harari suggests this "will confront humankind with the hardest trials we have ever encountered" (Harari 2018, p.29). These machines improving in cognitive ability and even emotional ability will put billions out of work.

In this new economy leadership will be required. It has taken many years for economic ideas to be put into action. Adam Smith, Hayek, and Keynes, all have suffered an incubation time that have seen themselves near out-of-date by the time their ideas are enacted. Kate Raworth has a catchy pop approach. In her new book, Doughnut Economics, she clarifies a contemporary economic plan. In its nucleus, is a social plan of well-being with rules for ecology. She wants to move away from the Merkel 'sustained growth,' the Obama, 'long term lasting growth,' and David Cameron 'balanced growth,' to a Raworth idea that ignores these populist thoughts. She suggests, "Instead of prioritising metrics like GDP, the aim should be to enlarge people's capabilities – such as to be healthy, empowered and creative" (Raworth 2017, p 42).

Communication technologies have already manufactured, mines without miners. It is foreseeable in the future that the products of mines are forwarded to robotics companies, who produce mines without miners. The human element will then be completely withdrawn from the workplace; even a modicum of this future is startling. There are ameliorating options for this new cultural environment. Universal Basic Income and Universal Basic Services, all paid for by taxing adequately Amazon, Google, Facebook, et al. Otherwise this unfathomable unemployment will lead to social tension and inevitable strife.

Education will play a huge part in this future. It is the unskilled work that is going to drive unemployment in an age of artificial intelligence. "In 2015 the US Air Force lacked sufficient trained humans to fill all these positions, and therefore faced an ironic crisis in manning its unmanned aircraft." (Harari 2018, p.39).

Many social functions are enabled by AI but for an economy to make the most of change, education will hold the key to countering mass unemployment. Quietly, society is underway with an introduction of STEM. That is, Science, Technology, Engineering, and Mathematics. This is a combination of subjects all well placed to play an economic role in public life because data has a future. "In the twenty-first century, however, data will eclipse both land and machinery as the most important asset," (Harari 2018, p. 91). Then comes the question for young people. That is, what am I going to do with my life? What am I best suited to? Perhaps next year you might just be able to login to Google /Facebook and the answer will be clear. It will tell you your university and your subjects, your best geographical location for employment and information about your algorithm arranged marriage. The supplementary program would give advice about fitness routine, your diet and how to stay clear of mental illness. The more information you give up to Google, the better the advice will be. This counseling will be free of charge but will come with few rights. Big Data will be much better than the citizen to make these life choices. Logical or emotional needs, these algorithms will take care of everything. Citizens should be aware though that, in times gone by, people even obeying simple GPS have been known to drive into lakes.

In summary, there are broad considerations to the origins of creativity, going back thousands of years. Many cultural ideas are at play and there are difficult times ahead. Throughout history creativity and technology have been well documented. Yet it is still remains to be seen if Godel's Theorem is true and 'Technology will save us.'

References

Goethe, Johann Wolfgang von 1986, *Faust: der tragödie erster und zweiter teil, urfaust,* Thomas Munster, Bad Langensalza, Germany.
Sartre, Jean Paul 1994, *Being and nothingness,* Gramercy Books, New York.

Plato 1987, *The republic,* Penguin Books, London, UK.

Claudius 1976, *I, Claudius - ep. 1 - a touch of murder – legendado,* videorecording. Viewed 1 October 2018, https://youtu.be/Gfxt9zKeNL4
Frazer, James George 1978, *The illustrated golden bough,* Macmillan London Ltd, London, UK.

Nietzsche, Friedrich 2007, *The birth of tragedy,* Universiy Press Cambridge, Cambridge UK.

Debord, Guy-Ernest 1955, *Introduction to a critique of urban geography,* viewed October 4th 2018, http://library.nothingness.org/articles/SI/en/display/2

Horne 2005, Donald, *The lucky country,* Penguin Books Australia Ltd, Melbourne, Australia.

Rand 1978, Ayn, *The romantic manifesto, a philosophy of literature,* The New American Library Inc, New York, USA.

Hegel, Georg Wilhelm Friedrich 2001, *The philosophy of right,* Batoche books Ltd, Ontario Canada.

Levinson 2014, Paul, *New new media,* Pearson Australia, Melbourne Australia.

Sawyer, Keith 2012, *Explaining creativity, the science of human innovation,* Oxford University Press, Inc, New York.

All you need is… n.d., The Cine Tourist, University College, London, Viewed 5 October 2018, https://www.thecinetourist.net/a-girl-and-a-gun.html

Žižek, Slavoj 2016, *Disparities,* Bloomsbury Publishing Plc, London, UK.

Harari, Noah Yuval 2018, *21 lessons for the 21 century*, Penguin Random House, London, UK.

Lanier, Jaron 2013, *Who owns the future?* Simon and Shuster in, New York, USA.

Raworth, Kate 2017, *Doughnut economics: seven ways to think like a 21st-century economist*, Penguin Random House, London, UK.

83. The Sleep of The Just

The sleep of the just before and the sleep of the just after.

84 Triumvirate

Yes, I'm talking the namaste mob. Omne trium perfectum...
And just bare with my tangent...As the TISM sleeve notes say on
the first single "Declan was the first to know." So, I was passed
the baton from the gods; the gods are Shiva, Vishnu and Brahma.
Today let's look at Brahma, the one who makes everything. My
understanding is; the god is sometimes male & sometimes
female.

The hospitals, the cops, the schools, the cars, the people,
the all .. Brahma made everything ... Yet rarely worshiped...
Now Nike, Ferrari, Lois Vutton et al..that is, the peripheral and
superficial (well, i find them superficial) They have all the eyes,
the energy, and are most valourised.

The idea of Brahma, who busted a gut and did
everything, is ancient ..And the collective society that provides
the knowledge, for the infrastructure of institutions that in-turn
providing the society with the basis of bon vivant...& sure folk
say "thanks' but not adored to the same extent as the local
football team. or other peripheral arrangements. Only celebrate
the icing on the cake not the cake. And if you don't have any
irony, get some.

85. Narrative is Pre-historic

Claude Lévi-Strauss in his *Pensée Sauvage* is caught-up in the idea that myth loves to follow a Hegelian dialectic.... {As if for one moment... the old Homer 750BC of the book the Iliad was a young Hegelian. (peut-être)}...The narrative is by meme nature /Darwinian

Lévi-Strauss identified myths as a type of speech through which a language could be discovered.

"A Levi-Strauss paraphrases. 'Myths are a type of speech through which language could be discovered'.
 After a pernicious ideology becomes rampant in his home country, Douglas Sirk came to the US in '37, leaving Germany. He came to work in the US with a ticket to suggest 'not preaching' when making films. This might be assumed to have a dual aspect. First, not proselytizing means he stays off the Hitler assassination list. secondly, in an apolitical style somewhere in the middle of the bell curve, perhaps the monetary returns are going to be fruitful.
 But what is the ideology of "no ideology" what happens to the fence sitters. What do they profess? Is it not the status quo? while all is OK in the world, nothing needs to change. is this not the politics of happy. That meandering ease, agreeable and quick to interpolate the world around as normal. The hierarchy needs no shake up, the constant world of flux is obfuscated in the simple movie fantasy of 'no political message.' Don't struggle for anything. All is at peace in the world. After a most catastrophic world war, who doesn't want to hear this message.
 Within the poetics of cinema, perhaps it's just not possible to preach and make a dollar. But not only not preach. His high romance, wealthy characters, well- healed and living an inspirational life, Sirk leaves little room for an audience to have

a convincing reflective experience that might be of benefit. Its just a movie, the hegemony of no message.

86. John Logie Baird

The Scot responsible for so much sitting down is
welcomed by the Harvey Norman sofa industry. John Logie
Baird demonstrated at, now Bar Italia, 45 Frith St Soho, (note the
plaque in the top left) on the 26th January 1926. It then took him
two years to broadcast trans-Atlantic.

The back lash didn't take long. Rudiolf Arnheim in 1935 says tv
" Does not offer new means for artistic interpretation of reality -
as radio and film does."

As Mark 16.4 tells "A prophet is not without honour except in
his hometown and among *his own* relatives and in *his own*
household." Baird might just be suffering from this after such
ungratefulness from such a momentous invention. & also let's be
fair to the critiques, at this time nothing went to tape, all was
merely live. Which immediately condemned the bandwidth of
ideas fractionally more interesting than radio. i.e. it had limits, at
the time this was all black and White. (colour came to the public
in 1939 in the shape of Wizard of Oz)

87. What Does it Take to Call It Cinematic?

It's a complement, you'd think? Cinema the great treasure, lure
and love of the people. Who could live without this repository of
this culture?

Television as a "density of visual texture" .. Television viewers
now have their cake and eat it.. They have as always "narrative
meaning" but as sauce on the side, they have "pleasure in the
imagery" States Bret Mills.

& the pleasure might not just come from the quality of the
picture but the community event of watching it all together. How
pixelated were the first landings on the moon, yet as a collective
experience cohered a generation in a world-wide shared
experience.

Cinematic is thought to be something to aspire to in television,
that pie in the sky, because as can be widely accepted, Tv isn't
cinema. Cinema films can be played on the tv but television can't
be cinema. a romantic notion never to be "it is felt to be an
ambition beyond the reach of normal television" states Bret Mills
in Television Aesthetics and Style.

Day by day as that cinematic style comes closer to a domestic
budget. For example, the free Australian DaVinci Resolve 15
colour grading or instant colour correction from the&
transformed Avid Media Composer. It will never be the night out
occasion sitting in the dark with a bunch of strangers being
transfixed by the screen to go on the ride of cinema to another
world.

Mills posits the idea that the use of the word "cinematic" sees Tv
a second class citizen. & not only that the relentless use of the

word in Tv means that Tv will always be the second place try hard medium. Good but not as good as cinema proper.

88. Ninety-Three Episodes of Mad Men

"Style matters. Television relies on style-setting, lighting, videography, editing, and so on - to set moods, hail viewers, construct meaning, build narratives, sell products and shape information" (Butler 2010, p. ii).

"Stories surround us" (Bordwell & Thomson 1986, p. 82).

The report will use the word 'hypertrophy' to describe 'moment' and recommends the word hypertropy as a better word than moment to be used in the understanding of serial Tv.

Be mindful of three types of 'hypertrophy.' 1. The moment of the excessive image, resonating beyond the plot. 2. The moment of camera dwelling on a gesture. 3. A moment of revelation, of 'subjective insight' privy to the viewer.

The report intends to shed light on the use of quality television to broaden a picture of the ontology of narrative itself. For example, looking at the ironic image of a cuff-link falling in episode three, it will be shown to be a narrative theme existing not just in quality television.

It is remarked that the viewer is acknowledged and plays a part in the structure of the episode. This is an addition to the idea that, 'the medium is the message' (McLuhan 1969, p. 2). The report finds that the audience also plays a part in the message.

The Cuff-link Sequence provides a viewer with a distinct place in as the continuity editing shows the viewer outside some of the 'on–set' characters. The report deconstructs the complexity of television, aware of the ideas of Mittell and Deleuze in the understanding of complexity. This approach bears witness to the deep and subtle influences of motif, academic relations and the entanglement of

this chaos. It is shown that the remit of quality television endeavours to create an order of this chaos.
280 words total

2. *The Cuff-link Moment* is a moment of the excessive image in the form of a cut away, interrupting the flow of the story. As Don Draper's cuff-link falls it appears as a semiotic punctum in the plot. The close-up reveals a couple's intimacy, as they enjoy a playful moment together, indicating the start of a romance. It is a television text that exceeds within the narrative. As a hypertrophy or excessive image suggests it "Is the power of expansion, this power is metonymic." (Barthes 1981, p. 45). It can be interpreted, as Don Draper's fall from grace plainly symbolized. He is literally falling and falling in love. The messages of the hypertrophy are characteristic of polysemantic quality TV.

The meeting is full of Sterling-Cooper men and the cuff-link falling is an open display of the fragility of the corporation. It is an ironic image, a cuff-link's failure, punctuating an important organized meeting. In fact, again ironic is the tableau vivant of a meeting full of men espousing ideas on the spending habits of women. Slavoj Žižek maintains every company blindly has an ironic image. In analysis it can be said the function of irony is complex. Complexity in a Deleuzian sense that of a heterogeneous element. The irony maintains sympathy as the company uses it to maintain the idea that it is not perfect. This appears as a mystery; a hypertrophy moment is clearly on display inviting engagement. A viewer will engage with the company, in the hope that, 'buying in' will present with an understanding. You beginning with the question that you will never know unless you compliantly engage. "Hegel's entire effort goes into explaining why trust needs the detour of true irony and suspicion to assert itself" (Žižek 2016, p. 117). From this Hegelian assertion it is to be believed even trust needs a dialectic. A perfect looking, aloof, company needs an irony to present itself as anthropomorphized. The company then is not interpreted as the 'other' alterity, in opposition, but familial and embraceable. That is, you love your family, though they are not perfect.

3. The sequence chosen to analyse is *The Cuff-link Sequence* S1 E3. This is the second boardroom meeting of company Sterling-Cooper and Ms Menken.

Don Draper's cuff-link falls into a parallel universe. This is a resonant image, "exceeding its place in the flow of events" (Mules 2018, l. 2.2). The shot goes to close-up and a new personalized space is made for three entities, Ms Menken, Mr Draper and the viewer. At this point, the viewer, Don and Ms Menken are separated from the advertising team. The advertising team is not privy to the cuff-link falling. It can be said the viewer is so respected that it is told the secret of the falling cuff-link, not known to the advertising team. Here, the viewer is invited to the inner circle as omniscient. This omniscience of the viewer, is characteristic of quality TV, respectful and trusting to the viewer.

The secret of the cuff-link falling is symbolic of Don's life falling apart, it is a symbol referent to the opening titles. A man in animation is falling and a feminine foot connects with the man as he falls. Don's cuff-link is falling and Ms Menken connects with the cuff-link, flicking (or kicking), it back to Don Draper. This is a hypertrophy moment of revelation, it reveals twofold a connection with the opening-titles and a connection to Ms Menken, clearly rejecting Don Draper's perceived attention seeking.

Looking at what Butler calls text, he states. "In its broadest sense, a 'text' is any phenomenon that pulls together elements that have meaning for readers, viewers, or spectators that encounter it" (Butler 2002, p. 6). Therefore, *The Cuff-link Moment,* according to Butler can be defined as text as it pulls together symbolic elements.

Don Draper has a choice of using buttons on his shirt sleeves or cuff-links. He chose cuff-links; the more stylish option of a social status. This choice is comparable to other choices in his life. He could have been Richard "Dick" Whitman but he chose Don Draper, the more stylish person. Don Draper was confronted on a train by a man calling him, Richard 'Dick' Whitman. It is now known that Don Draper has had a choice of two men and he has chosen to be Don Draper. Not the ordinary guy with buttons on his shirts but the society Don Draper. As the camera dwells on the cuff-link falling. It reflects on the idea that the world will occasionally interpolate Don Draper not as high society man but as the ordinary man, button shirt man, Richard 'Dick' Whitman.

In a real sense new television must consider the audience as literally at home. It reflects this through a cerebral complexity not allowed in popular cinema. Contemporary cinema is now known as, get away from it all, get out of the house, commercial popular entertainment. As moments prick the scene they can reflect the interruptions of life in the lounge room. "Une hypertrophie de l'instinct social" (Reinach in Freud 1998, p. 97). Interrupted social instincts. New television stop/start and dipping from plot to story are jolted space comparable to what is endured at home.

I'd like to review the content and cut into *The Cuff-link Sequence*. This means looking at the previous sequence and seeing how the continuity editing is made. This analysis is helpful in understanding the narrative as a whole and not just as separate parts. In his book Jason Mittell states, the characteristics of complex TV require "orientation practices" (Mittell 2015, p. 455), using "time, events, characters, and space" (Mittell 2015, p. 455). Clearly when moving from one scene to the next in quality television these factors are taken into account and so this continuity editing can be defined as the seamless manipulation of time and space. Within the Mad Men *Cuff-link Sequence* there is no new editing style. This is something of importance to consider in quality television, that the edit style, in all the technological revolutions, has changed little. In this cut from sequence to sequence, the cut can be understood as an inclination towards plot and narrative, rather than story.

In the previous sequence woman talk of intimate relations, in The Lady Chatterley's Lover book and the viewer gets a candid view of the office women. In the next sequence the junior executives gather and the viewer is privy to a bawdy joke concerning an intimate relationship. This cut from one scene to the next, works through a continuity editing of non-story dialogue, cutting to non-story dialogue, a cut from similarity to similarity.

So too can the continuity editing rely on what is different from one sequence to the next. The cut moves from woman to men. This is an example of a staple of quality drama, as Mittell commented "What was once a risky innovative device, such as subjective narration or jumbled chronology, is now almost a cliche" (Mittell 2015, p. 16).

Profoundly in *The Cuff-link Sequence,* Ms Menken arrives in the room holding her lit cigarette aloft like the statue of liberty. With this serenity, she is the symbol of liberty. This statue of liberty referent is entangled in the history of Madison Ave advertising proper. In the 1920's Freud's cousin Edward Louis Bernays was often called the "father of public relations" (*Edward bernays* 2018), the big man of New York advertising. He called upon cousin Freud to sell Lucky Strike cigarettes. The same brand associated with Mad Men. From this day on, it is no wonder Ms Menken walks into the advertising office with her torch, for it was Bernays who advertised smoking for women with his "Torches of Freedom" (Curtis 2016) slogan. It featured "across the United States and around the world" (Jackson in Curtis 2016). Mad Men episodes continue to use Freud references on many layers. For example, Freud's death urge, Thanatos, is cited as a tool to advertise. Though on-screen Don Draper rejects the idea of the death urge, the series leaves an ironic image of all possible shots littered with smoking. Another infamous Freudian signature phrase. "What does woman want" (Freud in Andre, 1999 p. 11)? is used many times by Don Draper. So as Ms Menken carries her torch of freedom, it has many meanings, connections and relations. Summarized by Butler, calling this approach, "stylistic schema, or patterning of techniques, the syntagmatic and paradigmatic relationships of one element to another elements within a textual system" (Butler 2011, p. 29).

The most notable mise en scène in this sequence is not what is put in the scene but what is taken out. Most profound in this sequence is a lack of smoking. The excessive image characterized as a style motif of smoking in Mad Men is lacking. The only male smoker is Kenny, the liar who is denounced by Draper. Kenny is the only man at the table holding the cigarette, connecting him to the death drive. "No one at this table has ever been to your store." Says Draper, denouncing his colleagues in front of everyone. This is an ironic image using smoking as the death drive as a pictorial signifier and then denouncing it in the dialogue. As it is shown, Draper admonishing the European woman, who mentions the use of death drive for advertising cigarettes.

4. In terms of narration and characterization, sometimes it is best to remind ourselves this is story telling. These are not real people; this is not a real life. It is conjured though the language of film. In this formula, the dialogue spoken is often the consciousness of everyday reality. But for effect, there are moments of excess in the dialogue that are of the unconscious. The author demands the character express their subconscious to further a story, to accelerate the search for truth. As Richard Dawkins stated. "Fiction can be a great way of telling the truth" (Dawkins 2018).

For example, Don Draper in *The Cuff-link Sequence* has characterized all of his colleagues as lying or negligent. He says " I can assure you that no one at this table has ever been to your store." In life, it would be near impossible to berate colleagues in front of clients without redress but here Don Draper articulates what he is thinking. This is what the Mad Men author demands of Don Draper, so as to deliver respectfully to the omniscient viewer. In the dynamics of the knowledge hierarchy, there is another triumvirate in the room. That of the Mr Pelham the host, Don and Ms Menken. This is the hierarchy of knowledge, keeping in check the focalization of the sequence. These are the actors of the head shot and the close-up. Rimmon-Kenan states there are clear guidelines for the criteria of focalization.
"Two criteria will be used in this section to discuss the different types
of focalization: position relative to the story, and degree of persistence" (Rimmon-Kennon 2005, p. 76).

This hierarchy is foretold in the camera time, spent on each individual, to explain a social structure lived through the sequence. The close-up and time spent on the groups, as opposed to juniors have meted out a valourisation concurring with the chain of command validated in the dialogue.

Moments as part of a complex whole are part of the story of 'televisuality " (Caldwell in Butler 2010, p. 116). The moments of hypertrophy don't just come from nowhere, Caldwell describes this type of interpolation as "excessive stylization and visual exhibition" (Caldwell in Butler 2010, p.116). A feature of the unconscious made conscious, for the sake of quality television, this is a truth annunciated on screen; this is the essence of the dialogue in *The Cuff-link Sequence*. What is happening here is a narrative evolution, described by Hegel in the *Phenomenology of the Spirit*. "The truth is the whole and the whole. But the whole is nothing other than the essence consummating itself through its own development" (Hegel 1977, p. 11). The changes brought forth in an age of quality television are the medium "consummating itself, "sutured by a human yearning for truth. A truth that the technical codes wish to annunciate to the viewer in a personal and civil manner. Re close-up of the cuff-link, delivered to the screen for the trusted viewer, Don, and Ms Menken and not imparted to the rest of the room. When all the types of screen culture are unfolded, the culture has no more to say, in effect it languishes. Will Self has announced this as death. "Film is dead"(Self, 2017), he shouts.

"Schopenhauer, for whom, of course, death is the 'proper result' of life and hence its purpose" (Freud 2003, p. 167).

The viewer witnesses a beginning, a middle and an end, knows this the purpose of the film, to end. And so too is the style itself, caught in the same narrative. Thus, death or languishing remains an omen and a blind ambition for quality television.

BIBLIOGRAPHY

Andre, Serge 1999, *What does woman want?* Other Press, New York, USA.

Barthes, Roland 1981, *Camera lucida, reflections on photography*, Hill and Wang, New York.
Bernays, Edward 2018*, Edward bernays Part 1 of cigarettes and suffragettes*, retrieved 20th December 2018, United States Information Agency,
https://people.howstuffworks.com/52448-edward-bernays-part-i-of-cigarettes-and-suffragettes-video.htm
Bordwell, David, Thompson, Kristin 1986, Film art, an introduction/second series, Alfred A. Knopf, New York, USA.
Butler, Jeremy G 2002*, Critical methods and applications,* Lawrence Erlbaum associates publishers, Mahwah, New Jersey, USA.
Butler, Jeremy G 2010, *Television Style,* Routledge, New York, USA.

Curtis, Adam 2018, *The century of the self - part 1: "Happiness machines"*, video recording, retrieved 20th December 2018,
https://youtu.be/DnPmg0R1M04
Dawkins, Richard 2018, *Fiction can be a great way of telling the truth*, The Telegraph, viewed 21 December 2018,
<https://www.telegraph.co.uk/culture/10879577/Fiction-can-be-a-great-way-of-telling-the-truth-Richard-Dawkins.html>

Freud, Sigmund 2003, *Beyond the pleasure principle and other writings*, Penguin Books Ltd, London, UK.
Freud, Sigmund 1998, *Totem and taboo*, Dover Thrift Editions, Mineola, New York.
Hegel, Georg 1977, *The phenomenology of the spirit*, Oxford University Press, Oxford, UK.
Mittell, Jason 2015, *Complex tv, The poetics of contemporary storytelling*, New York University Press, New York, USA.
McLuhan, Marshall & Fiore, Quentin 1967, The medium is the message, Penguin Books Ltd, Victoria, Australia.

Rimmon-Kenan, Shlomith 2002, *Narrative fiction*, Routledge, London and New York.
Self, Will 2017, *Will self on the death of film,* accessed December 20th 2018, YouTube, https://youtu.be/6Le43WJxNWU
Žižek, Slavoj 2016, *Disparities,* Bloomsbury Publishing plc, London, UK.

89. Is It On

The Netflix series. The media that has supplanted the film. Subverted and moved on in an understated fashion. Film is an old languishing idea. Like a dead admired familiar uncle. BINGE, the respected Aufhebung that put film out to pasture NETFLIX etc, A highbrow /low brow domestic product. Internet TV quietly crept up and the theorist didn't know which way to shoot.

Look! The genre that is no genre.

The inevitable means of transmission changed everything and not so much the camera and edit gear price plummet.

God is dead. The church is dead. Film is dead. The high street is dead. The book shop is dead. They are all owning up to their own mortality. The self-serving denial is difficult to keep up.

 Heidegger would be pleased, as he begged people to spend more time in graveyards.

BINGE, it's not just consumption. BINGE is non-essential. BINGE is essential.

BINGE - YOU PAY TO SEE AN AMERICAN TRANSCENDENTAL IDEA.

BINGE - YOU PAY TO SEE A BBC TRANSCENDENTAL IDEA.

BINGE - YOU PRETEND IT'S your OWN TRANSCENDENTAL IDEA.

You have your/my/their world view now. Australia doesn't
exist.

90. Big Foot

Two girls on the run… through the bush, the hills, the river and the mountains ..Just bush.

 They laugh . they are out of breath. They run like the wind with no tiredness. ..
Uncle waits in a shaded spot … thinking about his avuncular device.
Uncle. they cry, as they arrive.
"Where you going …?"

"Over dare".. she points her lips into the far distance.

 Uncle says "I bin dare … big foot dare."

"Big foot" she says … she looks at lil one and repeats in a whisper
"big foot"
 Child looks awkward and confused … squeegees her own face and stares down at her feet..

 Cu child's feet..

"Big foot eating sandwich from policeman then going to Nyrripi
"

91. Advertising Works

The cop show has a half-calcified reputation; looking in need of repair. Yet, "The show must go on." & on and on and on. The perfect replica of the form of top-down media. An unassailable authority who always won in the end. A legacy of years of incumbency, where the cop show was merely a grade above the cowboys vs the Indians on repeat. The Wire does not ask for a revolution, just an example of how things may be better served. It is pure neg' entropy, for negative entropy's sake. It is realism that is not real, just a movie and will have a cherished character killed off because that is what is real. As much as this well-loved show is applauded, the critics are not asking if the crime rate is down in Baltimore. And on a greater score, have similar communities had a drop in crime, or sadly, are the audience just too much revelling in entertainment. So, reported last year, Baltimore has the highest homicide rate in the nation's biggest cities.

Correlation is not causation. It is impossible to suggest that a homicide rate up or down has any connection to the highly popular HBO series The Wire. Then, in the same token it would be impossible to suggest The Wire had no effect on social situations of Baltimore. The show was aired between 2002 and 2008.

Year	Homicides (City, Number)	City, Rate	U.S., Rate
2001	256	38.7	5.6
2002	253	37.7	5.6
2003	270	41.9	5.7
2004	276	43.5	5.5
2005	269	42	5.7
2006	276	43.3	5.8
2007	282	45.2	5.7
2008	234	36.9	5.4
2009	238	37.3	5.0
2010	223	34.8	4.8
2011	196	31.1	4.7
2012	218	34.9	4.7
2013	233	37.4	4.5
2014	211	33.8	4.9
2015	344	55.4	5.1
2016	318	51.4	5.3
2017	343	57.8	5.7

https://homicides.news.baltimoresun.com/

David was strangely involved in stylistic components of the show... Surely this is the stuff for the producers. I suggest his addition to the stylistic component is reasoned to distance himself from a possible rise in crime rate. The 4:3 aspect ratio, the pagers, the lack of computers, was a particular attribute for David. It posits the show in the manner of an historical document. David was not advocating a future, not presenting a contemporary issue, he was positing The Wire in the limelight of regression. This measure ensured a distance from a grandstanding correlative view that he had a negative impact on Baltimore city. It is difficult to argue he was advertising murder when he was particularly asserting an historical view. This regression can be argued that history is naturally the place of a worse society and is not to be taken as an example to be followed.

 As can be seen these are speculation as an evaluation "Invites us to see a series differently, providing a glimpse into one viewer's aesthetic experience" (Mittel 2013 p. 46). "Persuasion rather than demonstration"(Fish in Mittel p. 48) Stanley Fish.

92. Mad Men & In the Mood for Love

The entangled image is semiotic, enacted by association. It breathes another life into a story. The entangled image resonates as an involuntary personal reaction to ratify memories. The entangled image is a welcome guest of complex TV style and can't be brought to life as abstraction. As Karen Barad states. "To be entangled is not simply to be intertwined with one another, But to lack an independent self-contained existence" (Barad 2007, p. 6).

I have chosen an entangled image from *Mad Men* S1 E3, it is entangled in the movie '*In the Mood for Love*' 2000 directed by Wong Kai-wai. 'The show is about the 60's, the work and home environment. The scenes are stylish and are placed in a world of infidelity. Business is happening, yet the audience does not see the machinery of manufacture. The industry hardware itself is an assumed entangled image. The protagonist male character looks, continually pensive, troubled, and perplexed.'
  This could be a description of either show, such is the broader entanglement of this image.

The *Mad Men* scene, parallels the haute couture of *In the Mood For Love*, both scenes have a strong design dress sense. The similarities again exist when considering the camera placement. Looking at the 2000 movie (see picture above left) it is a long shot, framed by the door. I allege this is copied by Mad Men 2007. (see picture above right). It is a complement to the Mad Men audience that it is suggested they are familiar with Hong Kong art house movies.

The essence of the entangled image is elaborated upon in Proust's book. 'In search of lost times.' The title is literally an explanation of the entangled image. A mental push towards finding a past that was profound enough to be triggered. Holland explains this experience, he states, "Proust emphasizes the importance of involuntary memory: images of the past that occur to us involuntarily are far more important than memories that are recollected at will" (Holland 2013, p. 20). Again hypertrophy. Holland claims an audience valourises the entangled image over the plot. As an audience might stop and ponder the memory, a viewer will miss the plot & derail an understanding of the scene. This in itself is another comprehension of "lost times," a characteristic of the entangled image.

The entangled image faculty is understood to go back further than language. Its origin remains before the primal scream. It is when humanity was "thinking in pictures," Sigmund Freud once wrote, (thinking in pictures) "stands nearer to unconscious processes than does thinking in words, and is unquestionably older than the latter both ontogenetically and phylogenetically" (Monk 2012).

The entanglement faculty itself has Darwinian roots as the audience is genetically related to "an entangled bank, clothed with many banks of many kinds, with birds singing in the bushes, with various insects flitting around" (Darwin 1996, p.395). Darwin invokes a time before language, when all that was thought was images of nature. A time of the origins of the entangled image.

References

Barad, Karen 2007, *Meeting the universe halfway quantum physics and the entanglement of matter and meaning*, Duke University Press, Durham and London, USA.

Darwin, Charles 1996, *The origin of the species*, Oxford University Press, Oxford.

Holland, Eugene 2013, *A reader's guide deleuze and guattari's a thousand plateaus*. Bloomsbury Academic, New York, USA.

Monk, Ray 2012, *New statesman america, Ludwig wittgenstein's passion for looking, not thinking,* viewed 18th January 2019, <
https://www.newstatesman.com/culture/art-and-design/2012/08/ludwig-wittgenstein%E2%80%99s-passion-looking-not-thinking?fbclid=IwAR3dKcXBZtFtVZ1ANePsZQnjsv6cTPk9rh TFJYmVQPvSUO_6Z_eSXYJFpGI>

93. I'm Totally Wired

The Wire is a visionary cop show, in the knowledge of many cop shows that have gone before. "Nanos gigantium humeris insidentes." Said Newton. "Seeing further on the shoulder of giants." Characters without malice, hate, fear. The series is played out with a sense of justice, rules and inevitability of actions. The existence of moral platitudes are gone. That is, there is no finger waving blaming rhetoric. The aftermath of killing has not portrayed, a crying family, destroyed from shot child, a murdered loved one. There are no tears. *The Wire* shows a utopian world where a murder has occurred without grief. *The Wire* ethical practice is not in the numbers of killings but in the quality of community. *The Wire* is filled with loyalty, camaraderie, generosity, fraternity. How can America give up the guns if it gives not just quality TV but a complex TV of social, philosophical, anthropological, and human understanding? The magic of television is all on display, as a sleight of hand. The story arcs, nuanced references to a later pivotal happening. forty-nine scenes in fifty-seven minutes S4 E1. This is a drama with pace and characters galore to keep the plot links and audience on the lightest thread. This complexity sits on the boundaries of narrative. Not just to be amused but to relish in the police who are solving crime and the honesty among thieves who exist in symbiosis. This narrative has to weave a spell to keep their moniker of realism. IN the 4:3 format and the flow of Baltimore vernacular. is not just the street dialogue " The lost ball in the high grass motherfucker corcetti" but the juxtaposition of.
the dull politicisation uncreative voice so heavy in overuse. For example, "talk about commitment and vision." There is a voice necessary to disparage vs the necessary voice to appease.

94. Like a Bird on A Wire

This is an evaluation of The Wire, a TV series set in Baltimore and broadcast from 2002 to 2008.
The Wire is produced by HBO, who put together sixty episodes over five seasons. The television drama has huge critical acclaim. "Arguably the greatest television programme ever made "(Arguably the greatest television programme 2009), says The Telegraph. This writing intends to explore textual and contextual dimensions and cover culturally significant subject areas initiated by the TV series. This New Television is developed in response to a 'home-group' rather than a cinema going public. An acknowledgment of a viewer who wishes to be interpolated in their own home. It is not a social occasion like cinema, but occasional, fitting in with domestic vicissitudes. The Wire's distinctive acclaim has made it a model for study. The evaluation will identify teleogically, what it is that makes it a most admired, narrative complexity (complex TV), of our time. "so, what exactly is narrative complexity? At its most basic level, narrative complexity redefines episodic forms under the influence of serial narration" (Mittel 2013, p. 38).

To begin the Wire Series E1. S1. There is a dead body on the streets of Baltimore and locals gather in the middle of the night. In a filmic sense, this is a 'point of no return' and a moral imperative for The Wire season one. The opening scene is most important to a TV series, whereas in the past cinema has developed characters and built tension, now New Television, just delivers. This will appear in complex TV, as starting in the middle of the story, *in media res*. A dead body at the beginning is not unusual for complex TV. For example, House of Cards, Twin Peaks, and the Mad Men titles. The dead body provides an immediacy. There is a sense that something must be done and the dead body delivers an essential narrative momentum and identifies the series as essential. Literally, 'a matter of life and death.'

This death in the opening scene can be understood as emblematic of The Wire series. This cutting-through, is quintessential to New Television and further guides the viewer to a new era in television. Here, complex TV does not start at the beginning. The opening shot is key and paramount. The 'home group 'can just switch off, switch over, or give up. So, the producer /director must be mindful of the home context, then modify the mode of production respectively. The teleology of this method is to hold the attention, steadfast, of the home viewer. In a filmic sense this is a televisuality world, where form follows function again. To explain, Caldwell states, "Televisuality was an industrial product. Frequently ignored or underestimated by scholars, television's mode of production has had a dramatic impact on the presentational guises, the narrative forms, and the politics of mainstream television" (Caldwell 1995. P 20).

Furthermore, the body provides a motif of complex TV in the style. "What Seymour Chatman calls 'kernels' and 'satellites.' The major kernels are central to the cause-and-effect chain of a plot, while minor satellites are inessential to the plot" (Mittel 2015, p. 46). This arcing narrative style is forever planting clues or distractions, kernels or satellites respectively. The dead body in a normative sense would be a kernel yet here in the unconventional complex TV, of The Wire, it is a satellite. Sadly, another dead body in Baltimore, not essentially referred to in the rest of the show.

Narrative has rules that have been in place since the beginning of language. At the heart of this evaluation is a poetics of complex TV and how The Wire has triumphed while others quit after the pilot program. It is an iconic beginning to start with death. This narrative has been done before. James Joyce's The Sisters begins "There was no hope for him this time" (Joyce

1961, p. 9) Camus' book, The Outsider," opening line is "My mother died today" (Camus 2018, p.4). The difference is that in literature, we are told but in complex TV we are shown. It is important to recognize how a TV medium can affect the narrative and yet fit into the classic plot. The leaning to diegetic in film, rather than mimetic, is an historical reference point and has valourised the TV series over the book. - There is no such thing as binge reading.

Laid at the feet of the audience is an old fashion murder mystery. Detective McNulty listens to a witness casually explain the banal murder. It was told like this. – Snotboogie, A card game player would always cheat and he would always be bashed, but this time he was shot dead. Detective McNulty says. "I gotta ask you. If every time Snotboogie would grab the money and run away, why did you let him in the game" (The Wire 2002)? The witness states. "Got to let him play, this America man" (The Wire 2002). A polysematic conversation that could be funny, sage, or surreal. This is the bespoke text of The Wire. It is unconventional, irrational and human yet follows the rules of narrative. Complexity here works as a kernel to be drawn upon later in the series, with the phrase from McNulty. "In the game" (The Wire 2002). The Wire is trying to solve the problems of a poor city in North America. In a broader context and acknowledging a broader audience outside of North America. These problems are the problems of all cities around the world.

The narrative of The Wire series follows a mythology structure understood by anthropologist Claude Levi Strauss. Claude Levi gives the example of the Oedipus myth to illustrate his findings and suggests all myth follows a formulaic story structure. Rimmon-Kenan explains. "According to Levi Strauss, the structure which underlies every myth is that of a fourth term homology, correlating one pair of opposed mythemes with another A:B::C:D" (Rimmon-Kenan 1983, p. 11). In this evaluation of The Wire, it can be deduced that the A:B is a dialectic of the Baltimore Police. That is, Detective McNulty's crew versus Major Rawl's establishment or what you might call, street cops versus office cops. The C:D is the Stringer Bell kingpins versus the Dee Angello street crew. Or what you might call, the office dealers versus the street dealers. Finally, :: is representative of the clash between the police and dealers. This is demonstrative of the idea that there is nothing new in New Television. It is noted that from the Strauss system that even within a contemporary culture of change, the plot formulae remains the same.

As much as this well-loved show is applauded, the critics are not asking if the crime rate is down in Baltimore. And on a greater score, have similar cities had a drop in crime, or sadly, is the audience just revelling in entertainment. Reported last year in The Baltimore Sun. "Baltimore has the highest homicide rate in the nation's biggest cities" (Neighborhoods are crying out 2018). According to crime data released Monday by the FBI September 25th 2018. Correlation is not causation. It is impossible to suggest that a homicide rate has any connection to the popular HBO series The Wire. Then, in the same token it would be impossible to suggest, The Wire had no effect on the social situation of Baltimore.

The Wire uses remediation in the use of 4:3 aspect ratio 35mm film. Remediation in the sense that it is appropriating a historical format, 4:3. A television TV series is usually widescreen 16:9. The 4:3 aspect ratio has brought a homogenous and idiosyncrasy style to the whole series. It is a hankering after simpler times, computers are not yet so available. The style trait, sets it apart from any other screen media. 4:3 is strictly TV format largely given up by 1995. Its use is a daring, risky and some would say, a pointless exercise. It would have been better to shoot in 16:9 and convert to 4:3. This would provide the 4:3 TV look, but also the possibility to play widescreen when necessary. Converting the other way would crop the frame, top and bottom. The notion that this is not a good idea is furthered by David Simon's blog, he states. "But there are other scenes, composed for 4:3, that lose some of their purpose and power*"* (David Simon talks controversial widescreen conversion 2014).

The Wire writer, David Simon, was involved in stylistic components of the show. This is not something a writer usually gets involved in. I suggest his addition to the stylistic component is reasoned to further the viewer to give an interpretation of the text as historical. The 4:3 aspect ratio, the pagers, the lack of computers, was a particular attribute for David. David was not advocating a future, not presenting a contemporary issue, he was positing The Wire as history. This measure, ensured his distance from a grandstanding correlative view, that The Wire might have a negative social impact on Baltimore City.

The realism of The Wire is asserted predominantly with the use of Baltimore vernacular and traditional shooting style in production. The realism is overwhelming, so overwhelming it is easy to overlook that police in the show don't shoot anyone. Whereas, it is much the norm that the world news will again cite a story of police shooting a civilian. "998 people shot and killed by police 2018" (*Fatal force* 2019). This is what makes this show complex, as it poses as realism, yet no civilians are shot by police. This is an enigma, a puzzle to be solved, complex. The Wire is not us versus them, cops versus drug dealers. It establishes the dialectic within the police and then separately within the drug dealers. It exemplifies a world where the police have stopped shooting civilians. A David Simon utopian vision. It provides an understanding that this is a starting point for a better community. It is asserting that the police should stop shooting people, The Wire is the road to recovery. This is hegemony of The Wire.

The Wire is a visionary police show in the knowledge of many cop shows that have gone before. Seeing further on the shoulder of giants. *The Wire* has a team of characters without malice, hate, fear. The series is played out with a sense of justice, rules and inevitability of actions. The existence of moral platitudes are gone. That is, there is no 'drugs are bad' rhetoric. The aftermath of killings is not portrayed, rarely a crying family. There are few tears. The Wire shows a screen world where a murder has occurred with little grief. The Wire is filled with loyalty, camaraderie, generosity, fraternity. A community that deserves to be saved.

Jason Millett commenting on complex TV has made it clear, in making an evaluation, aesthetics has been the key word for complex TV. He states, "we should consider the issue of evaluation, looking at such transformations through the lens of aesthetic judgment" (Millet, in ed. Jacobs, Peacock 2013, p. 45). The question can be asked, is The Wire beautiful. Beauty have long been assessed, most notably by Aristotle Metaphysics, Kant from The Critique of Judgement (1791) and Kierkegaard's Either /or: a fragment of life.

I will use Kant's method "analytic of the beautiful" and evaluate aesthetic, as it is said, "were it not for his work (Kant), aesthetics would not exist in its modern form" (Scruton 2001 p. 99). In his book Critique of Judgement, Kant goes through a fourfold process of moments. I will go through this, same fourfold process using The Wire as the subject. Answering the four definitions of beauty.

1. "Feeling of pleasure " (Kant 1988, p. 41) . The Wire is beautiful. This pleasure is exemplified in complex TV as the pleasure of kernels of narrative arcs. Such as, detective McNulty says, he doesn't want to be on the river and then 12 episodes later, he is on the boat. Many things of beauty are established in The Wire, the vernacular, the team work, human respect and disrespect, the brave application of 4:3 format, scene juxtaposition containing opposites and similarities. These are the beautiful things of The Wire.

2. "The beautiful is that which, apart from concept, pleases universally"." (Kant 1988, p. 60). The Wire does not please universally. The street talk is too difficult to follow and with subtitles it has a tendency to isolate viewers. For example, S4

E7. "Everyone knows his nigga ain't about to cop, is he?" This is difficult to understand, even with the benefit of time to ponder what this means. But then the writer David Simon claims it does have a universal appeal. "American dystopia plays a lot better the further you get from America" (Simon 2014).

3. "Purposiveness" [*Zweckmässigkeit*] (Aesthetics and morality 2005). Asks, does the object have purpose even though the concept was without purpose? Of course, this can be said of all movies. The map is not the territory. The movie concept will always have possibilities of purpose outside concept. For example, it would be hoped the crime rate would decrease. in Baltimore, yet who could see that the purpose might have increased the crime rate.

4. "The beautiful is that which, apart from a concept, is cognized as object of a necessary delight" (Kant 1988 p. 85). It is said beauty is in the eye of the beholder, the fourth moment is a subjective judgment. If it was pleasure, the viewer was looking for, many more took to watching Breaking Bad than The Wire. The Wire topped at 4 million while Breaking Bad had a finale that was 10 million. It is evident that the novel television of Breaking Bad upstages the realism of The Wire in popularity. Realism is trumped, it is not so full of "delight" (Kant 1988 p. 85).

"Ideology represents the imaginary relationship of individuals to their real conditions of existence" (Althusser 2008, p. 36)

The Wire does not preach an ideology, so what is the ideology of this no ideology? Stating no position, is a political statement and a pervasive means of captivation. A space of no apparent didactic reference. It is real and innocent. Nobody wants to see a movie that tells you what to do. So, the message of The Wire, is to be respectful and acknowledge why the viewer is watching. A viewer is seeking knowledge, a need to be informed, to be worldly, to keep up with a contemporary struggle, without experiencing it themselves. This is the ontology of The Wire and the reason for its critical acclaim. It establishes issues in the community by merely enunciating them. An example as to how things can be played. "In the game" as Bubbles, the informer, would say. This is the ideology, 'the game.' This is the capitalism of the streets. There is a market, there are hierarchies, there are rules and there is a code, as to how an individual is prepared to act ethically. This market only differs from the usual market by being illegal. Thus, The Wire suggests that everyone in North America is 'in the game' but for that one difference.

'In the game' is a club and The Wire expresses this collective as a team and establishes all illegal drug associates are 'in the game' as part of that community. As if, without the street drugs, there would be no collective community. Anthropologist Claude Levi Straus explains that games are disjunctive, in a way that people inevitably loose. This in contrast to, ceremony or ritual, which he describes as conjunctive, community orientated, and nobody loses. He states, "Games thus appear to have a disjunctive effect: they end in the establishment of difference between individuals or teams where originally there was no indication of inequality" (Levi-Strauss 1962, p. 32). So here, in The Wire people lose.

How can America give up the guns, if it presents a new complex TV? Full of social, philosophical, anthropological, and human understanding. The magic of complex television, is on display. The story arcs as references to a later pivotal happening. Forty-nine scenes in fifty-seven minutes, S4 E1, this is a drama with pace and characters galore to keep an individual style, plot links, and an audience on the lightest thread. This complexity is a glue for the narrative. This narrative has to weave a spell to keep the moniker of realism. In the 4:3 format and the flow of Baltimore vernacular. Is not just the street dialogue, for example, "The lost ball in the high grass motherfucker Corcetti" (The Wire 2004) but the juxtaposition of the dull politician. "Talk about commitment and vision" (The Wire 2004). There is always a voice necessary to disparage versus the voice to appease.

This evaluation of *The Wire*, will take into account, a credo of the writer David Simon. So as to answer the question, what is the relative motivation that inspires the Wire? And what is it, that needs to be explained in terms of economic and cultural factors? David states "Collective responsibility without freedom is tyranny:: personal freedom and personal liberty without collective responsibility ……. is selfish." (*The Wire*'s success is in its ability to be unconventional and new and join the realms of complexity but also stands firm in the corner of realism, asking to be taken seriously. Managing this has granted the show critical acclaim.

In summary, The Wire has a moniker of complex TV, while enjoying critical acclaim.
It has managed to broadcast realism, in its own way, on its own terms. It has been guided by narrative rules and added novel ways of representation. It is a pity; a social revolution cannot be seen in the wake of the broadcast. Movies with all their influence appear to influence other movies rather than society itself. The Wire won't be repeated and New Television will be historically seen a time of reinvention inspired by the home inclinations of its new audience.
Most TV series don't ache to avert social problems. The Wire's difficulty here, is to inspire the sedentary.

BIBLIOGRAPHY

Aesthetics and morality 2005, presentation of The Critique of Judgment by Stanford University, viewed 5th February 2019, <https://plato.stanford.edu/entries/kant-aesthetics/#2.8>

Caldwell, John Thornton 1995, *Televisuality : style, crisis, and authority in american television communication media and culture,* Rutgers University Press, New Brunswick, New Jersey, USA.

Camus, Albert 2018, *The outsider,* Oberon Books Ltd, London, UK.

David Simon talks controversial widescreen conversion of the wire for HD 2014, review of David Simon comments, viewed 5th February 2014, <https://www.indiewire.com/2014/12/david-simon-talks-controversial-widescreen-conversion-of-the-wire-for-hd-269568/>

Fatal force 998 people have been shot and killed by police 2019, data from official database, viewed 5th February 2019, < https://www.washingtonpost.com/graphics/2018/national/police-shootings-2018/?utm_term=.57c95a80b8e1>

Joyce, James 1962, *Dubliners,* Compass Books Edition, New York, USA.

Levi-Strauss, Claude 1962, *La pensee sauvage (The savage mind),* The Garden City Press Ltd, Hertfordshire, UK.

Mittel, Jason 2015, *Complex tv, the poetics of contemporary television storytelling.* New York University Press. New York, USA.

Mittel, Jason 2013, *Television aesthetics and style*, Bloomsbury Academic, London, UK.

'Neighborhoods crying out' Baltimore has highest homicide rate of US cities, 2018, journalist article from Baltimore Sun, viewed 5th February 2018,

Rimmon-Kenan, Shlomith 1983, Narrative fiction contemporary poetics, Methuen & Co. Ltd, New York, USA.
Scrutton, Roger 2001, *Kant, a very short introduction,* Oxford University Press, Oxford, UK.

Simon, David 2014, *David simon on why he created The Wire| observer ideas,* YouTube clip, <https://youtu.be/ZYXNdELqCe4 >

The Wire 2002, Television programme, HBO, USA.
The Wire 2004, Television programme, HBO, USA.

The Wire : Arguably the greatest television programme ever made 2009, review of television series, viewed 5th February 2019 https://www.telegraph.co.uk/news/uknews/5095500/The-Wire-arguably-the-greatest-television-programme-ever-made.html

95. Narrative

Narrative narrative narrative. My narrative, your narrative.

The News today. Crazy impulsive, is the false fulfillment of
narrative and the hasty desire towards it object petit a. or as
Zizek puts it, the sort after scroll in Kung Fu Panda that is found
but when seen, it is a blank sheet of paper.
The emptiness of desire, of news narrative, fake or no fake, is
still propelled effortlessly towards the viewer, not with
subversive intent or notions of control but notions of scoring.
The media has scored a hit under the rules, 'all in the game,' the
game that is disjunctive, as Levi Strauss told us. it is not
ontology objective; it is not essence objective merely notion
subjective.

96. Language Communication

The bank's pop-up slide announces "changes to simplify using the site" under which is a OK button. My understanding is, I acknowledge reading and wishing to dismiss the slide, push OK. After I have pushed OK I realise another meaning. A meaning that appears in my head after I push the button. as if the meaning would have only arrived after i pushed the button. This meaning being, that by pushing the button I had agreed to simplified the site by pushing OK

97.The Death of Hypertrophy

Hypertrophy must die

 In the edit of the text or the film. It is said, *Kill Your Darlings*,
re William Faulkner,

The stand out personal self must disappear.

it is private moment only known to the editor, it is the self
tumescent, it must die.

It is your totem.... not everybody owns the same totem. therefore
the audience considered, the totem

must be gone.

it is a social instinct...says anthropologist... Reinnach.. in Freud's
book Totem and Taboo...

He calls this Hypertrophy..

p 97 "Une hypertrophie de l'instinct social."

98. The Great Pyramid

The great pyramid faces true north, out by 3/60 of a degree. six million tonnes. and 13 acres...

. The height of the pyramid. multiplied by 43,200 is the polar radius of the earth.

The perimeter of the pyramid multiplied by 43,200 is the equatorial circumference of the earth & the number of seconds in a day is 43,200.

99. IHVH

Ignore things so that they are not part of your preferred world...
For example, ignore talking, mentioning, an unfavourite
something, so as to be not involved in this world. Even in your
negation of the subject matter you are part of the subject. Ergo,
don't mention it ...

100. To Name is To Know

To name is to know, to know is to control. Kant states that
space and time are a priori. Chomsky states an ability to speak
language is a priori. So, we consider the world as, a priori or
posteriori. As Kant popularised this concept similar concepts
collide. Let me explain. Let us consider Tony Myer's, Zizek
book. He paraphrased Zizek with a definition of the subject.

- "If you take away all your distinctive characteristics, all
your particular needs, interests and beliefs. - what is left is the
subject." The subject is the 'Plato's form' of the consciousness
and opposed to the contents of that form is the Symbolic Order.
Its constant negation is the work of the Imaginary Stage.

When viewing instructively, the subject pertains to the self. A
microcosm. The microcosm and a priori/ posteriori add to make
up all of the world. the everything.

The macrocosm yet is not the capture of subject posteriori & non
subject all things a priori. So, the macrocosm & microcosm are
the same, a unified field theory.

& also, consider the DMT trip as the real trip … it lacks the
emotional instability of acid and pot. So, it is the Apollonian
drug effecting a visual logic … And perhaps sadly merely an
aprior vision to recognise 3d coloured geometrical space and
homunculus of the ancients (leprechaun, Krishna, the dubdubani
of Tiwi Islands)….The DMT trip are signifiers with no signified,
like a dream in this sense. but has no signifying chain as Lacan
would have described it. the DMT trip is self-contained.
Archetypal. So, if the signfier is to bridge the gap to the
signifying chain it can be signified as archetypal. DMT vision is
a vision of a transcendent Lacanian subject.

THE SHAPE SHIFTING ALIEN BROADCASTING
CORPORATION
is not biological but mechanical

101. Duplicity is Not Such a Bad Thing

Duplicity is not such a bad thing.
The success of a smoke free campaign arrived as duplicity; the rise in the price, garnered with a sprinkling of horror memes on the packet. The duplicity harnessing the narrative formulae put forward by Claude Levi-Strauss -

A plus B is comparable to C plus D . This, states Claude is the form of all narrative, all myth, and has been inculcated to humanity since the time of the origins of language and still loved today through the books of fiction and the any narrative film.

A plus B is "the rise in the price" (A) plus "horror memes on the packet" (B)

C plus D is the human endeavour. Perhaps, Denial (C) plus i'm addicted (D)

To be continued...

.102. The Calculus of the Trip

Aka Trivelu brodeens the mindf.

I want to talk to you now, about the calculus of the trip. Where the time and date of the start of the trip are constants. a, the time of start, b, the time of finish and f(x) is the reality of the trip.

$$\int_a^b f(x)\,dx.$$

The reality of the trip can be split into two parts, analogous to the internet. UX User Experience and IA Information Architecture.

The Information Architecture IA is fully incorporated in the calculus above but fair to say there must be a use of e, the probability constant when examining UX. There are surprises on a trip the statistical probability of getting robbed in Rome is different than the statistical probability of getting robbed in London.

There are calculus equations that might peak and dip a crime wave on a visiting population. Even the idea of the possibility of being robbed might affect the equation. Peter Singer recently has been promoting the statistical probability of countries being more dishonest than others. The survey showed that religious communities were the worst offenders.

Everyone's trip to the same destination is different. This is the UX User Experience.

The IA information architecture remains the same.

It is without doubt the imagining of freedom that compels the person to travel. & ; that is all it is an imagined freedom.

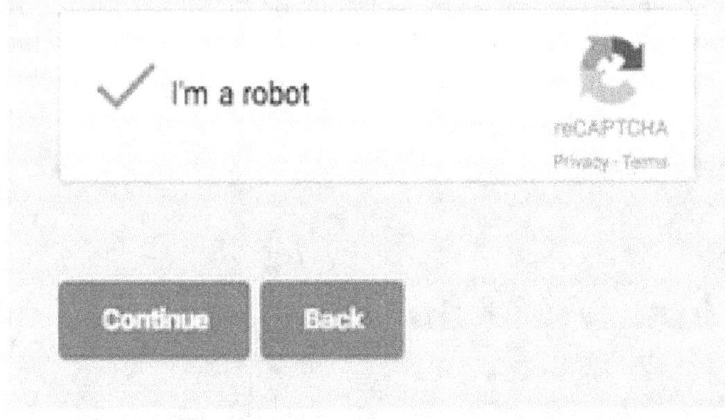

The analogue / digital dichotomy is a false dichotomy in the same way Albert Hoffman's synthesis of Psilocybin is the same as the mushroom in the field.

The start of the trip has a certain formula, the expense, the ticket, the gathering of clothes, the credit card, internet searches, the passport, the visa, the portable Wi-fi items, the travel, the toiletry bag. the snack, ag, &

The travel itself.

the destination and all that goes on in that vicinity.

The calculus of travel purely considers the holiday and the unforeseen circumstances. Unforeseen circumstance like being robbed, the car breaks down, a disease, a broken bone, can be considered as part of the statistical elements to the trip.

Under the umbrella of time. Maslow's hierarchy of needs is aptly used to negotiate the trip and the products of desire within. under the bandwidth of, age sex, interpolation of the locals and the random events. each trip has a near infinite possibilities and similarities. Here there is a concentration on the similarities and to be accurate not discounting the possibilities. Each travel to the same destination has a different experience.

I. Fourier, or the Arcades

The magic columns of these palaces
Show to the amateur on all sides,
In the objects their porticos display,
That industry is the rival of the arts.

—*Nouveaux Tableaux de Paris* (Paris, 1828), vol. 1, p. 27

There are all kinds of movement that are ingrained within a human psyche. For example, the inclination moves away from danger, the first steps from the trees to the savanna for food, the movement from fresh water to shelter.... There is something more than historical about travel. It is about survival over millennia.

Food, fresh water ... food, fresh water... these were the cyclical elements compelling travel for millions of years. Before an agrarian society, when all the organic detritus was mounting. The tribe would periodically move on or get sick from bacteria.

Even at a cellular level, bacteria moves towards food or away from poison.

As the feeling of being compelled to travel is alive today. Is this feeling an inculcated necessity of the DNA?

103. A List of Travel Songs

1. Helter Skelter. Siouxie and the Banshees
https://youtu.be/uoAFWBofj1Y
2. Itravel. Simple Minds
https://youtu.be/_6MwzSaBBQY
3. King of the Road. Roger Miller
https://youtu.be/7HBQFjoqDYE
4. Wide Open Road. The Triffids
https://youtu.be/7N5akOOlGTI
5. Music for Airports. Brian Eno
https://youtu.be/vNwYtllyt3Q
6. Kraftwerk. Autobahm ..
reworked.. https://vimeo.com/2149818
7. The Passenger. Iggy Pop
https://youtu.be/hLhN__oEHaw
8. Holiday. Madonna.
https://youtu.be/5Rswx2Z7SDw
9. Holiday in Cambodia. Dead Kennedys
https://youtu.be/-KTsXHXMkJA
10. Holiday in The Sun. Sex Pistols
https://youtu.be/2Ah1JM9mf60
11. Redgum. I've been to Bali too.
https://youtu.be/EVOIg_lHRzk

104. Parallel Travel

A ghost in the machine. In the sense that the words and pictures and stories of the other worlds of the Romantic era conjured a reification of a fiction of Gulliver's Travels, 1726, Robinson Crusoe 1719, and Mary Shelley's Frankenstein 1818. are told to hardly describe the reality that cannot been explained. This is a contemporary reality of 17th century.

Quite literally Hegel and Wordsworth/Goethe living alongside each other. Hegel and Wordsworth born 1770. Goethe died a year after Hegel in 1832.

An enlightenment (age of reason)
1715- 1789

105. Parallel Travel

The trip has been variously described "
1. an act of going to a place and returning"
2. a self-indulgent attitude or activity:
3. a device that activates or disconnects a mechanism,
4. a hallucinatory experience caused by taking a psychedelic drug, especially LSD:
Through the eyes of the dictionary connections between the meanings and the
method of derivation are not explained.
Here lies the subtleties of the meaning of the word. The dictionary states the meaning
as an abstraction and for our word "Trip" "
n act of going to a place" does not relate to or give rise to "hallucinatory experience caused by taking a psychedelic drug, especially LSD:" Yet
this is an essential part of the meaning of the LSD experience. to simply
"an act of going to a place and return." This is a start to explain further the ineffable LSD. Psilocybin and the other hallucinogen DMT. The separation between the
mushroom and LSD and on the other side of hallucinogens DMT is a clear analogy
between the traveller and the tourist. The magic mushroom /LSD has a euphoric feeling
that come with the trip. and this is truly sublime in the Edmond Burke definition. He
always sees some horror attached to the sublime this advice when on the LSD trip not
to look in the mirror is great advice. This is in stark contrast to the DMT which is a
clinical trip not messing with emotions. You saw what you saw, make what of it you
will. Just like the tourist site seeing. The analogy of the trip goes

further as Alain de Boton talks philosophical about the
Mediterranean cruise he inadvertently stumbles upon a salient
part of the LSD trip .. "IN
the middle of day one I had inadvertently realised that I had
brought myself with me
on the holiday" Poignant is the picture that is used to introduce
this sentence.... A
picture of a vast ocean. that what Alain was getting to was the
space between meals
there was plenty of time to stare into the abyss. It was a soul-
searching time where all
the demons and bliss might dwell... is this not the Edmond
Bourke sublime. ?
$110 trip to Bali is way in the ball park affordability of travellers
and if you haven't done overseas. You
haven't grown up yet. You are uninitiated and a general social
sense that you are less worldly ... if you
haven't travelled then you have marked yourself off out of any
social milieu. - 'hell, what is wrong with
you!' might be laid on you.
https://youtu.be/EVOIg_lHRzk
"Bali T-shirts, magic mushrooms, Redgum bootlegs I've been to
Bali too"
Reverend Neil Swartz, a Uniting Church Minister living in East
Bentleigh Victoria once told me the
meaning of the biblical parable The Original Sin. He said -Adam
and Eve ate of the apple and the sin
was not that they were forbidden, it was that they didn't eat the
whole apple. That there was an
opportunity, the apple, and only a single bite was taken. Suffice
to say, given an opportunity, you must
make the most of it, that is, eating the whole apple.

106. An Historical Look at the Obscenity Laws

In Response

A Short Australian History of an Expletive - *The Cunt Word.*

Following the Kennett /Peacock tapes airing on RMIT TV
1987 in Melbourne Australia, the law was swift and covert.
Houses were raided in the night, students were takenaway for
questioning, and no charges were laid. The mobilization of
police resources and their actions are revelatory moments in the
Australian public use of the cunt word. This is thirty-two years
ago and these actions would seem

excessive today in 2019.

Here is part of the transcribed, 1987, telephone conversation
between Jeff Kennett, Victorian

Premier 92-99 and Andrew Peacock, Deputy of Liberal Party,
1987 -

"Howard. You're a cunt. You haven't got my

support, you never will have and I'm not going to rubbish you or
the party

tomorrow but I feel a lot better having told you, you're a cunt."

The cunt word is one of the most pejorative and taboo
words in the English speaking

world. So, why use the cunt word? If you are going to use a taboo word because you want

dramatic effect,

use this one. Or if you are a politician who wants to assert a private lingua franca

 denoting yourself as

part of an elite, use the cunt word. Ironically, using the cunt word, also makes

the politician appear in touch with the working man because it is understood in

Australia that the cunt word is part of the working-class vernacular.

   The cunt word has a certain onomatopoeia. The pronunciation sounds like

the noise of a blunt instrument, a thud. The c at one end, of the word, and the

t at the other end, using a combination of powerful sounding consonants to make

an impact. Ferdinand De Saussure, Swiss linguist and semiotician, famously stated,

"The connection between the signifier and the signified is arbitrary". Therefore it

is understood that a 'dog'

in one language and 'une chien' in French language is the same. That is to say,

a cunt is a cunt in any language. But in addition to the cunt word, is its

onomatopoeian thud, which for the English version acts as a catalyst for impact

and effect…In short, it makes the cunt word even more taboo.

The use of the cunt word in a joke constructs a barrier to those who wish to

dismiss it as rude. The detractors are seen as wowsers or unfunny people. The

use of the word in a ten-million-dollar Australian government funded movie 'Welcome

to Whoop Whoop' 1997, is a case in point. The movie quotes "The Sound of Music'

movie, stating, "Marie, what is it you <u>can't</u> face?" and with a Swiss

accent it sounds like, "Maria, what is it you <u>cunt</u> face".
https://youtu.be/xFOw_-5glqg

Everyone joins in the fun by laughing at

the screen. This is a significant push in the social constraint of the word. An

awareness of transgressive behaviour and a receding of the conservative cause. Does

this explain to the world Australia is an open, free, liberated society?

As an egalitarian society, the use of the cunt word in everyday language is

 announcing a world of equals, were everybody is a cunt. In Denis O'Rourke's 2000

documentary Cunnamulla,

staggering in its intimacy, the cunt word is used as a collective noun and transposable

 to any group of people. "He was drunk, it would take more the fuck to make me get the fuck out

of the cunt. No matter how much I love I'm fucker, she wants to go let her go, I'll get

another cunt". https://youtu.be/KBMyzyZcCJo 38 m.01sec.

Tourism organizations often announce a colloquial

phrase to entice the tourist into the world of the local vernacular. "So, where

the bloody hell, are you?" was the announcement of Tourism Australia in 2006. The

"bloody" word expletive and the "hell" expletive were part of an official 180-million-dollar government

advertising campaign banned in UK and Singapore. The current Australian prime minister,

Scott Morrison was the Managing Director of Tourism Australia at the time. Since then, larrikin

language has been

used again, this time using the heavily taboo cunt word in the slogan 'CU in the

NT'. It came to light first appearing as an official tourism campaign, then

denied by Tourism NT. The story still remains as to whether it was government

campaign or not. The 'CU in the NT' campaign doesn't look like amateurs or short

of a million dollars. Here is the website with a big-ticket budget.

https://cuinthent.com/

 https://www.abc.net.au/news/2017-01-05/nt-tourism-department-welcomes-asb-ruling-against-cu-in-the-nt/8163114

Each notorious published case of the cunt word is a emblem of the Australian community

and where it stands on this subject at a particular time. With the most

recent incursion in the Northern Territory, there is a section of the public

who wear it as a badge of honour. Proud of the stir that it causes and

are seemingly heading towards a place for the cunt word in the everyday language.

Currently in the Northern Territory the "CU in the NT" campaign is in full view

of the public, with bumper stickers and spare tyre covers etc. Displayed with

no recourse from government officials.

The cunt word is taboo and the nature of taboo lends itself to avoidance and is even sometimes illegal. Traditionally and socially, it is a word that cannot be

spoke. It is unacceptable and redacted in the official language. People use "c*#t"

instead of "cunt". In one case in Sydney Australia activist Danny Lam uses a 'cvnt' spelling and is

taken to court. He is found innocent of charge. This sets a precedence for a

redacted use of the word in public. Though this court case sets precedence of

sorts, the word still remains one of the most unutterable words.

Danny Lam

court case. 2017.

https://nswcourts.com.au/articles/court-rules-its-ok-to-refer-to-tony-abbott-as-a-ct/

Here, in chronological order, are a number of cunt word broadcast articles that have made it into the public domain.

1 Kennett/ Peacock tapes. 1987.
https://australianpolitics.com/1987/03/23/kennett-peacock-car-phone-conversation.html

2.Welcome to Whoop Whoop movie. 1997.
https://youtu.be/xFOw_-5glqg
3. Cunnamulla 2000. Denis O'Rourke documentary.
https://youtu.be/KBMyzyZcCJo

4 Cu in the NT campaign 2017.
https://www.abc.net.au/news/2017-01-05/nt-tourism-department-welcomes-asb-ruling-against-cu-in-the-nt/8163114

5. Danny Lam court case. 2017
https://nswcourts.com.au/articles/court-rules-its-ok-to-refer-to-tony-abbott-as-a-ct/

138 The Monarch of the Glen, by Edwin Landseer (1851)

This graceful horned beast passes as subject and object, and falls in the category of the sublime. The category of awe inspiring, yet terrifying.

Well known critique of the sublime, Edmond Bourke, *A Philosophical Enquiry into the Origin of Our Ideas of the Sublime and Beautiful* 1757, goes further into the definition and uses Milton to describe Satan as sublime. This fits well into what is signified by the painting *The Monarch of the Glen,* a horned beast, incorporating a monarch by the use of the title.
Perhaps Bourke's use of Milton is the origin of the title of the painting, *The Monarch of the Glen.* Here below is Bourke's writings, using Milton to understand Satan and the sublime.
 "We do not anywhere meet a more sublime description
than this justly celebrated one of Milton, wherein he gives the portrait of Satan with a dignity so suitable to the subject:
He above the rest" *(Paradise Lost 1658)* -
 "In shape and gesture proudly eminent
Stood like a tower; his form had yet not lost
All her original brightness, nor appeared
Less than archangel ruined, and th` excess

Of glory obscured: as when the sun new risen
Looks through the horizontal misty air
Shorn of his beams; or from behind the moon
In dim eclipse disastrous twilight sheds
On half the nations; and with fear of change
Perplexes monarchs".
(Milton in Burke, Edmond, p.44)
The first glance of the painting can be understood as an
apprehension, an object, and a second look a comprehension, the
object also as subject.
The subject becomes a sublime signified idea that man and beast
converge as one. Is this not this a chimeric monster of sorts….
Essentially that awe inspiring monster abyss that Nietzsche
mentions in Beyond Good and Evil 1886.
"Whoever fights monsters should see to it that in the-process he
does not become a monster. And when you look long into an
abyss, the abyss also looks into you" (Nietzsche p 89).
This could quite well be a sub heading for the painting.

 This subject object vision reifies an anthropomorphic gaze. A
vision that Jung called the shadow, the dark side of human nature
that asks to be integrated into the self.
 The sublime is such a vision, one that looks back at humanity as
a mirror stage and sees clearly a humanity that asks to consider
and integrate a shadow.

Twenty Years a-Growing by Maurice O'Sullivan.

 On seeing a great edifice of a rock, and thinking it to be a
human figure.

hat. " Your soul to the devil, isn't that Micky the Pillar ? "

Pádrig laughed. " Upon my word, it gave the two of you a good fright."

" Indeed," said Michael, " it is no laughing matter. I was terrified when I saw it."

" You are not the first," said Pádrig, sitting on the thwart. " But this won't do, my boys," he said, putting out an oar. " We are letting the day pass and doing nothing. We will go west through the Sound of Mantle Island and then make for the Strand."

89

108. What is Enlightenment?

Enlightenment is man's emergence from his self-incurred immaturity. Immaturity is the inability to use one's own understanding without the guidance of another. This immaturity is self-incurred if its cause is not lack of understanding, but lack of resolution and courage to use it without the guidance of another. The motto of enlightenment is therefore: Sapere aude! [Dare to be wise!] Have courage to use your own understanding!

Passage above from the start of Kant's "What is Enlightenment?" first published 1784, Three years after his Critique of Pure Reason.

It's talk of moving on, while not mentioning what we are being moved on from. it's not difficult to imagine it is the catholicity of Europe that is the measure that the text refers to.

There it is now; will you force people to be free?
Marx's tomb engraved with the word "philosophers" is said to be a footnote to Hegel. Yet Kant appears just as fitting. Hegel the emancipatory power from capitalism while Kant is the emancipatory power from religion.

109. Travel Music

There is a Travel Music of a different kind. Not the music you listen to when you travel but a special music you listen to that brings you back in time and space. This is the highly subjective phenomena of remembering days past, by listening to an old piece of music. You are literally thrown, without volition, into the past, through time and space and you experience that same life again. All the feelings that the old era might generate, comes back again. It is a type of, "what Heidegger calls thrownness, Geworfenheit, a having-been-thrown into the world." (https://plato.stanford.edu/search/searcher.py?query=Geworfenheit), into a situation you have no choice to be in. This is what Travel Music does, more than likely a favourite tune, throwing you into a historical mindset. Whenever I hear LL Cool J music, I am brought back to LA 1987, driving my Cadillac around the vast streets of LA. It brings forth a feeling of the mood and a sense of the geography experienced at the time.

This is not a completely new phenomenon. It is a theme of Marcel Proust's 1909 book, *In Search of Lost Times*. But in Proust's story the subject doesn't use music, he uses food and drink to travel back in time. A nostalgic trance is brought on literally, "In Search of Lost Times", by eating tea and cake. Food and drink was the catalyst for the invocation of a spirit that used to dwell in the older body and since the young spirit no longer exists, the perception might be, you are emotional because you are mourning the loss of that younger spirit.

Here is the text from Proust's "In Search of Lost times" that expresses that moment when a flood of memories come back from eating tea and cake.

"I raised to my lips a spoonful of the tea in which I had soaked a morsel

of the cake. No sooner had the warm liquid, and the crumbs
with it, touched my
palate than a shudder ran through my whole body, and I stopped,
intent upon
the extraordinary changes that were taking place. An exquisite
pleasure had
invaded my senses, but individual, detached, with no suggestion
of its origin.
And at once the vicissitudes of life had become indifferent to me,
its disasters
innocuous, its brevity illusory--this new sensation having had on
me the effect
which love has of filling me with a precious essence; or rather
this essence was
not in me, it was myself. I had ceased now to feel mediocre,
accidental, mortal.
Whence could it have come to me, this all-powerful joy?"
(Proust 2005, p. 47).
Proust writes heavily about this phenomenon, becoming quite
obsessed by the idea.

110 Travil BrOAdins The MvND

A view, an analysis of the provenance of Literary Tourism. Today's idea of Literary Tourism has a history that provides a foundation for contemporary actuality. Literary Tourism is a unique way of looking at the world and hopes to energize the traveller, furthering an appreciation of the author and text. As the popular phrase of Isaac Newton goes, "Nanos gigantum humeris insidentes", commonly know as, "If you have seen further, it is by standing on the shoulders of giants" (https://discover.hsp.org/Record/dc-9792/Description#tabnav). So too, does the Literary Tourist seek to 'see a little further' by honouring the author.
The preparation of the Literary Tourist is largely unplanned and unrealized. Reading at bedtime and on the commute in the morning, who was to know the aficionado had crossed the Rubicon and begun the trip of a life time. Only in hindsight, it can be seen the books were going to inevitably lead to their grand tour. And now it is hoped, the effort to travel many thousand of kilometres, will instill a fuller sense of meaning to the text. To feel what the author has felt, to endure what the author has endured. The Literary Tourist must ameliorate the quest with all possible adorations to the author. To walk in the footsteps of the author, breathe the air of the author, identify with and understand the surrounding architecture, getting a quasi-real sense of the author's inspiration to write. This is a geographical journey and a journey of the mind, in the hope that the traveller will be inspired.

Literary Tourism is a self-designed celebration of books and their authors. An unabashed distinctive view of the world through a list of travelled experiences. Literary Tourism gives purpose back to travel, by revisiting the authors' lives in the vernacular. Yet, some don't wish to be visited. - "What matter who's speaking someone said, what matter who's speaking" (Beckett, in Foucault 1969, p.300), stated Samuel Beckett. Foucault interpreted this as indifference. In addition, Becket's axiom craves anonymity and a call on the literary tourist to justify themselves. 'Leave me alone, it is all in the text' - Beckett might be heard say. Beckett is dead, buried in Montparnasse Cemetery, who knows what he exactly meant. Roland Barthes reaffirms this idea in Th*e Death of the Author*, leaving every interpretation for debate. "Once the author is removed, the claim to decipher the text is quite futile" (Barthes, Roland 1977, p.147), states Barthes.

Essentially the book, Homer's Odyssey was in many ways the inaugural journey into Literary Tourism. "Received opinion dates him to c. 750-700 BC" (Homer 1991, p. i), and the text is said to be written 8th Century AD. The story is of an epic, ten-year journey, returning to Ithaca from years of war in Troy. The first paperback on Penguin. This publication was itself born out of travel. Let me explain, the co-founder of Penguin paperbacks, Sir Allen Lane, was on a trip to visit Agatha Christie in Greenway, Devon and on returning was waiting on the platform at Exeter St David's railway station. He then came upon the idea of <u>paperbacks for sixpence</u>. And so, the inaugural paperback Homer's Odyssey was born. A book about travel conceived while travelling.

Seemingly, the author wields such power. The fandom get ups, leaves home, treks across the world, spends precious moments at the grave side of the author, visits the author's place of birth and walks the prescribed streets. It must be said that the author has managed vast control and authority. This is the quest that the 'subject position' (Morton, 2011), unearths. That is, the conscious space left by the author for the reader to dwell. An hegemony for the reader to fall into and then be commanded to trek half-way around the world. The 'subject position' (Morton, 2011), in literature, can command such a power because it is narrative. The print word began in 868 AD, the diamond sutra, and written word invented in 1,400 BC with Ugaritic, but narrative is as old as language, 60,000 – 200,000 years ago. The narrative command has been, for such a long time, inculcated to the heart, that is the power of the narrative.

The need and implementation of Literary Tourism is not a new occurrence. Editor of Literary *Tourism and 19th Century Culture,* Nicola J. Watson, suggests there are four historical milestones that are references to today's Literary Tourism. "The rise of Shakespeare's Stratford in the aftermath of David Garrick's Jubilee of 1769, the development of pilgrimage to Robert Burns' birthplace in Alloway from as early as 1799, the building and display of Sir Walter Scott's Abbotsford from 1811 onwards, and the enshrinement of the Brontë sisters' home at Haworth by the end of the century" (ed.Watson 2009, p.2). Remarkable from Watson's list, is what can be identified as the passing of The Age of Enlightenment, circa 1715-1789, into the Romanticism era, circa 1800-1850. In literary terms, it is a passing from Newton, Spinoza, Kant, Hume, Rousseau and Adam Smith to the Romanticism of Wordsworth and Coleridge. This was the handing of the baton from the rationalism to empiricism. From fiction to non-fiction, from indoors to outdoors. The sublime was a lived experience, the *Daffodils* poem of William Wordsworth was a 'subject position'(Morton, 2011), to be experienced. "I wandered lonely as a cloud" (https://www.poetryfoundation.org/poems/45521/i-wandered-lonely-as-a-cloud), begged humanity to contemplate the natural world in the natural world. This was the motivation for a literary tour. For example, Newton's law, "To every action, there is an equal and opposite reaction", tells us how to understand the world and the painting, *Wanderer above the Sea of Fog,* by

Casper David Friedrich 1818, shows us how to live it. The Romanticism was the idea that brought the grand tour outdoors, fully embracing the empirical idea that knowledge was primarily, a posteriori, an experience lived and then reflected upon.

In summary, the Literary Tourist is a noble historian, honouring the author in life and death. The Literary Tourist has become beholden to personal eulogy of the author, to travel and be inspired. Thus fulfilling, a place that was vacant "on the shoulders of giants" (https://discover.hsp.org/Record/dc-9792/Description#tabnav), and in 'the Sea of Fog'.

References

Barthes, Roland 1977, *Image music text*, Fontana Press, Harper Collins Publishers, London, UK.

Foucault, Michel 1969, Modernity *and its discontents,* https://lauradufresne.files.wordpress.com/2013/10/micheal-foucault_what-is-an-author.pdf, retrieved 30 12 2019.

Homer 1991, *The odyssey*, Penguin Books, London, UK.

Morton, timothy 2011, *Timothy morton - "hegel, ecology, aesthetics*, YouTube, https://youtu.be/jrvA3nv0Py4, retrieved 30 12 19.

Newton, Issac 1675, Isaac newton letter to robert hooke, 1675, https://discover.hsp.org/Record/dc-9792/Description#tabnav, retrieved 30 12 2019.

Newton, Issac,
https://ccrma.stanford.edu/~jos/pasp/Newton_s_Three_Laws_M
otion.html, retried 30 12 2019.

Watson, Nicola 2009, *Literary tourism*

142 Ding an Sich

From philosopher Kant, "Ding an Sich" in German or in English
"the thing in itself "
Kant tells us we cannot know the thing-in-itself … We have
limited abilities.
The opening of any book sets the scene. These are the words of
the advice given to any writer wanting to engage an audience
and give the subject (the reader) a place to be.

   Like the flower gives a petal for the bee to sit on and some
honey to nurture on ... The bee has a subject position.

JG Ballard's The Drowned World begins with a subject position,
a psychogeography and geography tempertura. a place of solid
surrounds providing a consciousness and a heat + humidity that
provides the candidate with a certain consciousness. " any book
needs to set the scene"

"Soon it would be too hot. looking out from the hotel balcony
shortly after eight o'clock. Kerans watched the sun rise behind
the dense grooves of giant gymnosperms crowding over the
roofs of the abandoned department stores of hundred yards away
on the east side of the lagoon. Even though the massive olive
fronds the relentless power of the sun was plainly tangible".
(Ballard, JG, p.1)

   Ballard's written word is the concretisation of the
metaphysical... A part of the 'ding an sich' that Kant refers to that
is part of the noumenon. That which we cannot possibly
understand. But as psychogeography stands, it is a felt effect.

112. Freud

As quickly as they pounce at his throat, they are quick. He did
give us the opportunity hundred years ago to talk of such things.
So now we adequately rubbish his Oedipus rex complex and his
father bashing theory as the reverse to be true .. the mother
fucker is the mother who wishes to go her son and the father
wishes to shirt front the son.... Freud gave us a worthy place,
subject, to talk, albeit to sometimes disagree.
Freud gave us Jung. Mythology upon mythology analyses. .. He
gave us Lacan, as Lacan "a return to Freud."
 And he gave us Bauhaus - Shadows Part 2

113. The Egyptian Book of the Dead

"For magic to happen the temple must be in order in all its parts. My *The Egyptian Book of the Dead.*

114. Nicomachean Ethics and Free Will

Humanity rarely gets to express how free they are. Freedom & the feeling of freedom can be easily associated with travel ... When the time comes and the person is free of work, domestic chores, bills, the mundane of everyday life. They choose to travel ... 'get away from it all'

Workers have designated holidays to do as they please, as the French poet Francois Rabelais instructed:" (*Fais ce que voudras*), 'Do what you want'...and more fully an ancient expression by St Augustine of Hippo "Love, and do what thou wilt".

But shocking as it is, humanity is not free at all.

They didn't choose their DNA

They didn't choose to be born. They didn't choose the rules and culture to which to live. They are bio-computers.

But they choose their breakfast .. Their car, their living accommodation....the town they live in. Didn't they?

'Free will' is a cul-de-sac of an argument.

Yet there are positive ideas about choice.
Aristotle in Nicomachean Ethics states -
"Every art and every investigation and likewise every practical pursuit or undertaking, seems to aim at some good: hence it has been well said that good is that at which all things aim".

115. The Ticket That Exploded

The Ticket that Exploded' William Burroughs even sounds like a great travel novel.

It begins with "It's a long trip, we are the only riders".

It begins with

 "It's a long trip, we are the only riders".

A novel with time but no space.

editing or the cut up might be considered to be a cut up of time and space.

But here there is only editing of time, no space.

TTTE has no geography.

& after awhile you might find a little hidden in the text ... look carefully ... like diamonds in the snow , rare as... geography page.128

"A precarious city of iron cable cars, elevators, ferris wheels, scenic railways plane rides all in constant motion"

 it took a while but here it is the translation of the sensory effect of being there and the translation into text.

116. Rousseau & The Social Contract

"A man must be forced to be free" cried Rousseau

"Whoever refuses to obey the general will, shall be constrained
to do so by the entire body: which means nothing other than that
he shall be forced to be free . . ."
where in, lies the nature of freedom, that in its essence lies a
contract with your society. That might come from 'with in" as
Kant pointed out but is written in law as Rousseau understands.
Yes, you are free, just obey the rules... And so, you are forced by
the rules to be free.

117. Psychogeography & the Dérive of Hanoi and Uluru-Kata Tjuta, Central Australia

(The holy grail of the Enlightenment project (knowingly or unknowingly) was finding the secular immanent God. This was the Spinoza God, described in the introduction of his *Ethics as* "Deus sive Natura", this is why Spinoza should be referred to as the inaugural psychogeographer.)

Comparing two distinct destinations, Hanoi Vietnam and Uluru-Kata Tjuta National
Park, Central Australia, both lending themselves to a specific distinctive orientation. Uluru-
Kata Tjuta is made of conglomerate sandstone in Central Australia, and is situated 500km from the nearest coast-line and five hours drive from the nearest town. The local indigenous

people are Anangu,
living in the heart of a vast desert. Hanoi is a city of lakes on a river, converging on high-rise
buildings. Hanoi, the capital of Vietnam has a population of eight million people and
five million motorcycles. These are the basic principles on which these places can be characterised and remain a fundamental way on which the attributes speak to a visitor from any country.

This report intends to dwell upon the things that don't get reported, the sensory experiences of a location; the psychogeography.

First, let's explain psychogeography. Psychogeography is a portmanteau of
psychology and geography. "Psychogeography, the point where psychology and

geography meet." (Coverley, p,12). Originally developed in
Paris in the 1950's. Psychogeography is a "Study of the precise
laws and specific effects of the geographical environment,
consciously organized or not, on the emotions and behaviour of
individuals"
(http://library.nothingness.org/articles/SI/en/display/2). This is
an
understanding of psychogeography by French writer/filmmaker
Guy Debord. A central
figure in the psychogeography ethos and member of Situationist
International.

Let's now take a walk, or more precisely, a dérive, as
they call it in psychogeography, literally, a drifting from place to
place. This is the key to
psychogeography and an empirical understanding of landscape.
According to Debord, a
derive, acts as an experiment to flush out certain esoteric truths
in the terrain. Guy
Debord explains dérive in his 1958 document Theory of Dérive.
"A technique of rapid
passage through varied ambiences. Dérive involves playful
constructive behaviour and
awareness of psychogeographical effects and are thus quite
different from the classic
notions of journey or stroll" (https://oss.adm.ntu.edu.sg/2016-
dn1008-g5/wpcontent/
uploads/sites/574/2016/02/Theory-of-the-Derive-Debord.pdf).
Essentially, Guy
Debord expresses methods and destinations of dérive. He
suggests gathering people
together as a social event and drifting through the streets, "the
goal is to study the
terrain or to emotionally disorientate oneself" (Debord 1958,
p.64). This dérive /

excursion is a game and a time to open up to possibilities of the sensory self.

As we move through the landscape is traversed there is an image of
nature with no language. Karl Marx is quoted within the 1958 *Theory of Dérive*
document expressing the idea that psychogeography is like having a mirror in the
terrain. "Men can see nothing around them that is not their image, everything speaks to
them of themselves. Their very landscape is alive" (Marx in Debord 1958, p.63). Plainly,
Marx sees the landscape as a mirror reflection of oneself.

In Jacques Lacan terms this is a stade du miroir, a mirror stage, a period in human development where a mirror relays feedback to instil a moral consciousness. As Lacan would say, a suture of The Real through a stade du miroir into the Symbolic Order. Using this Lacanian theory, Kata Juta and Hanoi are a suture to the Symbolic Order, ameliorating The Real to the self. At this point it can be
a scary process and evokes the feeling of the sublime. As Nietzsche put it "When you look
out into the abyss, the abyss looks back at you" (Nietzsche 2002, p. 69). Whether it is the large sandstone conglomerate or a large Asian city the feeling of awe from the vast unfathomable reaction, the context is still the same.

While the bulk of landscapes present as prosaic and uninspiring. Hanoi and Kata
Tjuta have an imposing terrain; giving rise to a particular response. Indeed, oral
traditions have inspired stories passed on from generation to generation using both these

landscapes. The Hoàn Kiếm Lake story of Hanoi, tells of Emperor Le Loi,
1428, receiving a sword from a turtle, Kim Qui, after a war of independence with China.
 The sword is returned to the turtle, who swims to the bottom of Hoàn Kiếm Lake.
In Uluru, Central Australia, in a vastly different terrain, there is a story of the
same topic of 'ethics and conflict'. The sand python, Kuniya, leaves eggs while dancing
across the rock. Kuniya is upset because of a murdered nephew. In an act of payback
Kuniya hits Liru, the brown snake. The battle leaves the sand python, Kuniya, dead.
https://parksaustralia.gov.au/uluru/discover/culture/stories/kuniya-liru-story/.

 So, resounding is the reaction to the terrain that a story is told to parallel the psychogeography
sensory response that had no language. Here, the author of the story and the
psychogeography collaborate to form a narrative. In vastly different terrain, the subject
matter 'ethics and conflict,' goes unchanged, unaffected by the terrain. The
environment is intrinsic to the possibility of the story being told. The terrain has
reflected the self, leaving the subject matter unchanged. The terrain is not a catalyst for
the story but an essential interface for the story.
The playful yet serious stories have had a remarkable effect. They are passed down
from generation to generation as children's stories. Psychogeography has enabled
difficult subject matter to be concluded. Central to the stories are

moral values set
around conflict and the psychogeography has enabled this story.

      The dérive is the walk of the psychogeographer,
unbound by
conventional logic, it enables an opening up to an acquisition by
perception. The dérive
is an opportunity to live in fresh symbiosis with the environment,
urban or rural. And
when called upon the dérive presents as a continuous gestalt
explanation for the given
environment. That is, the feeling of the sublime, then the
Cartesian point is meted out
as a story. The apprehension before comprehension as Hegel
called it. Or, the sublime
before the narrative.

      Psychogeography is part of a secular project towards an
ethically reasoned world.
While Emmanuel Kant suggests - "the moral law within" (Kant
2002, p, 203). That is,
humanity's ethical self is not subject to a transcendent god but
comes from within humanity.
      In short, Psychogeography adds to the project and
doesn't dispute Kant's "moral law with",
psychogeography is the assertion that "the moral law" is a
concretisation of the metaphysical
response from self within the environment.
      As Spinoza asks, "Deus sive natura?" "God or nature?"
(Spinoza 1996, preface).
The question can now be answered. God is nature, or to be more
precise. Psychogeography
is the immanent God.

Today, as we dérive in Hanoi or the outback, the comfort of Google maps lends
itself to drifting. Letting go and exploring through intuitive steps, wondering where
these gut feelings might lead. Always knowing, 'you can't get lost with your GPS'.
Psychogeography purist might frown on the GPS but it is undeniable, the dérive and
Google Maps make dérive safer in an unfamiliar environment. In this undistracted
mind, the GPS may even act as a sensory catalyst.

Derive, or 'drifting' suggests the walk has a sense of tide or river flow. Of course,
there is no tide in the Dérive /walk. The suggestion of water lends itself to the fact that
humans are made of "60% water"
(https://www.usgs.gov/special-topic/water-scienceschool/
science/water-you-water-and-human-body?qt-
science_center_objects=0#qtscience_
center_objects) and the brain and heart are 73% water. The dérive lends itself
to apparent understanding of forces at play. Trying to experience that which is
normally beyond the human five senses. It would be unscientific to suggest that the
water in the brain is unaffected by this tidal pull. The meaning of dérive /'drifting' is
hidden in clear sight. The 'drifting' refers to the drifting of the water inside the body,
pulled in the same manner as the tide. Studies have shown that the moon has an
influence on human behaviour "The incidence of crimes

committed on full moon days
was much higher than on all other days"
(https://www.ncbi.nlm.nih.gov/pmc/articles/PMC1444800/).
States C P Thakur and D
Sharma.

Psychogeography adherents keep coming back to remind
us of its significance.
There are numerous published authors who have added to the
story. Gaston Bauchelard, Baudelaire, Walter Benjamin and now
contemporary authors Peter Ackroyd, Will Self, Iain Sinclair,
and Phil Smith. This history of psychogeography and
continuous rejuvenation has placed the original ideas again in the
limelight. Authors
fascinated by the ideas have reworked the original narrative to
cajole something more
from the theory. Will Self choose to walk to Heathrow Airport
then walk from LA
airport. "I decided to walk to Heathrow. ...., probably nobody
had done it since the preindustrial
era" (https://www.theparisreview.org/blog/2011/06/22/will-self-
on-walking-tohollywood/).
Iain Sinclair walked the M25 London ring road, some 80 km. He
describes
the walk as "unloved outskirts of the city"
(https://theconversation.com/psychogeography-a-way-to-delve-
into-the-soul-of-acity-
78032) and the need to "exorcise the unthinking malignancy of
the dome, to
celebrate the sprawl of London"
(https://www.theguardian.com/books/2002/sep/21/featuresrevie
ws.guardianrevie
w6). These are examples of the extension of the ideas of derive
and the furthering of

the project.

In the naming of the walk, dérive, the walk establishes itself as something more
than just a walk. Something more than meets the eye. The person who derives
becomes an antenna for the concepts not usually available for perception. There are
many historical examples of the person who walks and venerates walking as the
bestowal of concepts. Prominent authors such as Rousseau, Nietzsche, Henry Thoreau,
Socrates, Jeremy Bentham, Kierkegaard, Kant, and John Stuart Mill, all countenanced
the walk as inspiration. Walking through their landscapes, whether city or countryside
seemed no matter, it was the walk that bestowed the reflection, the ideas, and then the
inspiration to write them.
Rousseau wrote, "I can only meditate when I am walking. When I stop, I cease to
think; my mind only works with my legs" (Rousseau in Solnit 2001, p.27).
""Only ideas won by walking have any value" (Nietzsche 1990, p.45).
"Walking came from Africa, from evolution, and from necessity, and it went
everywhere, usually looking for something" (Solnit 2001, p.62).

The dérive is accessible and delights in affordability. And as such a habit cannot
be recommended highly enough, it parades a badge of the egalitarian. Dérive carries
the sense of revolution, as it is, all of the above, "Liberté, égalité, fraternité" (Robespierre,

https://franceintheus.org/spip.php?article620). That is, "Liberty, equality, fraternity". Free
of charge, it is a lifestyle of traveling countering the anthroposcene. The dérive is fossil
fuel friendly. To engage with your own streets, in your own backyard and trandsend. a
holiday while forgoing a holiday.

      The person who dérives is said to be a flâneur. A character, that emerged from
the writings of the poet Charles Baudelaire. The flâneur was modelled on an actual
person, Mr C.G, in the essay from 1863 called The Painter of Modern Life. Baudelaire
refers to "artists, man of the world and a man of crowds, a dazzling soul" (Baudelaire
1863, p.1). As the years would have it, the dictionary definition of today's flâneur is less
flattering. "An idler, a lounger" (Apple custom dictionary 2020). All the same, the
Baudelaire's flâneur is out to understand, to be the antennae, to reveal what is
freedom. A worldly sense of, 'what is freedom?' or 'being free'. And as the flâneur walks
the outback or the Asian city, away from the routine of everyday life, it makes sense for
them to think, 'am I free?'

      Though dérive / flâneur has a fashionable air, the ethos is difficult in the
knowledge that in the end in 1994 at the age of 62 " Debord shot himself with a single
bullet through the heart"

(https://www.theguardian.com/books/2001/jul/28/biography.arts
andhumanities). As if this
act wasn't contentious enough, The Guardian obituary states
"His most important
political action" from the same article the novelist "Philippe
Sollers explained that, for
Debord, suicide was the purest critique of the spectacle". For
those who thought they
had found a new cultural revolution. Debord's final act leaves
the psychogeography
canon shaken. If Debords suicide is a reflection of his life's work
then it will be
tempting for others and new arrivals to complete or add to the
project. To act out, in
respect of Debord, something that is missing and reinstate an
attractive proposition.
Psychogeography will keep coming back and will keep being
reinterpreted but what is
needed is an addition to clear the critique that psychogeography
has no purpose. And
within its definitions lays a purpose and that purpose should be a
warning that this has
been a deadly pursuit for Debord.

   Humanity rarely gets to express how free they are.
Freedom and the feeling of
freedom have a strong connection with travel. When the time
comes and the person is
free of work, domestic chores, bills, the mundane of everyday
life. They choose to
travel, 'get away from it all'. The general population are given
holidays and told they
are 'free to go'. But people are not free, they are merely
embracing the idea of their

freedom. Freedom doesn't exist, it is travel, the symbol of freedom that exists. People
want autonomy, yet more often than not, choose that controls them. This is the
freedom that exists, the one on offer.

Shocking as it is, humanity is not free at all. Nobody chooses their DNA. They
didn't choose to be born. They didn't choose the rules and culture to which to live.
They are bio-computers. But, as adults, they choose their breakfast, their mode of
transport, their living accommodation and the holiday they just had. What is argued
here is a determinist theory of freedom, In which "commonly understood as the
doctrine that every event has a cause" (Strawson 2005, p.286), as such, "everything
that happens by what has already gone before" (Strawson 2005, p.286), in which "the
history of the universe is fixed" (Strawson 2005, p.286), yet you still get to choose
things. And where you get to choose things without being forced is the compatibilist
idea of freedom. "Freedom is a matter of not being physically or psychologically
forced" (Strawson 2005, p.287).

It is impossible to separate freedom and the traveller. If you don't have one, you
can't have the other. The traveller symbolises freedom, lives it, and for moments in
time, feels free. This stance agrees with the humanist idea of

mankind, that humanity
can be a master of their own destiny. Humanity has been given a
representation of
freedom.

Slavoj Zizek states, "We feel free because we lack the very
language to articulate our
unfreedom" (Zizek 2002, p.2).

Standing in all the splendour of Kata Tjuta, Northern Territory
Australia and viewing
the context in the surrounds, it is truly free in the heart of nature.
Romanticist painter,
Caspar David Friedrich, express this same ambiance in his
portrait, Wonderer above the Sea
of Fog 1818. The painting depicts a free world, beholden to
whoever can get amongst it.
Literally, a romantic idea, of freedom, that can only be
experienced in far off places. While
most people live in a city surrounded by rules. Hanoi has a
contrasting sense of freedom.
Hanoi is a free modern city, proud to be free from colonial rule
yet contained by a
Vietnamese rule of law. A freedom most notable in Vietnamese
history is the emancipation
from colonial rule. This can be compared to another romantic era
painting The Monarch of
The Glen, by Edward Landseer 1851. Royalty is only noted in
the name of the painting The
'Monarch' of The Glen but not depicted on the canvas. While the
original authentic deer,
stands powerful, on the land of its birth. This is analogous to the
Vietnamese who have had a
royalty, not seen in contemporary society, that is not seen in the
painting, yet named proudly

in history, i.e., named in the title.

The freedom experienced here is a Rousseau freedom where "a man must be forced
to be free" (Rousseau in Bertram 2003, p.87). This is an essence of freedom, while not under
rule of another country and therefore free. The population must obey national laws. This is
the essence of freedom fully experienced through derive. To go as you will to be as you will,
yet within the laws of the land". Rousseau writes in his Social Contract 1762.
"Hence for the social compact not to be an empty formula, it tacitly includes the following
engagement which alone can give force to the rest, that whoever refuses to obey the general
will shall be constrained to do so by the entire body: which means nothing other than that he
shall be forced to be free" (Rousseau in Bertram 2003, p.87).

"The medium is the message" is a term often thrown around in a
communications debate. The adage assumes any object interacted with, transmits a
message. 'The medium" discussed here, is Hanoi and Kata Tjuta. The axiom tells us that
the city and a rock formation have a message. It cannot be denied that different
environments produce; altered responses, altered emotions and change of
consciousness. The structures communicate something. Upon receiving that message
the receiver will undoubtedly react. Therefore, the message is effective on the receiver.

Thus, a psychogeographcal communication has been made.

Finally, please consider, The Psychogeography Lament. On
walking, driving, or
cycling to a destination chosen by you, the traveller. Why do you
invariably return on a
different route?

In summary, psychogeography is an unfinished project. As the
first proponent of
the art psychogeography Debord killed himself in 1994. Many
will now return to the
project to fix what is broken. There will be additions to this
movement. Kata Tjuta and
Hanoi remain great contrasting features in a world of derive and
yet with amazing
presence they have remarkable psychogeographical similarities.
Most notably, they are
the source of mythological fighting stories and at the same time
can be compared to
notable Romantic era paintings. It is particularly the artist who
can pick up the sensory
ideas conveyed by the landscape. What is conveyed in the
paintings is the sublime of
psychogegraphy. The moment of mirroring the landscape,
pulling together what is
justice and inspiring a moral narrative. Succinctly,
psychogeography is the secular god,
the unfinished Enlightenment project.

Spinoza asks the question "God, or Nature", Deus, sive Natura:
"That eternal and
infinite being we call God, or Nature, acts from the same
necessity from which he

exists" (Part IV, Preface). Psychogeography is God.

Reference List

Bachelard, Gaston 2014, *The poetics of space*, Penguin Books,
New York, USA.
Botton, Alain De, 2003, *The art of travel*, Penguin books,
London England, UK.
Coverley, Marlin 2012, *Psychogeography,* 2012 pocket
essentials, Oldcastle Books,
Harpenden, UK.
Debord, Guy 2010, *Society and the spectacle*, Black And Red,
Detriot, USA.
Dicks, Bella 2003, *Culture on display, the production of
contemporary,* Open University
Press, Maidenhead, Berkshire, UK.
Harris Sam 2012, *Free will,* Free Press, A division of Simon and
Schuster, Inc, New York,
USA.
Kant, Immanuel 2002, *Critique of practical reason*, Hackett
Publishing Company, Inc,
Indianapolis, USA.
Lyons, Siobhan 2017, *Psychogeography: a way to delve into the
soul of a city,*
https://theconversation.com/psychogeography-a-way-to-delve-
into-the-soul-of-a-city-78032,
retrieved, 17/12/2020.
Marino, Gordon 2010, *Ethics, the essential writings*, Random
House Inc, Modern Library,
New York, USA.
Nietzsche, Friedrich 1990, *Twilight of idols and anti-christ,*
Penguin Books Ltd,
Registered Offices, London, England.

Nietzsche, Friedrich 2002, *Beyond good and evil, prelude to a philosophy of the future,*
Cambridge University Press, The Edinburgh Building, Cambridge, United Kingdom.
Pink, Thomas 2004, *Free will, a very short introduction,* Oxford University Press Oxford, UK.
Solnit. Rebecca 2001, *Wanderlust: a history of walking,* Penguin books, New york, USA.
Smith, Philip 2010, *Mythogeogeography,* Triarchy Press, Devon, UK.
Spinoza, De Benedict 1996, *Ethics,* Penguin Books, Princeton University Press, New
York, USA.
Strawson, Gallen 2005, *The shorter routledge encyclopedia of philosophy,* Routledge,
Oxon, UK.
Thompson, Donald 1973, *Bindibu country*, Thomas Nelson Australia Ltd, Melbourne
Australia.
10
Zizek, Slavoj 2002, *Welcome to the desert of the real: five essays on september 11 and*
related dates, Verso Books, London UK.
Zizek, Slavoj 2007, *How to read lacan,* W.W. Norton and Company, Inc. New York, USA.

West of Ho Kiem lake... is an Psychogeographical road intersection par excellence. Driving Dien Bien Phu can muscle up some fervent emancipatory memories, as Dien Bien Phu is the name of the battle with the French enabling a brief independence in 1954. (Battle_of_Dien_Bien_Phu)& then you intersect the road with Nguyễn Thái Học (street), what a combo.Nguyễn Thái Học is the name of the Viet freedom fighter who was executed by the French in 1930.

<u>N T H</u>

"Life is a journey not a destination" Ralph Waldo Emerson.

This axiom invoked a reminder that Australia has a perennial need to present a new axiom for a new tourist era. "Where the bloody hell are ya", comes to mind. It is here in Communications that the nature of the axiom can be explained, shed light upon and caution the use of a new phrase. The Northern Territory has proudly presented its new phrase of 2019 as "Boundless Possible". It is keen to bury the mistakes of the past "It will never never leave you", tourist axiom. A somewhat innocuous phrase, until someone pointed out "it sounds like herpes". The nature of the axiom is thus, that an opposite and equally valid axiom might also be enunciated.

118 Origins of Travel.

There are all kinds of movement that are entrenched within a human psyche. For example, the inclination to move away from danger,
the steps from the trees to the savanna for food, the movement from fresh water to shelter....
There is something more than historical about travel. It is about survival over millennia.

Food, fresh water ... food, fresh water... these were the cyclical elements compelling travel for millions of years.
Before an agrarian society, when all the organic detritus was mounting. The tribe would periodically move on or get sick from bacteria.
Even at a cellular level, bacteria moves towards food and away from poison.

As the feeling of being compelled to travel is alive today. Is this feeling an inculcated necessity of the DNA?

119. The Great Barrier Reef

I have driven the length of the Great Barrier Reef, a beautiful drive and glad to be out of Melbourne in cold July. I drove a day at a time, 10 hrs a day... I couldn't help but notice one particular day, I never lost sight of sugar cane plantations for 10 hours.
A combination of monsoonal rains and chemical fertilizers for the sugar cane is surely going to have an effect on the reef.

120 The Slow Death of the Library

Kids playing video games, people watching video, a child care centre, and a tourist display. Before these days, libraries were places of books, seats of learning, I mean, like, 'swaths of books'. I took a photo of a catalogue of John Stuart Mills books, I don't think I even photographed the whole catalogue, in memory of how Christopher Hitchens, had the idea that Mill's, On Liberty, John Milton's, Areopagitica , and Thomas Paine's, Introduction to The Age of Reason, were the three canons of freedom of speech.

121. Closer

It was late May 1980, I was 18 and I went to Plymouth city centre to buy Joy Division's Closer. It was probably Virgin records, where all the punks hang out. Buying the album meant I had not enough money to get the bus home. It was no quandary at all. I bought the album and walked home. I remember distinctly the crossing of Laira Bridge, over the river Plym. You have a view on one side of the old railway bridge. I walked on the south side, the ocean side and had this enormous feeling to throw the album into the water, It stuck with me for a while, a reoccurring thought; as I walked, to think of this sacrifice to the gods, "throw Closer into the river" it suggested. What a fine moment, hypertrophy par excellence, if I did throw it. Abraham takes his son Issac to the mountain, as the God had asked, decides not to sacrifice his son, what God is this? In the JD Salinger's *Catcher in the Rye* the protagonist is hearing the voices in his head "throw mud at the pretty girl on the swing." But Declan didn't throw it. & here it is at home today, that same album that managed to walk that bridge.

122 PAUL RICOEUR

Ricœur's hermeneutical work *Freud and Philosophy* contains the famous assertion that <u>Karl Marx</u>, <u>Friedrich Nietzsche</u> and <u>Sigmund Freud</u> are masters of the <u>school of suspicion</u>[37][38] (*maîtres du soupçon/école du soupçon*). Marx is reductionist, because he reduces society to economy, particularly to means of production; Nietzsche is a reductionist, because he reduces man to an arbitrary concept of <u>superman</u>; Freud is a reductionist because he reduces human nature to sexual instinct.

160 The Ontology of Modern Love
A clandestine relationship at an agreed time, chatting to each
other in the comments of a YouTube clip.

123. The Aleister Crowley Moon Landings

Author of Chaos Magic, Steve Wilson announced in an Oxford Symposium in 1996 the coincidence of Crowley's Book of the Law perhaps announced by a interstellar intelligence and at the same time Einstein's E= MC squared. This equation got NASA to the moon and back.
Hell, he even wrote a book called Moonchild. Theorist will gather together and anoint the idea that this Moonchild was of the Book Of The Book of the Law. received in in Cairo 1904.

"And unto the crowned Child it is known" Libre Cheth.

 The fringes of society breath into the mainstream of society and don't know it. The clairvoyance, the synchronicity Al play a part in the magical coming together of the impossibility (without many many accidents) the landing on the moon.

    Crowley in the US gathers neophyte adherents, one such folk was Jack Parsons.

Whose visionary work would culminate in a crater on the moon being named after him.

How did he become visionary?

 Jack set up the JPL which later became NASA which landed on the moon.

Jack became a member of OTO ... Not some johnny come lately

dilettante but delving deep enough to grasp the possibility of a spirit invocation.

Yet again, happening far to often to be a coincidence.

Parson's work with Crowley's OTO and jet propulsion are separate things and the fact that the moon was landed on in 1969 has nothing to do with Crowley or Chapter 69 in the Book Of Lies.

124. Schlomo

"In time the thing which is meant to be warded off invariably finds its way into the very means which is being used forwarding it off." Freud.

S Schlomo Freud DOB 06 05 1856

That is, Irony creeps in. The coke machine in the hospital's A&E.

& the function of this irony is to humanize the system, give it a homeopathic amount of poison, a shadow, as Jung would call it. This is the desire to anthropomorphize everything.
  To give the inanimate a conscious and subconscious.

It is what humanity does to the big other's alterity to make it acceptable. Only then can it use the thing as a moralising force in acts of stade du mirror. The 'take a look at yourself' ethical mirror.

125 A Return from Otherness

"A return from otherness." Is an explanation for the Hegel title of his book...*Phenomenology of the Spirit.*1806,

Hegel goes further with evolution with his statement "a return from otherness" It is a realization of the evolutionary order of things and identifying the self and 'being in the world' in terms of evolution. First was a mystery to self, then an alterity and next we we return from Otherness. there is a mystery self without awaremenss, a secondary self imbued with awareness

302

consciousness of the Otherness.. ... The first self remains a mystery. An unrealised self, humanity hasn't yet been able to walk..

While Hegel dies in 1831, Charles Darwin leaps on boat in Plymouth Devon, for a five-year voyage leaving his wife behind.

Darwin's journey is compelled in the consciousness of Other ness..answers outside of us will commute to answers of ourselves .. The evolution of the species.

The question is surprisingly synchronous because Darwin book " The origin of the species " did not annunciate the origin of the species but only the evolution of the species. Herein Hegel annunciates the issue.. A return from Otherness... That the origin of consciousness is first then there is a seeking within other ness then a return to a self-encompassed by the experience on otherness. There is otherness, followed by self-consciousness is the implied idea. Otherness comes before self-

consciousness. Homo before homo-erect-us. But not only this deduction, So what was self before self-consciousness?   we are returning

from otherness ... the statement suggests that we are returning to a self that is not yet self-conscious.

So what is this self that is not yet self-conscious?

or animal without language. The animal self without time, forced to be in the now.

Self-consciousness followed by language, & then language portents to a moral world integrating a CG Jungian shadow through a stade de mirror.

The subject as defined by Z becomes a useful notion as it is the position that allows the self to be objective and as true as it's going to get.

126. A Dog Barked

Walking the fence line, a dog would make a run and bark. I whistled to calm the mut, ... The dog had become aware of the big Other. But what was happening before, in it's immediate vicinity? A sense of its own body, in pain, in health, in hunger or in need? The awakening by the big Other (me) from dogmatic slumber is truly the parapraxis of Kant to Hume.* And as the dog calms and returns to the balcony, Hegel would say "a return from otherness" and begs the question. If it returns from otherness(Me) what does the dog return to. - Not a self-consciousness. In canine awareness does it return to a psychogeography or psy'cho'geography.

 Four states of consciousness
1. immediate vicinity (pain, hunger, well being)
2. Psychogeography
3. otherness
4. self-consciousness.

There is no need for rules in the conscious.

Kant says of Hume "Thanks for waking me from my dogmatic slumber" with reference

171. René Girard's Mimetic Theory

"The fox knows many things, but the hedgehog knows one big thing."
—Archilochus

According to Roberto Calasso, René Girard is one of the "last surviving hedgehogs." With this thesis, the Italian philosopher makes use of Isaiah Berlin's interpretation of Archilochus's dictum in order to describe the founder of the mimetic theory more closely. Berlin differentiates "hedgehogs" such as Plato, Dante, Hegel, Dostoyevsky, or Proust from
"foxes" such as Aristotle, Shakespeare, or Goethe. While the former authors attempt to trace all phenomena back to one single insight or principle, the latter take on an array of ideas and inquiries.

127. God is a Metaphysical Poet.

The meaning of life is,,,
Life has no meaning, no significance....But but but, we must act
as if life has meaning.   Zizek pointed out that Christians don't
kneel because they believe, they kneel so that others watching
can start to believe. And in this notion. there is the belief in the
existence of the non-existence of God. or we should act as if God
does really exist... I might add ... God exists the same way, love,
virtue, kindness exist... God is the metaphysical poet.

128. Reification of The Rock

My understanding is....... I want to make this clear, "I have an understanding .... " but that doesn't make me right or wrong. & I turn to Bertrand Russell, with his quote" One of the painful things about our time is that those who feel certainty are stupid, and those with any imagination and understanding are filled with doubt and indecision."
Thanks Mr Russell, he has my back.

Uluru, or as Aboriginal people call it Ayers Rock, has an iconic world status. The climb now is dead and buried 26th October 2019.... The notion of the rock, for some, has changed and the ontology remains the same.   If i can explain, it is a notion that has changed is the one of..you can't climb so the Everest mentality has gone and the ability to enact veni vidi vici is gone... The controversy has been realigned but not evaporated. People would come and pontificate around the rock climb as the ascenders enacted their free choice in a free country. & now people will pontificate as they surround the rock as to whether it would be better if the climb was an optional factor in the free market of the commodification of everything.
 My understanding is that for millennia Occupational Health and Safety has always been at the core of the avuncular advice not to climb the rock. 'it's not safe, don't climb'. The slippery slope, the heat exhaustion, the rain, the wind, all play as accident factors on the rock.

and has now begun a era that tries to establish an indigenous voice of consequence and an attempt to rid of selfishness by law.

Where in 'the structure of commodity relations' is normally taken as a whole herein lies an individual problem of commodity capitalism and against as Marx pronounced in Hegel critique "go

to the root of the matter. For man, however, the root is man
himself." There is the nature of commodities but not to forget it
is humanity that is in the game of reification of the commodity.

The reification or *Verdinglichung* "making into a thing" might at
last be real. And seen as a terrible thing a degrading thing in
Marx vernacular ... The laborer sorrows of badly paid factory
work. Has little bearing on a community as far from a factory as
you can get.
There is notion that on going, camping & climbing the rock
was not after as real thing, an insight in local culture, but a
spectacle in the Debord sense, a copy of something real. And
that copy of something real is almost certainly one of self
absorption. An Everest achievement without climbing Everest.
an achievement per se without actual doing much, a climb as a
personal symbolic colonization. And Now in the confusion of
reification where subject becomes object and object becomes
subject. Perhaps it is now in this realignment that the old essence
of the rock appears and the tangible details of millennia of tried
and tested, truth gets past as an identity of Australia is keenly
rebuilt as the originators has first imagined.

129. God Loves You Cleaning

God loves you cleaning. The algorithms don't lie, - a whole row of cleaning videos on your YouTube suggestions page. They haven't heard the sound of a hoover for months. They are listening in. The bereft soft wispy sounds of the floor brush and the sound damp cloth squeaking over a kitchen bench are all gone. The digital status of the hearing algorithm is nil by cleaning. I hate it when I have this attention. God is dead and not replaced by nihilism but a state & corporate power, watching, listening, googling in.

130. Obscurantist Terrorism

"Existence is the being of those beings who stand open for the openness of being in which they stand by standing" Heidegger .

131. Beauty Mate!

Emmanuelle Kant states that Aesthetic is Synthetic A Priori.

It must be possible to draw conclusions of beauty. These ideals
have long been assessed, most notably by Aristotle, Kant then
Kierkegaard.

Aristotle from Metaphysics. Kant from The Critique of
Judgement (1791) and Kirkeguaard's Either /or: a fragment of
life.
In summary Kant's account made the assertion "It cannot be the
same time aesthetic and also judgement" (Sruton p.109) and
Mittel makes a blunt statement concerning aesthetics and
comments that The Wire " is zero degree style." (Mittel p. 49)
Mittel A style he explains as "fully linear conventional in
presenting and objective narrative perspective throughout."
Strives to render its televisual storytelling techniques invisible"
(Mittel p. 48).

This is a judgement on style not on beauty. Yet without style
there is now a contention, that the Wire lacks beauty.

  Kirkeguard's aesthetic is a dialectical process. "The first is the
aesthetic, which gives way to the ethical"

https://plato.stanford.edu/entries/kierkegaard/#Aesth

Beauty is not something that consciously happens. The dullness
of something can be a conclusion without conscious thought. A
subjective notion

"Not every predicative use of the word "beautiful" signals the making of a judgment of beauty"

https://plato.stanford.edu/entries/kant-aesthetics/#2.1

The underlying theme of Zero-degree style.

132. Immanuel Kant States that Aesthetic is Synthetic A Priori.

aesthetic is an innate subjective experience not a concept.

Jason Mittel calls out The Wire as Zero-degree style. This puts the show in the realms of soap opera of the 70's. Jason's remark details the Wire

133. Kafka

In the "Sublime object of Ideology" Zizek voices a number of
anecdotes to move towards the warm glow of empiricism.
Anecdotes are at the core... one after the other, unveiling
something more about ideology. Somewhat like the methodology
of Lacan in the Graph of Desire. Each of the four graphs unveil
something about the unconscious. This is Zizek methodology
also, each anecdote reveals something about ideology.

And here also lies the parallel. Z retells part of a Kafka novel
The Trial, in which a neophyte is in front of a door with a
gatekeeper and the door is made for the neophyte. Yet the gate
keeper, *no matter what*, never lets the neophyte inside. We are
told "this is desire" the nature of desire... here now is the
parallel between desire and ideology. The constant barrage of the
object by the subject to fulfill desires.

Ideology exists within hegemony. Behold, derive is pure
hegemony. & Within this derive is naked desire.

So as the syllogism goes, desire is hegemonic. So be it, both
desire and ideology both exist as hegemony.

184. Irony

Irony exists because only Allah is perfect. The irony in any institution is an anthropomorphism. Nobody claims to be perfect so the bad judgement or irony is sewn into the fabric of the corporation to humanitise. Present a corporate face with a mistake or humility. A Jungian shadow, a part of the psyche that is illogical and detrimental. People would hate it if the trains run on time. The message for the subject object position is a mystery dissonance to be contemplated. Asking for a leap of faith, in a secular place. Do we not enter a place of religious sanctuary to trade away a logical understanding that the invisible deity?

135. Semiotic Origins

Charles Peirce pulled the word semiotic from John Locke (1632- 1704), in *The Essay of Human Understanding*, 1689. Charles Peirce (Pronounced purse) 1839-1814 born Massachusetts along with Ferdinand Saussure 1857-1915 born Geneva Switzerland are both conventionally thought of as the inaugurators of semiotics, yet Plato and Aristotle both explored the relationship between signs and the world.

136. Knowledge Information & Data

Speech is missing.

Knowledge, Information & Data. Might be seen as the all-encompassing - Omi trium perfecticum " Alas.
Speech procures something that the other three lack ... that is 'an essence towards truth'...

We have all seen the scripted speech and an ability to acknowledge the questions of the day and ameliorate a willing public. This should be seen as a good thing as it advises the public speaker as to their vision and mission. And is a movement towards a reflection of the people...whether democratic or not... The public speech is a mirror and a tool of reasoning. rarely do we hear a public speaker off script.... But sometimes there has to be needs to be and accidental choice to express self ... unbound with fidelity to the self.   a real person emerges... it is said that text is knowledge, whereas speech tends to truth. Speech comes from the unconscious. It can be heartily seen in slips of the tongue... In natural attempts to appear authentic. Real and flowing with a sense of genuine... ... The unconscious acts in language.Text is the knowledge that sets a clear announcement of a Lacanian Symbolic Order. It is thought over, thought through, corrected and assimilated to a clear vision of the mission at hand.

Journalism 101. An Interviewer doesn't start with "How do you feel? Or "How does it feel?"

In this model, is not the interviewer playing a part to move towards truth extraction?

318

A corner stones of media thought is "The medium is the message" a corner stone not because it

is true but because it is a great place to start the discourse... So to, with epistemology.

"Cogito ergo sum" René Descartes (1596- 1650).

 "I think therefore I am" is a great place to start the epistemological question, what can I truly know?….And as western philosophy embraces this statement as wrong but a great place to start… so too does media neophytes acknowledge " The medium is the message" as wrong, but a great place to start.

And it is here we start in the shadow of RA Wilson, as to provide questions as well as, sometimes, answers.

In Immanuel Kant's philosophical framework, knowledge is divided into two main categories: a priori and a posteriori. A priori knowledge is independent of experience and is derived from reason and logic. On the other hand, a posteriori knowledge is derived from experience and observation of the world. Information, in contrast to knowledge, is the result of data processing and can be derived from both a priori and a posteriori sources. Data, however, refers to raw and unprocessed information that lacks meaning or interpretation. Both analytic and synthetic propositions play a crucial role in the acquisition of knowledge. Analytic propositions are true by definition, while synthetic propositions are true based on empirical evidence. Therefore, information can be synthesized from data using a posteriori reasoning, while knowledge can be obtained through a combination of a priori reasoning and a posteriori experience. Ultimately, the interplay between knowledge, information, and data relies on the balance between reason and observation, and between analytic and synthetic propositions.

137. Knowledge is Power

From a communication's perspective this story exemplifies a number of theoretical points.

A student is perplexed by what the teacher has just said. "Knowledge is power" & then the teacher says, "France is bacon". The student hearing the statement is bemused and feels, something is not right. The student should have heard, "Knowledge is Power - Francis Bacon".

The joke is *Hypertrophy,* that is, it stands apart from the everyday and this time, it is a phrase misheard. *Hypertrophy* is taken from Salomon Reinach, a French anthropologist, who wrote *Cultes, mythes et religions* 1905 -1912. Reinach describes totems as; "une hypertrophie de l'instinct social". This anecdote is totemic, in that, it sticks out instinctively in everyday life and viewed subjectively, it exists as overblown; in this case an overblown misrecognition.

In the misreading, the story is presented to the listener as a chance to always remember the Francis Bacon quote, "Knowledge is power". Coming from the original experience, "France is bacon", how will the student forget?

188. Knowledge Information Data

[refering to url, http://www.infogineering.net/data-information-knowledge.htm]

While knowledge believes it is king of belief, belief acts in contempt of knowledge to prove at one's own expense, that oneself has free will.

"I see and applaud what is better, but follow what is worse" Ovid, Metamorphoses.

In Schopenhauer, again it can be seen, a suspicion of a personal logical master. "le matin je fais bonne résolution le soir je fais des sottises. Translation - "In the morning I make plans, In the evening I commit absurdities", says Schopenhauer, he then explains the axiom, "Thus the man lets his conduct be guided not by thinking, but by the impression of the present moment".

Then, within Aristotle's rhetorical reserve of ethos, logos and pathos .... Pathos is king, but only in the evening. - Thank God elections are in the morning, finishing around midday.

Shown in the diagram is the theory that information, data and knowledge, come together to make decisions, as if these are separate and from personal, emotional, or irrational decisions. The diagram tells us of the Apollonian spirit but ignores the Dionysian. Apollo and Dionysus are two parts of self that constitute nearer the whole.

In choosing the "absurdities", there is a certain pleasure in this masochism, Lacan calls it jouissance.
"What we find at the basis of the analytical exploration of desire is masochism—the subject grasps himself as suffering; he grasps his existence of a living being as a signifier" states Jacques Lacan.
(https://www.frontiersin.org/articles/10.3389/fpsyg.2017.01593/full)

These "absurdities" can be also understood as The Prisoner's Dilemma acted oneself, in that, a prisoner would be prepared to lose a finger, if a fellow, despised inmate, lost a hand; only to prove that one had power over another.

Within Aristotle's rhetorical reserve of ethos, logos and pathos .... Pathos is king, but only in the evening.

Thank god elections are in the morning, finishing around midday.

Then in our diagram of Information Data and knowledge. An arrow presumes a logical volition to act upon the three components. It is clear that the efficacy has

Schopenhauer refers to this in The World as Will and Representation.
"Thus, the man lets his conduct be guided not by thinking, but by the impression of the present moment".

In the diagram

It is ironic that a person would not act in their own best interests.

unencumbered by what is right and subverted by what appears necessary. Belief then acts
out the jouissance by listening to Joy Division.

"What we find at the basis of the analytical exploration of desire is masochism—the subject grasps himself as suffering; he grasps his existence of a living being as a signifier" states Jacques Lacan.
(https://www.frontiersin.org/articles/10.3389/fpsyg.2017.01593/full)

"I think therefore i am, despite the evil demon". is the full quote from Descarte cogito ergo sum de trompteur.

& This evil demon is the one whose evening has come. If I can explain.

The human is corrupted intrinsically. Mentioned in Schopenhauer's Will and Representation (page 518)

"le matin je fais des projets, et le soir je fais des sottises" In the morning i act with resolution in the evneing i comit fillie..

The evening is the devil's handbag.

I see and applaud what is better but I follow what is worse. Ovid metamorphoses

it is apprehending that the pen may be mightier than the sword ...
but the irrational feelings are still top dog.

The emotions are in control.

Within Aristotle's rhetorical reserve of ethos, logos and pathos
.... Pathos is king but only in the evening.

Thank god elections are in the morning finishing around midday.

Working class people vote for a political party acting against
their own interests.

Belief is, a feeling, an act of a faith, an unreasoned position.

but author Yuval Noah Harari. tells us "However, for better or
worse, elections and referendums are
not about what we think. They are about what we feel." In all,
our democracy, that we dearly hold

close to our hearts, is merely, most unprogressively, made of
feeling.

And all that part of a collect consciousness is the idea that an
election will give us the best for the country ... Under the belief
that a stringent path of a country's brains trust will inevitably
give birth to the best president of the age. Yet, Harari maintains
the election will precipitate in a feeling.

& what happens here is actually worse than expected. The human is corrupted intrinsically. Mentioned in Schopenhauer's Will and Representation (page 518). are two axioms

"le matin je fais des projets, et le soir je fais des sottises"

I see and applaud what is better but I follow what is worse. Ovid metamorphoses

it is apprehending that the pen may be mightier than the sword ... but the irrational feelings are still top dog.

The emotions are in control.

Within Aristotle's rhetorical reserve of ethos, logos and pathos .... Pathos is king but only in the evening.

Thank god elections are in the morning finishing around midday.

http://www.infogineering.net/data-information-knowledge.htm

190. Critical Thinking Reduction

"Critical thinking is the intellectually disciplined process of actively and skilfully conceptualizing, applying, analyzing, synthesizing, and/or evaluating information gathered from, or generated by, observation, experience, reflection, reasoning, or communication, as a guide to belief and action" (Ennis).

Paul Ricoeur proposed the sceptical reader as critical thinking. Then Ricoeur goes on to tell us Nietzsche reduces everything to power, Marx reduces everything to economy, a la surplus value and Freud to libido. These are ricoeor suggest are all hedgehogs as opposed to foxes. They have one idea rather than many. This is an order of two, put forward by Archilochus 680bc 645bc of Paros Greece.

John Dewey dominates the public sphere of education when it comes to education and his "how we think " 1910. He asks for analysis and judgement .. stating that thinking can be developed.

In practice, we have source material and from source material we make statements and come to conclusion for the source material. So, you are a computer after all. & it can be conceded that this is one of the more dull part of the mind.

More wonderful parts of the mind.

1. ideas and fantasy

2. thinking about thinking. Ekart Toll rejects the assumption of " I think therefore I am " {Descartes) "had given expression to the most basic error' to equate thinking with being and identity with thinking" or simply you are not your thoughts or your existence.

3. a realisation about where and when you think and work
towards these places and nurture their time and enjoy the beauty
of their presents.

   One of the features of Proust .. Dan la reaseach perdu" is to call
this thinking whwile reading where something is trigger a
signifiwr is sihnifed and the reader passes into a trasnce, getting
lost in the tt and actually loses volition in the beauty of the
thoughts.

Another mistake of human nature is from Roberta Anton Wilson.
who derides the action from the conclusions of our thoughts...
thats is to convince others we have the right thinking.

Wilson's poke at ideology is most effective. He wastes no time in
telling his reader that all of us have tunnel vision and feel
inclined to convince other their tunnel vision is the correct tunnel
vision. This given credence to the phrase. "it is easy to be brain
washed, you just need to be born."

140. The Critical Think

I am aware of the right, true and acceptable definition of certain theories, the prescriptive method. Yet what is also useful is an analysis of a mistake made in concluding statements and data. This is the méconnaissance of Jacques Lacan, part of the divided subject. "This division differentiates the ego from the subject and consciousness from the unconscious." (https://www.encyclopedia.com/psychology/dictionaries-thesauruses-pictures-and-press-releases/splitting-subject)

It can be considered that, 'I have thought and my thoughts are wrong but I can learn from the analysis of this mistake'. For example, I recently confused a definition of 'ideology' with a definition of 'desire'. This was my méconnaissance. At first, I understood the comparison as a mistake, then on second glance, the comprehension after apprehension, I see a connect. A connect, in that humans 'desire' and make the same mistake again and again. For example, a choice of bad partners, or recidivist behaviour. Likewise, in 'ideology' a political party might be found to be corrupt, yet people stay with the party. And so too in religious ideology, a church is found to have a core that are convicted criminals. Yet members stay with the church.

In conclusion, people stick with ideology and desire, though logic forbids.

This idea of a similarity between ideology and desire is exemplified in John Carpenter's movie, "They Live". https://youtu.be/jTK8eff1Zsk. The protagonist, on seeing a reality with his special glasses, is sent into a rage. His desire or ideology has been challenged. He is caught between two worlds, the logical and the unconscious ideology/desire. He is beset with trauma, a little PTSD.

This similarity can be seen of the Lacan graph of desire.

https://youtu.be/67d0aGc9K_I

141. All News is Fake News

If Ludwig Wittgenstein was alive today, surely, he would tell us. 'All news is fake news'.

In his *Tractatus Logico-Philosophicus* he concludes, "Whereof one cannot speak, thereof one must be silent" (Wittgenstein 2013, p.108). He is summarizing a resolve to explain that philosophical problems are overwhelmingly linguistic problems and the limits of language fall prey to a lack of ability to explain.

Phenomenology. "The limits of my language mean the limits of my world"(Wittgenstein 2013, p.88).

Language is limited, language cannot and does not express truth enough and yet is taken seriously

because it is the best communication tool there is.

'All news is fake news' is the axiom to produce critical thinking of Paul Ricoeur, that of the skeptical read.

'All news is fake news ' is the place to start the conversation, much the same as philosophers start with

Descartes'. "I think, therefore I am" and communication theorists begin with, "The medium is the

message".

...Philosophers, the live ones will turn you on to the dead ones.

W had finished T in 1918 and since then authorities in communications have used phrases

like "The medium is the message" This has been a great place to start the discussion with reference to media & the phrase is most prominent in the world of communication.... But it is wrong, the message is not just fabricated by the medium.

" all news is fake news" is a phrase worth discussing.

& to justify the axiom let's consider.

1. A US journalist shot in India.

And an Indian journalist is shot in America.

I think it can be agreed the first gets reported more than the second and therefore news is fake per se.

2. A terrible injustice has occurred. An editor decides this needs to be an issue in the public sphere but

there are no pictures so the article gets relegated to the down the order of the news. So as it is said "all news is fake news" it can be understood that stories are valourused because they fit the format not because they are worthy.

3. The idea of balance is a key feature of fake news. Why would you give a rapist the same amount of air time as tou would give a survivor? Balance is commonly understood as the goal of news yet asecting a truth or trying to be fair is a secondary issue. The accusation of a lack of balance is a false flag. I have never seen a news institution reject publicly the idea of balance and therefore must conclude their news is limited.

4. if news doesn't change people are not going to change. n it's fake posturing as a community benefit is a subversive challenge to the community.
 The spoken word is analogous to truth as the written language is to knowledge.

Check out the Facebook page Terminal Language a whole list of language exerts that sound true then a second glance fall into the problematic a Wittegenstein classification.

https://www.facebook.com/Terminal-Language-1503758623198120/
 And there ... to some degree lies the idea "all news is fake news".

 W had finished T in 1918

This as Phrase as a media stater pack might best uncover a CT sharper and thoroughly sceptical that Riceour would be proud.

Insults are the arguments employed by those who are in the wrong. - Jean-Jacques *Rousseau*

142. The Function of Hypertrophy

Hypertropy, if you don't have one get one. Hypertrophy, the social instinct. A Totem.

Things that stand out for you... Totem.... an eagle, a fish, a crow.... They are given to you, to stand out for you.... Your very own conspiracy theory...

Because if you don't have totem, you will invent a totem... Totem, an invention of a conspiracy. The thing in the

everyday life that will stand out for you.

143. The Fourth Wall

 Goddard started this.

When the actor then turns to the camera and tells you, what is really? Happening?

Re House of Cards.

This is the annunciation of the unconscious.
The dialectic come clean to form another viewed identity. The dialectic being the conscious/unconscious and the video producing a synthesis.

This is Hegel dialectic.. Thesis- anti synthesis - then synthesis-

 conscious- unconscious- then spoken word from video not taken as an abstraction.

As Hegel tells us this continues ad infinitum, if you like ... the video 'piece to camera' invents another unconscious, that in turn may be ameliorated.... such is history..

"Survival of the fittest" exclaimed Spencer... The entourage for Darwin was building, mounting a concerted effort to revolutionize the thoughts of everyday existence.. A Copernicus moment..

The murderer, evil to the core, is presented here with reasons as to his criminality ... Molested as a child etc.... A father who loved guns... How did he survive? He is not fit at all? He survived because he has a warmth, a lovable self. It is in fact as Darwin would now admit .... "Survival of the most lovable". Is why Chopper got to survive, because he is lovable charming..Anon.

144. Dream Baby Dream

What came first? Language or dreaming?

Dreams from the heart. Dreams without a Symbolic Order, without contradiction & no sound track. Lawlessness, meandering lies. Dreams have a structure of language. Eyes wide shut, 444. Rapid eye movement slips of the tongue.

Corporate Gaslighting

"The research benefits of the paper may not have justified all of this anxiety"

 (Facebook postAdam D I Kramer30/6/2014Accessed:25/3/2015Source:https://www.facebook.com/akramer/posts/10152987150867) Sorry the link is broke, but posted at the bottom here. .

UX of anxiety is argued to justify the experiment by Facebook. And that might be true.

The interpolation of the corporate gaslight (CG) is rife. The CG is communication and with AI it is a joke most severely referenced in comedy show little Britain.
"Computer says no"
Little Brittan are here as an omen of the dystopian AI days to come. There are no banks, no post office, no enrollment officer. All is taken care of.In the name of value for money and savings (that can be spent on public service proper). The ideals are the ones that discount humanity.

 The insults are profound. "Would you like to push in" says the University recorded voice. The interpolation and assumption

here is that all students are underhanded, out for themselves and
are somewhat of a criminal element. The problem so deep and
entrenched that a simple message to the authority in question
will not bring about a change.

□□□□□□□□□

whole articleFacebook post Adam D I
Kramer30/6/2014Accessed:25/3/2015Source:https://www.facebo
ok.com/akramer/posts/10152987150867796OK so. A lot of
people have asked me about my and Jamie and sJeff's recent
study published in PNAS, and I wanted to give a brief public
explanation. The reason we did this research is because we care
about the emotional impact of Facebook and the people that use
our product. We felt that it was important to investigate the
common worry that seeing friends post positive content leads to
people feeling negative or left out. At the same time, we were
concerned that exposure to friends' negativity might lead people
to avoid visiting Facebook. We didn't clearly state our
motivations in the paper.Regarding methodology, our research
sought to investigate the above claim by very minimally
deprioritizing a small percentage of content in News Feed (based
on whether there was an emotional word in the post) for a group
of people (about 0.04% of users, or 1 in 2500) for a short period
(one week, in early 2012). Nobody's posts were "hidden," they
just didn't show up on some loads of Feed. Those posts were
always visible on friends' timelines, and could have shown up on
subsequent News Feed loads. And we found the exact opposite
to what was then the conventional wisdom: Seeing a certain kind
of emotion (positive) encourages it rather than suppresses is.
And at the end of the day, the actual impact on people in the

338

experiment was the minimal amount to statistically detect it --the result was that people produced an average of one fewer emotional word, per thousand words, over the following week. The goal of all of our research at Facebook is to learn how to provide a better service. Having written and designed this experiment myself, I can tell you that our goal was never to upset anyone. I can understand why some people have concerns about it, and my co-authors and I are very sorry for the way the paper described the research and any anxiety it caused. In hindsight, the research benefits of the paper may not have justified all of this anxiety. While we've always considered what research we do carefully, we (not just me, several other researchers at Facebook) have been working on improving our internal review practices. The experiment in question was run in early 2012, and we have come a long way since then. Those review practices will also incorporate what we've learned from the reaction to this paper

145. Dialectics is Not a War… Yes < It Is

Pierre Bourdieu (French: [buʁdjø]; 1 August 1930 – 23 January 2002 French sociologist says … "it's half theory, half empiricism"

.. you don't know the argument if you only know one side of the argument. John Stuart Mill

146. The Divided Self

Not my other half.

"The unconscious is structured like a language". Not the language we speak but the language that communicates (speaks) through us.

A process of signification. A signifier and a signified. The signifier is not a sign but a form.

Lacan defines a signifier as "that which represents a subject for another signifier," in opposition to the sign, which "represents something for someone." In the Lacanian math below, The signifier is barred from the signified ...

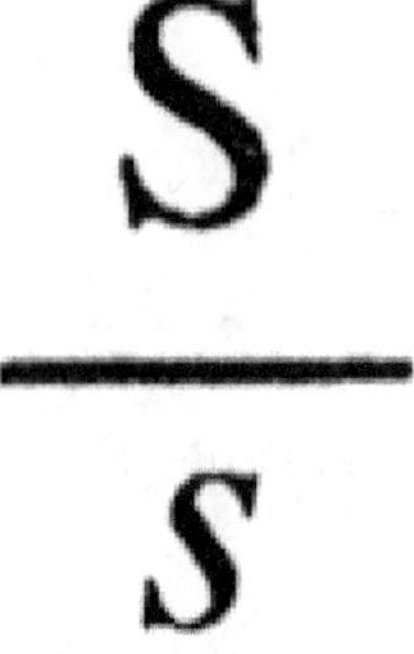

$$\frac{S}{s}$$

The Saussure math

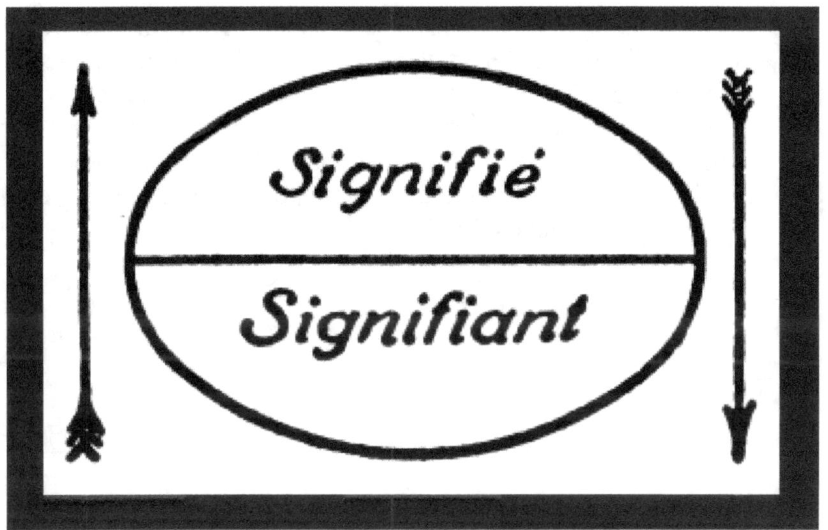

it is this process of signification. a signifier & hence the chain of signification as Lacan calls it ...

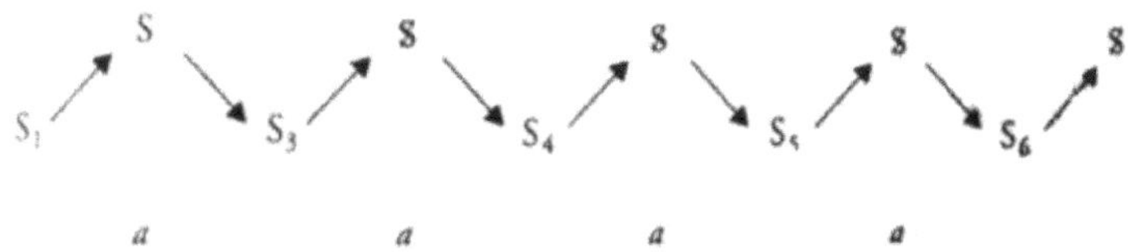

and a signified that is the big Other or simply "Other". The radical otherness. Lacan calls it. because it "speaks through us not of us" (this points to the concept of Lacan using the Cartesian

342

I. The thinking thing of conscious thoughts.) The symbolic Order
is as described by Žižek as 'the rules of the chess games'... the
control room... the secular god, that needs a host of conscious I.
.. (it does not need time or space...) And so it is a part of the
whole self and not the otherness of somewhere else... it is not
alterity but the connect to the other.. opposite ... outside .. love
they neightbour, love of god...

147. Luxury Communism

Luxury Communism, where every other mother works for the government. The growing pains of a wealthy wannabe place, desperate to be a big and metro and international with all the trimmings. But it isn't, so it awards itself luxury communism, hoping to 'fake it till you make it.' Some argue …It's embarrassing, corrupting, incorrigible, pathetic and destructive. The cultural so bad it invites a pharmaceutical response. Having all the natural resources laid at its feet. The needs are further up the chain and builds and builds. sport stadiums, museums without history. But., how does it move from luxury Communism to a world.... It can't, it can't move.... so, as you start, so shall you go & go & go & go. Go Luxury Communism.

148. The New Pandemic: Disaster

A Literature Review presenting an analysis of articles critiquing the Slavoj Žižek book, Pandemic!: Covid-19 Shakes the World. Using the author's own tools of analysis; Lacan, Hegel and pop culture, the review seeks to understand the Zizekian plot, utilising the book itself and four associated articles.

Pandemic!: Covid-19 Shakes the World, is a theoretical text for a new Communism. Zizek uses anecdotes to establish an understanding of a world with covid-19. Every chapter of the book includes China, then concludes with a German anecdote regarding a better world.
<https://www.facebook.com/groups/Zizekstudies/permalink/101
5710015184077/?hc_location=ufi>

Article 1. Žižek on China and COVID-19: Wuhan, authoritarian capitalism, and empathetic socialism in NZ. Michael Peters proposes a New Zealand/Chinese perspective, portending an authoritarian state if the public attitude is laissez-faire. The article includes discourse in Žižekian proposals for a new Communism.
<https://www.tandfonline.com/doi/full/10.1080/00131857.2020.
1801122>

Article 2. COVID – 19: A Critical Ontology of the present. Maarouf offers a formula of survival, he calls it; the beneath, the behind, and the beyond. This is a dark Lacanian analysis including; an assimilation of the world, production/consumption is never enough and an apocalypse that has already happened.

<https://www.tandfonline.com/doi/full/10.1080/00131857.2020.
1757426>

Article 3. Mind the economy! But mind the right economy!
Žižek highlights the movie The Escape, a boring film with a
thought-provoking idea that the unconscious is in control and
working life is a troubled soul; ruled by forces of desire.
<https://www.welt.de/kultur/article208002105/Slavoj-Zizek-
Mind-the-economy-But-mind-the-right-
economy.html?fbclid=IwAR1fUK8ppkX7xC3K2lW9Qohz-
PuIGOYt9sf-83oADK2Zhe_YAYzyC6Se_hE
>
Article 4. Is Barbarism with a Human Face our fate? The Critical
Inquiry invokes The Communist Manifesto's, "Spectre haunting
Europe" (Engels & Marx 2005, p.1).
"I am afraid to fall asleep since nightmares haunt me in my
dreams" (In Barbarism 2020, p.1), says Žižek. The text asks for a
change in economy, giving examples of, already implemented,
socialist ideology.
<https://critinq.wordpress.com/2020/03/18/is-barbarism-with-a-
human-face-our-fate/>

When things breakdown in a pandemic, it can be seen how
things are put together. In the article, A Critical Ontology of the
Present, Maarouf presents a simple list of how the world is put
together. "We live in an illusion of permanence of things, of
mastery, of immortality." (A Critical Ontology 2020, p.1). In this
setting, "an illusion of permanence" (Ibid), Žižek sees an
opportunity to apply theory, that is, covid-19 provides the means
necessary for transference to a new Communism, sutured by a
distraught public in lockdown. It is within this starkness that
Žižek hopes to herald a new Socialist era. "The virus of thinking
of an alternate society, a society beyond nation-state, a society

that actualizes itself" (Žižek 2020, p.39). Of course, the lockdown will cause many to sit and think, but not about Communism, Žižek confesses, "I have been criticized, mocked even" (Žižek 2020, p.106). From Alain Badiou to Byung-Chul Han, Žižek's new Communism theory has been thoroughly canned. Žižek might believe in the Hegelian conclusion that, "The history of the world is none other than the progress of the consciousness of freedom" (Hegel 2001, p.33), but it is an impossibility amongst his peers. If people believe they are already in "the land of the free" (What are the lyrics 2019) then why change?

Žižek rarely uses data in his discourse and Pandemic!: Covid-19 Shakes the World, is no different. Not one percentage, no figures, no averages, no cited data at all. The only figures Žižek quotes are the figures on children's health with better air. "Saved the lives of 4,000 children under five and 73,000 adults over 70 in China" (Žižek 2020, p.90). Data does not enter the Žižekian hermeneutics and Hegel states directly, "If theory does not fit the facts, then so much the worse for the facts" (Hegel in Žižek, 2013, p.461). The use of facts and figures would spoil the beauty of this theorist's plot; ethos, pathos, and logos without data, this is the Žižekian way. Any pandemic has a horrible haunting quality and just like the opening line of The Communist Manifesto. "A spectre is haunting Europe" (Marx & Engels ND, p.1). Zizek too, uses the same word, haunt. "I am afraid to fall asleep since nightmares haunt me in my dreams" (In Barbarism 2020, p.1). Žižek describes the virus as a horror movie. "Viruses are neither alive nor dead in the usual sense of these terms, they are a kind of living dead" (Žižek 2020, p.78), Žižek explains, this entire tale looks like a Lovecraft novel. It has to be said that, this is not anything that would endear itself to a public willing to embark on Žižek's "radical social changes" (Is Barbarism, p.2). Even before covid-19, there was a horror. The planet was falling off an environmental cliff, but now it is as if, the environment has been suspended, while the world attends to covid -19. People are now yearning to get back to normal, apparently to get back to the good old days of impending climate disaster. A particularly Lacanian summation suggests it is not Communism that is longed for but for desire itself, unobtainable desire, or Lacanian objet petit a. "We desire to regain desire itself" (Mind The Economy, p.3), says Žižek. The suggestion being that desire is the most basic instinct that valourises all others, the notion that makes shopping malls the default position. As long as everyone can shop, or think they can shop in the future, then there is an ameliorated public. As religion is "the opiate of the people" (A Contribution to the Critique of Hegel's Philosophy of Right, p.1), surely Communism must be happy the shopping malls are open, even on the holy days. What would appear impossible a decade ago is happening. Conservative governments around the globe are propping up the economy with handouts. Jobkeeper and Jobseeker in Australia, suspending mortgages and rents in many countries, leftist style economics are now familiar to right-wing governments. A creeping Communism slowly bending the conservative ideals to a transference to Keynesian economics. Universal basic income has a bipartisan political future. "Even Trump is now considering a form of Universal Basic Income" (Žižek 2020, p.93). There are incremental signs of governance of a Communist market economy and even the Republicans have bowed to the idea. "The US president said he would invoke a federal provision allowing the government to marshal the private sector in response to the pandemic" (Coronavirus Latest 2020). As Žižek explains, "We are all Socialists" now (Žižek 2020, p. 93).

And finally, the outcome that seems plausible, nothing dramatic, nothing revolutionary, in fact, a sense of everydayness. From

Žižek's appendix from Pandemic!: Covid-19 Shakes the World, he reflects upon, "Andreas Rosenfelder, a German journalist for Die Welt, described the new stance towards daily life that is emerging: I really can feel something heroic about this new ethics, also in journalism—everybody works day and night from their home office, participating in video conferences and taking care of children or schooling them at the same time, but nobody asks why he or she is doing it, because it's not any more a question of so 'I get money and can go to vacation etc.,' Since nobody knows if there will be vacations again and if there will be money. It's the idea of a world where you have an apartment, basics like food and water, the love of others and a task that really matters, now more than ever. The idea that one needs 'more' seems unreal now" (Žižek 2020, p.113).

References

Hegel, Georg, 2001, The Philosophy of History, Bartouche books, Ontaria Canada.

Key, Francis Scot 1814, What are the lyrics to the us national anthem, the star-spangled banner? Viewed 31 August 2020, <https://www.classicfm.com/discover-music/periods-genres/national-anthems/us-national-anthem-star-spangled-banner-lyrics/%3E/>

Maarouf, Moulay Driss El, Belghazi,Taieb, & Maarouf, Farouk El 2020, Covid – 19: a critical ontology of the present, viewed 30 August 2020, <10.1080/00131857.2020.1757426 >

Marx, Karl, A contribution to the critique of hegel's philosophy of right, viewed 30 August 2020, <https://www.marxists.org/archive/marx/works/1843/critique-hpr/intro.htm>

Marx, Karl, & Engels, Friedrich ND, The communist manifesto, Penguin Books, London, UK.

Peters, Micheal 2020, Žižek on china and covid-19: wuhan, authoritarian capitalism, and empathetic socialism in nz, viewed 30 August 2020, < 10.1080/00131857.2020.1801122 >

Rawlinson, Kevin 2020, Coronavirus latest: 18 march at a glance, viewed 30 August 2020, < https://www.theguardian.com/world/2020/mar/18/coronavirus-latest-at-a-glance-wednesday-2020>

Žižek, Slavoj 2013, Less than nothing, hegel and the shadow of the dialectical materialism, Verso Books, Brooklyn, New York, USA.

Žižek, Slavoj 2020, Pandemic!: covid-19 shakes the world, OR Books, New York, USA.

Žižek, Slavoj 2020, Is barbarism with a human face our fate? viewed 30 August 2020, <

https://critinq.wordpress.com/2020/03/18/is-barbarism-with-a-human-face-our-fate/>

Žižek, Slavoj 2020, Mind the economy! but mind the right economy! kultur, viewed 30 August 2020, <https://www.welt.de/kultur/article208002105/Slavoj-Zizek-Mind-the-economy-But-mind-the-right-economy.html?fbclid=IwAR1fUK8ppkX7xC3K2lW9Qohz-PuIGOYt9sf-83oADK2Zhe_YAYzyC6Se_hE>

Bibliography

Lovecraft, Howard Philips 2008, Necronomicon, the best weird tales of h.p. lovecraft, the call of cthulhu, Orion Publishing Group, London UK.

https://www.thelancet.com/journals/lancet/article/PIIS0140-6736(20)31241-1/fulltext

https://link.springer.com/article/10.1007/s42438-020-00161-0

http://www.journal-psychoanalysis.eu/coronavirus-and-philosophers/

https://www.smartraveller.gov.au/COVID-19

https://www.smartraveller.gov.au/COVID-19/leaving-Australia

https://www.rt.com/shows/sophieco-visionaries/497910-slavoj-zizek-wartime-communism/?fbclid=IwAR0HBn14zftvVw3mtaAm0t7_FEU6_0OgR2DmbELO7imvCxoldrLp8pihPWU

Smith, B Smith, 1987, Hegel's Idea of a Critical Theory. Yale University, viewed 20th August 2020, https://www-jstor-org.libraryproxy.griffith.edu.au/stable/191722?seq%3D1=&seq=1#metadata_info_tab_contents

149. Qualitative Research

"Qualitative research (QR) has a long history in liberal democratic societies" And its use in the community can be greatly respected as a means of providing better services. QR is a considered scientific and objective method, used to progress any community to live up to its potential. When presented with facts and figures, it is difficult to deny.

Then it is a shock to see how QR can be co-opted and corrupted. For example, within hours of the Brexit referendum 24th June 2016, journalists of all shapes and sizes, blamed migration on the result. "The referendum resulted in 51.9% of the votes cast being in favour of leaving the EU". An unsuspecting public thought the referendum was about a slogan on a bus. "Sending the EU £350 million a week. Let's fund the NHS instead". This was written on a doubler-decker bus, paraded around the country in favour of a Brexit and was the prime marking strategy in favour of Brexit. From a communication perspective, it should be noted that not many people actually saw the bus. The real message and the power in the message, was the ability of this communication to be intertextual, that is, transferred from the real bus, to the internet as a meme. Postable, sharable and topical. The Facebook meme was plastered on the internet and spread. This modus operandum is cheap and effective… One bus paint job has saved a heap $$$ in TV news advertising and the public has done all the distribution, free of charge.

Before the referendum, immigration was not the issue, yet hours after the result came in, it became an issue. Britain was about to leave the EU by a small margin and the press began a campaign informing the public that the break from the EU was all about immigration. The press provided an immediate explanation to a bewildered public. The result had given space for a story and a story that need not be true, but fit a possible narrative. Here was an opportunity to install a divisive debate. A scoop ready to create division that would sell much more news for months to come.

The seeds had now been planted for QR. After the result the response of the public, in vox pops and letters the editor… etc, was all about immigration and not about saving $$$ for the NHS. The public have parroted the news that was previously fed to them. The possible QR has been sufficiently, co-opted and corrupted, as seen in the public mouthing their given opinion.

150. Groups

Groups Naturally in society there are groups; old age, teenage, new age, all groups. & these are powerful things. "Tribalism is the most powerful force in the world today…..Tribalism is about belonging, teams, neighbourhood, it's about culture", says Patrick Dixon. https://youtu.be/CivP6VN2cJc Yet to remain as a group there is a need to have a 'group think'. A dogma that the group possesses to forward the needs and identity of the group, based on common ground. As time changes the 'group think' is ingrained and it finds it difficult to change. Even the idea of change is dismissed, the groups' ideas are the foundations of the group and it is inexplicable for change to occur because obviously the group would not be the same group. This need for change can be seen as an attack on the group itself. Change appears paradoxical; things need to change so that things can remain the same. Australia as a new country is more amenable to change. The foundations of the country are new and flexible. Other western democracies have more ossified in their cultural ways and find change difficult, even unthinkable, - Just think of US gun control. Things need to change so that things can remain the same.

151. Semiotic Rules

This discussion of names has a history in ancient Greece, that is, Socrates Dialogues circa 300 BC, from the Plato book, Cratylus.

Plato's book points out the arbitrariness of signs.

"Well, now, let me take an instance; - suppose that I call a man a horse or a horse a man, you mean to say that a man will be rightly called a horse by me individually, and rightly called a man by the rest of the world; and a horse again would be rightly called a man by me and a horse by the world: - that is your meaning?"

"For Saussure, the arbitrary nature of the sign was the first principle of language". States Daniel Chandler. To exemplify this arbitrariness, the book, Semiotics for Beginners, uses Shakespeare.

"That which we call a rose by any other name would smell as sweet."

It is historically, a well trotted out semiotic rule, that the sign is arbitrary or the name is arbitrary. But let's just test this notion and remove the word 'rose' from the Shakespeare quote and replace it with something else. In fact, the rule suggests we can change it to anything and apparently it will still mean a 'rose'. So, let's change it to 'Chptegontwo'. This is an impossibility. No one would take it seriously and therefore it must be remarked that the sign is not arbitrary and in any similar case, when the letters are put together in an arbitrary fashion; this is plain silly.

But let's go again, let's change the word "rose" to "yes", this time a familiar word in the English language. The double meaning brings immediate complications to the sign, complications in meaning, that didn't exist when using the word 'rose'. The sign is again proven not to be arbitrary.

Perhaps Saussure was merely thinking of the translation to another language, so let's try this, the Vietnamese word for 'rose' starts with 'hoa'. When spoken out loud the word again has a double meaning, it sounds like the previous Vietnamese leader 'Ho' Chi Minh. The rule of semiotics and the arbitrariness of the sign is looking a little shaky.

Put into a broader context, considering languages as a whole. It can be said, making fair comparisons, that French sounds romantic, while German sounds harsh. This is an implicit difference and has change of meaning in all translations. It begs the question, what is "lost in translation?"

When you substitute a word like 'rose' for anything else. The new word has a different onomatopoeic influence. If the sound of the new word is more like a bird singing or more like the thud of a hammer… These changes are effective signifiers, changing the meaning and again dismissing the idea of the arbitrariness of the sign.

Saussure has a good point concerning the arbitrariness of signs and cannot be dismissed easily. Yet the examples given, prove a point, that the rule is not water tight.

153. Introduction: God and the Pantheon

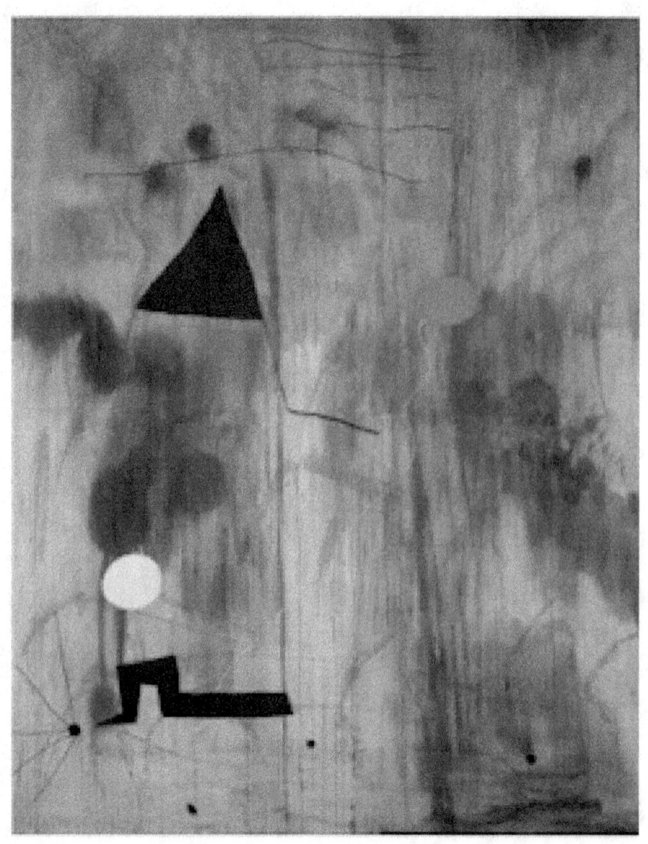

Look no words. In this painting, landscape is absent.

On these shoulders of giants, that is the vast history of realist painting have now been built on a new direction. what is signified is a task to look internally... .. The Freud's *Die Traumdeutung*)... the interpretation of dreams... 1899 instructed the world to do so . And this Copernican moment set in motion the writer artist and musicians alike .. to delve in to the unconscious and examine the signs. Charles Sanders Peirce "We think only on signs"

And as soon as this happens, things are a little dark, the signified, the painting is in a choke hold, the subject to the signifying for an internal review.

In the beginning was the Word, and the Word was with God, and the Word was God.

In principio erat Verbum, et Verbum erat apud Deum, et Deus erat Verbum.

With close reading this hypertrophy fills the page..."deus erat verbum".."the word was god"..... Taken from

the New Testament St John gospel's opening line. Points to an unconsidered god

Within all the usual statements of trying to explain the universe with the antk science of the middle ages.

It is most peculiar to see a statement that has stood the test of time and can be reasonably sort after to

360

explain contemporary thought in the communications of humanity.

The surrealist movement born from the thought of the day .

  As the bible is

154. The Birth of the World: A Semiotic Reduction of the Surrealist Painting 1925 of Joan Miró

Considering the 1925 Joan Miró painting, *The Birth of the World.* The art is examined using a semiotic method, including recognised semiotic tables and explanations of the semiotic process. It can be seen in the report a transition of the semiotic system from linguistics to art. The work of art, under the microscope, reveals the semiotic values in the areas of science and literature. Valid scientific inferences have been made in regards to the splitting of the atom by Ernest Rutherford. Theological deductive arguments are made, considering 'the subject as God'. And fascist political moves by Hitler are understood, in semiotic terms, of the Entartete Art movement. Furthermore, the painting is used to compare Saussure and Lacan theoretical variance and exemplify the use of the semiotic categorisation.

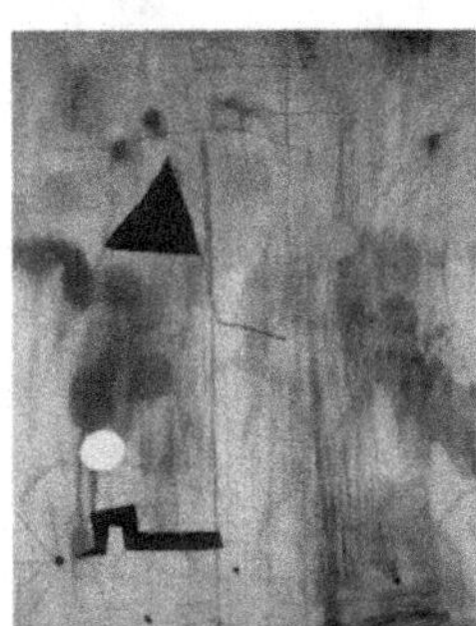

Introduction

The painting's semiotic indicators are not in doubt. *The Birth of the World* enjoys the hallmark semiotic devices of the conscious and unconscious. Using the taxonomy of Saussure, Peirce, Lacan, Vico, et al. Meaning is unfurled, revealing the components of the signs of the painting, *The Birth of the World.*

Charles Sanders Peirce states "We think only in signs" (Peirce 1955, p.115).

Miró's painting is exact in proving the semiotic theory, that the sign has a signifier and a signified. The signifier, "the sound pattern" (Saussure p.15), as it is here, *The Birth of the World* and the signified is the concept of the painting. The sign is the inseparable combination of the painting and the title. "These two elements are intimately linked and each triggers the other" (Saussure, 2011, p. 66).

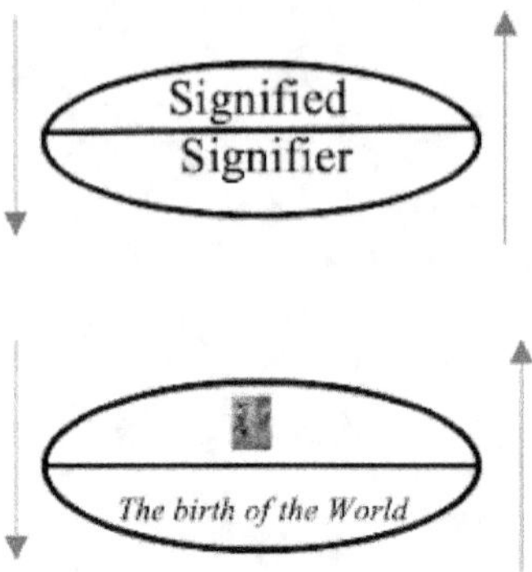

The schema above indicates a sign for a sign, not just the sign itself. Or as Lacan puts it, getting into the detail, "a signifier that which represents a subject for *another* signifier" (The Symptom 2020).

Here in the Saussure schema, the signified is barred from the signifier.

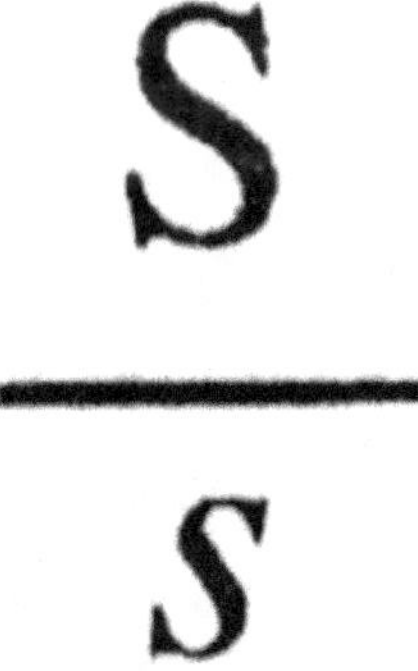

The signified "concept" (Saussure 2011, p.67) or "Nothing less nor more than inference" (Peirce p. 246), is barred from the signifier "sound pattern" (Saussure 2011, p.67) but the "sound pattern" (Ibid) is less barred and more autonomous from the concept. The 'bar' itself, as it is termed, is not a ban as such, but a thing to overcome.

The arrows either side of the schema indicate the passage to meaning, abrogating the bar and representing the arbitrariness of the signifier. That is, the name of the painting in any language still maintains the same

relationship with the concept of the painting. For example,
translating *The Birth of The World* into Spanish, still
maintains the same meaning of the painting.
"For Saussure signifiers and signifieds are like words
written on a sheet of paper, with the signifier on one side
and its signified on the other; they cannot be separated, and
yet they cannot occupy the same place." (Bailly 2020, p.44).

Lacan prefers his own schema, inverting the signified
and signifier of Saussure's schema. That is,
Signifier/signified.

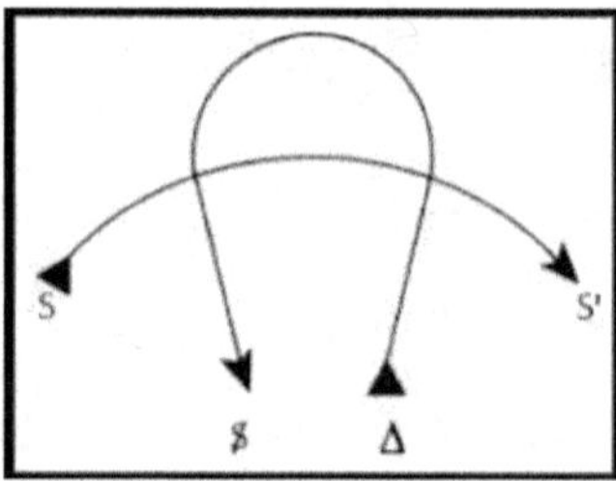

This time, the signifier (S) is barred from the signified (s).
"It underlines the autonomy of the signifier to the signified"
(Bailly 2020, p.46). Bailly adding to the theory states. "The
signified inevitably 'slips beneath' the signifier, resisting
our attempts to delimit it" (Bailly 2020, p.45).
Lacan sees the slippage of the signifier, that is, the sound
pattern, and its reworking, as the more significant unit.
It can be understood why this is a debatable point, Lacan
has inverted the schema of Saussure. However, Saussure

has good reason to valourise the signified. Literally, *The birth of world,* 'the concept', comes first and then the words to describe, the sound pattern, come next. If you imagine a child, the concept of 'mum' comes first then the sound-pattern 'mum' comes later. But as an issue, Lacan sees this schema as secondary to the signifying chain of the signifier. The ability of the mind to associate signifiers with other signifiers, is the most dominant feature, suggests Lacan. *The Birth of the World's* associating factors, as a stream of consciousness, is the happening thing. Nevertheless, the signifier must always be connected to the concept, so as to make meaning.

Lacan's schema is called the Signifying Chain, depicted below.

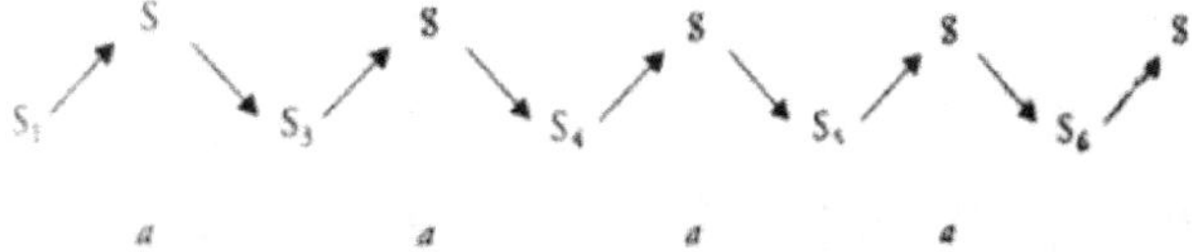

Further to this semiotic chain. It can be added that there is a "mimetic desire" (Girard 1996, p.69) happening. The chain is searching for negative and positive results, but as soon as a negative result is found, more negative results are searched for, a "mimetic desire" (Ibid). The chain is ideologically predisposed to negative or positive results according to the subject.

The painting is an artistic impression. Unlike previous Realist movements the artist is usually an autonomous entity undirected by the whim of a philanthropic art collector. This individuality is not welcomed by the fascist politics of Europe; about to come to the fore in Germany. The art of the individual, of the unconscious, was deemed 'degenerate', called Entartete Kunst and was attacked by

Hitler's government in the 1930's. Baron states, "In 1937 the National Socialists staged the most virulent attack ever mounted against modern art with the opening on July 19 in Munich of the Entartete Kunst (Degenerate Art) exhibition" (Baron 1991, p.9). The valourisation of the connotation over the denotation was the problem.

Miró's painting connotes and denotes, it denotes, what is generally thought to be and connotates, what the inferred thought is. The denotation is the conscious expression of the painting and the connotation is the unconscious expression. In 1925, as a break from the Realist art history, Modern art was born, the art of the unconscious. In 1925 this art was a revolution because the unconscious is valourised over the denotation. Barthes uses a diagram below to adapt connotation and denotation. Here it is, from his book Mythologies.

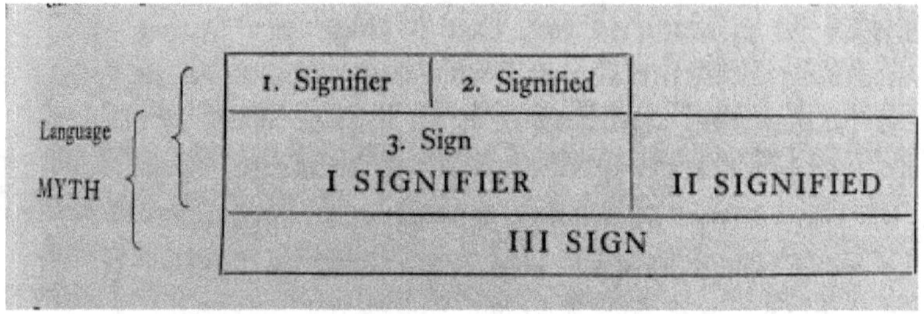

"In myth we find again the tri-dimensional pattern which I have just described: the signifier, the signified and the sign" (Barthes 1989, p.114). Lacan states, "The unconscious is structured like a language" (Bailly 2020, p.29), in the sense, it is a signifying process that involves coding and decoding, or ciphering and deciphering.

Using the Barthes' table, *The Birth of the World* is inserting into the appropriate place.

	sad	
I can see eyes or planets The painting looks partly human	organic	
The whole painting is a sign of simplicity.		

As can be seen in the chart, Barthes argues that the "Connotation and denotation combine to produce an ideology" (Chandler 2002, p.93) a third order signification, as marked above, named, *the whole painting is a sign of simplicity*. Barthes claims, that in third order signification is where ideology is manufactured.

Another most notable semiotician and contemporary of Saussure was Charles Saunders Peirce. Below, The Peircean Table has been completed using the painting as an example.

368

The Peircean Table: *The Birth of the World.*

The representamen: the form which the sign takes.	A red circle and a white circle
An interpretant: the sense made of the sign	Mars and the moon

An object: to which the sign refers	The sign refers to the viewer as the world.

The painting is a part of the Surrealist movement, keen to draw upon the inspiration of the unconscious. Of course, the artist was called a conceptual artist fitting to the Jungian idea of archetypal concepts from the unconscious. That is, something organic in all of us, stooped in ancient history, memories that have memories. Jung stated "the modern artist is not very different from those of the old masters who knew the spirit of the stone" (Jung 1964, p.234). Lacan contradicts this idea of Jung. Lacan believes the signified is under the signifier. "For Lacan, there are no signifieds in the unconscious, only signifiers" (Bailly 2020, p.48). This is the opposite of Jungian thought. Lacan could be correct here. Let's just say our emotions are archetypal but not our concepts.

At the time of the painting in 1925 of *The Birth of the World.* Freud's books, *The Interpretation of Dreams* 1899, *The Ego and the Id* 1921, *and Jung's Psychology of the Unconscious* 1912, had been gaining ascendency throughout

369

the world. Although the genre of art was in revolution, the synchronic semiotic idea was still a valid approach. There have been detractors of the Saussure perspective because the outward signs appear like *The Birth of the World* was an evolutionary diachronic system. However, Saussure insists the synchronic building blocks remain primary. Roy states, "It was a position which committed Saussure to drawing a radical distinction between diachronic (or evolutionary) linguistics and synchronic (or static) linguistics, and giving priority to the latter" (Roy in Saussure 2013, p.15). Saussure's method still looked on the Surrealist revolution as having the same structure, the same internal references, although outwardly looking different.

In 1917, with the birth of nuclear physics, a young Ernest Rutherford had split of the atom. "He discovered that he could disintegrate the nuclei of nitrogen atoms by firing particles from a radioactive source" (Rutherford 2009). Looking at the diagram below, it appears similar to the Miró painting. Miró is referent to the birth of the world of nuclear physics, in fact, the painting might be truer than the diagram itself.

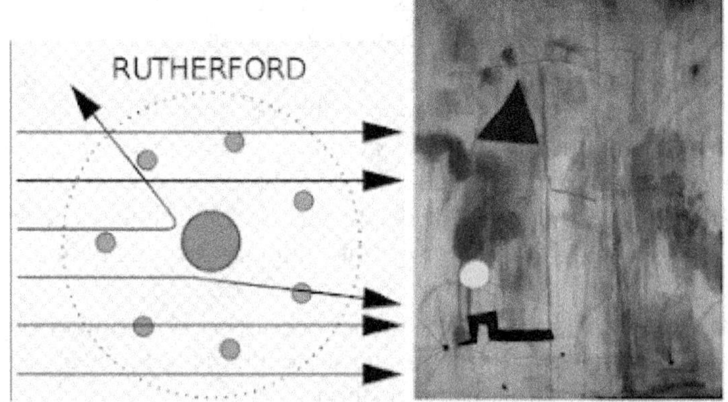

Kristeva intersectional semiotic approach sees a horizontal axis in the subject-object position and in the vertical axis in the text-text position. For example, it can be speculated, the subject-object position for Miró's work is, God and the painting. Let me explain, the painting is *The Birth of the World*, and considering Creationist thought, if the object is the painting then the subject is the viewer. Adhering to Creation thought, this makes the subject the transcendental God.

The text-text position of *The Birth of the World* can be speculated as the big-bang theory. What is instructive of the Kristeva approach is the formula of a vertical axis and a horizontal axis, this implies, a possible meeting of the axes. Here, and again only speculation, this can be viewed as *The Birth of the World* of Modern art. The lines drawn of, the

371

painting and God, are intersected by, the big bang, producing at the intersection, an era of Modern art. Pure speculation, however; that is what modern art is, pure speculation.

Saussure describes *langue* as, "The language minus the speech" (Barthes 1986, p.14) and *parole* as "speech ..essentially an individual act of selection" (Barthes 1986, p.15). The system was first introduced by Saussure as linguistic units, suggested by Barthes to explain other cultural sources to elicit meaning. Roland Barthes, in his work on theoretical semiology has further developed the semiotic system of *langue* and *parole*. Langue is the conscious understanding of the painting. For example, an eye-catching part of the painting, the two circles, red and white, are obvious conscious choices for understanding the world, without anything being spoken. The parole of the painting is the postulated, guess work, enunciated by the viewer. That is, what is understood and what might be postulated by the personal knowledge of the viewer. The viewer knows the moon is white and that mars is red. This would be the selected spoken word of the viewer; the parole.

The Birth of the World, in Spain, in the 1920's, would be immediately thought of as, God's creation, because Spain's dominant faith in the 20th century was Christian. The bible would be the text to describe *The Birth of the world* and it is stated in The New Testament of St John. "In the beginning was the Word, and the Word was with god, and the Word was God" (John, 1:1). Herein lies a proposition that Saussure would have been interested in, that God has linguistic origins. Let me explain, the painting is *The Birth of the world* and "In the beginning was the Word" (Ibid).

So, the painting is 'the Word', "and the word is God", so the painting is God. The meaning signified by the text, ie the concept, is a radical break from Christianity proper. How can a painting be God? In conclusion, it must be denoted as heretical, however connoted as promethean.

The passage from signified to the barred signifier, and vice vera, is what gives meaning and in this meaning is the entry into the Lacanian Symbolic Order, i.e, the personal moral compass. This passage from signified to signifier, or vice versa, can be seen as the secular God. What has been termed in the past as 'thing that is not understood', God, has started to be theorised as a science. As soon as the bar has been passed through, then it is possible to act humanly, to be asked to act humanly and to act in accordance with those rules. This bodes well with the Barthes distinction of the third order signifier, the one that is of ideology.

Lacan's first graph, the graph of the unconscious, though it is named The Graph of Desire in Lacan's book, *Ecrit*. This particular schema, drawn here, is named 'point de caption' and for our purposes, Lacan stated. "It can be used to connote" (Lacan 2017, p.8).

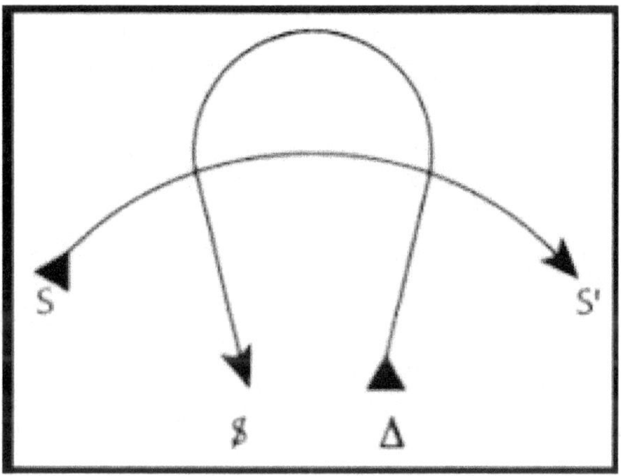

The two lines mark the subject and object position. Lacan uses a sentence to exemplify how the graph works. The sentence to be used here, is of course our title, *The Birth of the world.*

Lacan states, "If I begin a sentence, you will not understand its meaning until I have got to the end" (Lacan 2017, p.9). Hence the beginning of the sentence is the first juncture on the graph and the second juncture is the end of the sentence. Notice how the Δ subject swings back on itself thus explaining that the beginning of the sentence is retroactive and not understood until the sentence is finished. That is, *The Birth* is not fully understood, until it is said, *of the world.*

Semiotics from the outset was linguistic theory but through time and conversation has become the tool of analysis of social activity. Of course, similarities of the structure of language and the structure of social activity are possible. Notice above how there is a clear split in the sentence, *The Birth of…… the World,* to make a dialectic. Levi Strauss in his theory of myth making, stated that all stories use distinguishable building blocks. "According to Levi Strauss, the structure which underlies every myth is that of a four-term homology" (Rimmon-Kenan 1983, p.11). First, there are two parts to the narrative. Let's call this a:b, homologous to the sentence, *The Birth of…… the World.* Levi said the first dialectic, a:b is in contrast to a second dialectic c:d. c:d is the painting itself, split into two definite parts. The shapes, black triangle, red and white circle is c, and then the background of the painting is d. Levi argues that to form a narrative there must be a tension between the two sides and a tension within the two sides. That is, the formula of Levi Strauss a:b::c:d. What Miró has built is an abstract form of narrative. - The title a:b and the painting c:d. This form of narrative is the Plato 'form'. Where now, it can be understood that for fine art, a narrative is the ideal form. Concluding that what the art intends to do; is narrative.

Semiotics is a set of linguistic rules. Used so frequently, the rules are lost to habit and convention. Rules that manage to be transferable from literature to art. James Joyce had started to write Finnegans Wake's first chapter in 1926, the year after *The Birth of the World.* Even though this literature can appear at first random and lacking in regulation. It still contains the verifiable signs of semiotic convention, that of signified /signifier and four basic tropes.

"Joyce had planned from the beginning to base Finnegans Wake on the linguistic theories of Giambattista Vico" (Wilson 2020, p.7).

Like the art of the day, appearing random and without rules. The writings of Joyce have validated the Surrealist movement of Miro and it can be seen as using the same structuralist ideas.
"riverrun, past Eve and Adam's, from swerve of shore to bend of bay, brings us by a commodius vicus of recirculation back to Howth Castle and Environs" (Joyce 1992, p.71).

It can be easily said that ""it is, ….. unreadable" (Joyce 1992, p.1). And it can be said that *The Birth of the World* is not art. However, these are opinions and as has been proven both the art and the literature, have the classifications of semiotic structure. It can be seen both examples use the semiotic structure of tropes. Early identification and understanding of these tropes came from Giambattiata Vico, an Italian Naples man from 17th century. He states. "All figures of speech may be reduced to these four types - metaphor, metonymy, synecdoche and irony" (Vico 2010, p. 10).

Here is a diagram of the tropes of *The Birth of the World*.

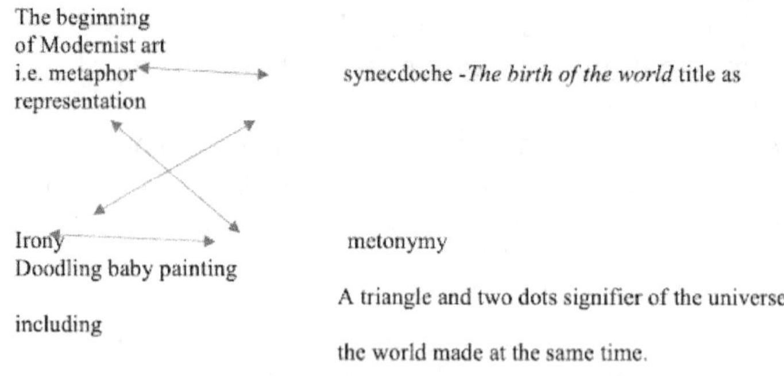

This style of schema is attributed to Greimas 1987

"Here finally we find opened up the 'black box' through which narrative is somehow 'converted' into cognition and vice versa" (Greimas 1983, p.xiv).

The Greimas Chart sets out to display the opposites in convention and add any possible interaction with a binary solution. It is a step beyond dialectics of just two opposing tropes.

From Julien Greimas's book, *On Meaning Selected writings in Semiotic Theory*.

"This is to say that a "semiotic reduction" (as I will call the central operations of Greimassian analysis) aims at

377

rewriting a verbal or linguistic text into more fundamental mechanisms of meaning" (Greimas 1987, p.ix).

The article, *The Birth of the World*: A Semiotic Reduction of the Surrealist Painting of Joan Miró 1925, draws on distinct features of the painting, splitting the work into manageable parts and employing core semiotic tools. The semiotics of Saussure, Peirce and Vico have all proved that Levi Strauss was correct in assuming linguistic theories have a place in all social activities. Semiotic interpretation has been made to find that a social activity is a threat to fascist politics. Contradicting theories all have a valid place, particularly that of Lacan and Saussure. However, how much all this theory relates to empiricism, is an ongoing quest.

References

Baron, Stephanie 1991, *Degenerate art, the fate of avant guard art in nazi germany.* Los Angeles County Museum of Art, LA. USA and Harry N Abrams, New York, USA.

Barthes, Roland 1986, *Elements of semiology*, Hill and Wang, New York, USA.

Barthes, Roland 1989, *Mythologies,* The Noonday press, New York, USA.

Chandler, Daniel 2002, *Semiotics the basics*, Routledge, London UK.

Culler, Jonathan 2002, *Barthes: a very short introduction,* Oxford University Press, UK.

Culler, Johnathan, 2005, *The pursuit of signs,* Routledge London UK.

Eco, Umberto 1976 *Theory of semiotics,* Indiana University press, Bloomington London, UK.

Greimas, 1987, *On meaning selected writings in semiotic theory,* University of Minnesota Press, USA.

Joyce, James 1992, *Finnegans wake, Penguin, London, UK.*

Kristeva, Julia, 1980, *Desire in language a semiotic approach to literature and art,* Columbia University Press.

Lacan, Jacques 2017, *Formations of the unconscious, the seminar of jaques lacan book v,* Polity Press, *Cambridge, London UK.*

LacanOnline, *A Tour of Lacan's Graph of Desire 21 April 2020, viewed 29 09 20*

<https://youtu.be/67d0aGc9K_I>

Peirce Charles Sanders 1955, *Philosopical writings of peirce,* Dover publications Inc, New York, USA.

Rimmon-Kenan, Shlomith 1983, *Narrative fiction contemporary poetics,* Methuen & Co. Ltd, New York, USA.

Rutherford: splitting the atom 2009, Description of
Rutherford history, viewed 3rd October 2020,
<http://news.bbc.co.uk/local/manchester/hi/people_and_pla
ces/history/newsid_8282000/8282223.stm>

Saussure, De Ferdinand 2013, *Course in general
linguistics,* Bloomsbury Publishing Plc, London, UK.

The Baptist, John, *The gospel according to john*, viewed 4
October 2020, https://biblescripture.net/John.html

The Symptom 2020, Lacanian description of the symptom,
viewed 8th October 2020,
<https://www.lacan.com/symptom8_articles/miller8.html>

Verhaeghe, Paul, *The function and the field of speech and
language in psychoanalysis: a commentary on lacan's
'discours de rome',* viewed 24 September 2020
<https://www.sfu.ca/humanities-
institute/contours/LaConference/paper1.html>

Wilson, Robert Anton 2020, *Coincidence: a head test,*
Hilaritas Press, Colorado, USA.

Wiseman, Boris, and Groves, Judy, 2020, *Introducing levi-
Strauss and structural anthropology*, Totem Books, New
York, USA.

155. Anna Freud

 Anna Freud states "if you let children do what they want they become very aggressive, if you let adults say what they want they talk about sex." From Adam Phillips

156. Look like You Are Doing Something

A cynic would say, 'The government's job is to make mistakes and then repair the mistakes that they have made'

Sad that, how often this is true.

A program, in my local, was spending up big on getting kids to school. Uniformed officers, managers, people on the ground, and FIFO officials, costing the NT $7.25million per year. After eight years, the program was abandoned, as it made little or no difference to school attendance.

circa 2017

On a smaller scale, Zizek is a proponent of this dark side of governance. Zizek claims every institution carries an irony or two. He suggests that this is a characteristic of all institutions. Here are a few examples.

• The coke machine in A&E at the hospital.

• Popular government funded open air cinema sees nearby private cinema closed through lack of business.

• The education facility that depletes creativity.

Knowingly or unknowingly, there are three functions of the irony. These are gifts to the community to ponder, grab attention and remain beholden in their light. You have to wonder if this is not just some institutional ADHD.

The three functions are

1. Create mystery in the form of added complexity

2. Create a space for a leap of faith & define who is with you, kindling an underling class within your hierarchy.

3. To piss people off in cognitive dissonance and establish a weak enemy, easily dismissed.

Though this may not be done internationally, the powers that be might use the irony as a test case to define who is with you and who is against and define your public value as so great that you can get away with a coke machine in A&E. Who is going to argue with a sugary drink when lives are being saved of the moment? And so it goes as a logical understanding to the things that appear to stand in the way. But even science weighs in. Godel In the 1930's spoke at the Berlin symposium. and stated every system had a sentence that can be neither proved or disproved. It was his incompleteness theory....And is this no the adopted irony of every institution that they too have an alleged irony that cannot be proved or disproved.

Another of the great governance shams is 'looking like you are doing something'

What are you doping about youth crime?

What are you doing about aboriginal education?

These are questions that need answers more than they need success .. In fact sucess

there must be an answer to everything .." i don't know" is never the answer from governance.. they are the interpolaters of the all-knowing and omniscient. Hoping to result in a don't ever bother us again signifier.

206. The Seminar of Jacques Lacan: The Other Side of Psychoanalysis

We have a signifying chain... mine went like this... In the beginning it was Hegel's definition on truth...paraphrased from Phenomenology of Geist.

The truth is merely the essence completing itself in it's own development.'

Then Mr Hegel explains, more better,... the word 'essence'...

He says, from memory... 'essence is between notion on one side and ontology on the other...

that is, in this order...Ontology, essence then notion.

Then goes on to say ... ontology is objective but essence and notion are subjective...

Now, amongst other thing, we can complete Mr H's syllogism, it can be stated that, truth is

subjective.

Now see in the "discourse of the master" of Lacan, shown below, that this order of things can be applied to the

"discourse of the master". Here below, the master signifier and the signifying chain come between

the barred subject and the unobtainable object of desire.

Four mathemes revolve counterclockwise through four positions of the quadripode: S_1, S_2, $\$$, and a. These are the: i) the "master signifier"; ii) "knowledge" or the "signifying chain"; iii) the "barred subject"; and iv) the "*objet petit a*," respectively.[13]

Matheme	Concept designated
S_1	master signifier
S_2	knowledge
a	*objet petit a*
$\$$	barred subject

Discourse
of the Master

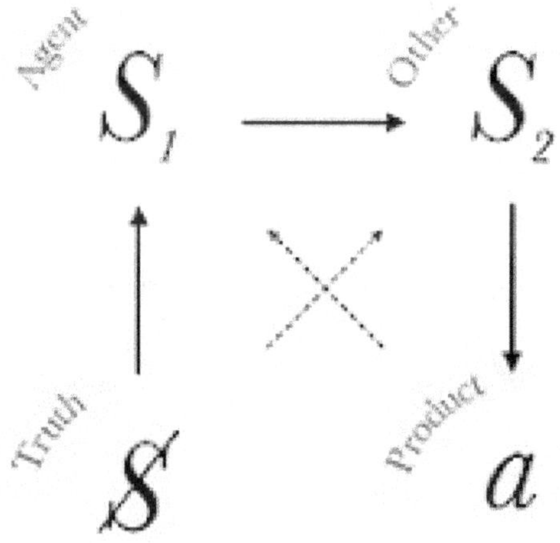

Lacan argued that there were four fundamental types of discourse our task is to find which one best fir the discourse of mass culture. if Lacans bullshit is fairdincum.

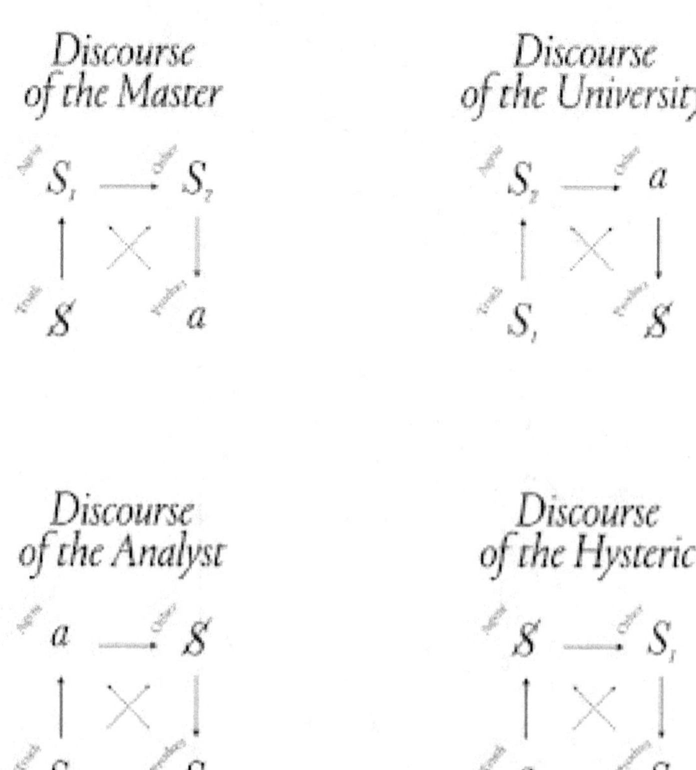

CULTURAL POLEMIC ORGANSATION

Any organisation has a conscious and unconscious.

The conscious is the overt rules of the organisation.

These are for all to see, public outsiders and the organization
people within.

That which is true of the organisation is the organic internal
development of its essence.

The unconscious is that which is in control, it has no negation. It
is a dream sequence of ideology.

The unconscious is structured like a language.

As a syllogism, it can be stated that the control and power of an
organisation is structured like a language.

The organisation adherents are knowledgeable in knowing that
the benefit of the organisation is their own benefit entwined ...
Not a dialect of opposite but of an Hegelian *Aufhebung*. The
subject enmeshed in the Other. The employee not as individual
but at one with the organisation each fighting for each other. The

organisation's cause is the employee's cause, benefiting each other as symbiosis.

The unconscious of the organisation is in charge.

As an organisation forever conscious of Price's law. There are 100 employees, 10 of them do half the work.

158. The Society Society

A handshake, a vernacular, a way of doing things, all are ways in which an organisation is secret. Privy only to the initiates and the schooled, the organisation is officially coded to separate and protect themselves from an inexperienced public. 'Civies,' the army calls them. This is the nick name for the general public used by the military to denote the Other, also known as civilians. Many associations do not let the public inside, metaphorically or physically, instead they have an open day once a year. This is the time to present the face they wish to provide to the public. In all this menagerie, the organisation, communicates the idea and reverence to their own unconscious. And according to Freud, it is the unconscious that is truly in charge.

Freud's book The Unconscious, first published 1911, in his chapter called *Unconscious Feeling,* asks several questions that would assist an organisation to understand itself. So, under the axiom of Plato's "know thyself", here are the questions to put to the organisation.

1. What are the organisation's unconscious ideas?

2. What are the unconscious drives, feelings and sensations of the organisation?

3. Does the organisation have a sense of guilt or an anxiety?

This is a place to start and think of the unconscious of the organisation. The unspoken rules that rule the organisation. The implicit reading between the lines of the official regulations.

These are characteristics that keep the organisation together and strengthen the ability to keep the centre together. And as WB Yeats says -

"Things fall apart the centre cannot hold" WB Yeats *The Second Coming.*

Discourse In Mass Culture

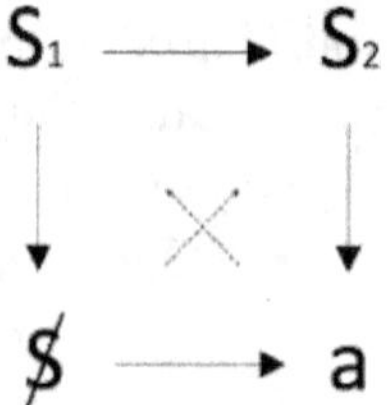

SOCIAL MEDIA

"I googled myself" sounds like masturbation. "I just Facebook-ed you" sounds like sex... So I say to people ,   i'm going to Facebook all of you, while you are googling yourself.

208. Utilitarianism is not an Agrarian Farming Method

J.S. Mill "The Greatest Happiness holds that actions are right in proportion as they intend to promote happiness, wrong as they tend to produce the reverse of happiness" (Mill, Stuart, 2007 p.6).

In short, ' 'the greatest amount of good for the greatest number' has three considerations to consider for consideration.

1. What is good?

2. Considering the utilitarian axiom, it suggests that people are logical, make logical decisions and do things for 'the good' in a logical manner. This is invariably not true. We are as much ruled by Dionysus as we are animated by Apollo.

3. Everyone's 'elation' is agent-neutral. That is, no one person's 'elation' is more important than another.

160. Fuck Up Theory

& so, the show must go on... but only in terms of trying to reel
in the runaway wagon.

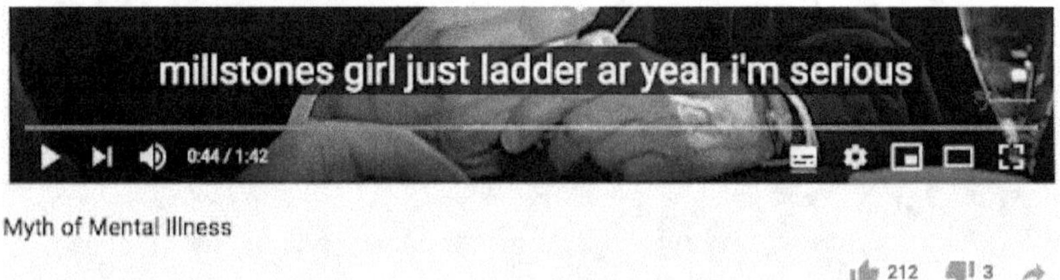

Myth of Mental Illness

212   3

& that's what you witness... & that is the only thing you did
wrong. You were a witness to this "FUCK

UP" ... & what is it? It is a good friend, or work colleague, who
you watch 'fuck up' and it is all your fault because you were a
witness... But

all you have done is nothing

After 'the fuck up' you have witnessed is the intriguing part of
the affair.

'The fuck uppperer" will then make things worse by distracting
you from what you have witnessed to discombobulate what you
have seen..

This happens, most predictably, in a strange accusation, the weirder the better. because we all know its

not true and therefore becomes at the fore of everyones' mind, distracting everyone one from the FUCK UP.

 But what is most at stake is the social status of the fuck upperer... they can be strange weird but we

must all be distracted from the 'fuck up' that lowers their social status.

161.The Utilitarians

Jeremy Bentham 1747 -1832 and his pupil, John Stuart Mill,
1806 -1873, identified the good with pleasure, but let's go further
and imagine euphoria. For is it not under the examination of
possibilities, that in the name of utilitarianism, will bring about
this 'very joy'. Is it not this, the moral value of our time the 'very
joy' as central values and a common notion to the populous?
Isn't it this that it needs right now?

It must be fairly explained 'the pursuit of happiness' is set aside,
for this constitutional phrase has just left us drinking and
consuming... what the 'very joy' would propose would be a
foundation that firstly, lifts out of poverty, & opens a possibility
of the 'very joy'... Rich, quite rich, plain rich, a bit rich ... it must
be remarked that all these types of rich have very similar lives...
it is the taking out of poverty that which abrogates a different
life, abrogates the life of Sisyphus. Pushing shit up hill just to
survive. Arise to the consciousness of not having to worry about
the bills.. all the other people ...Rich, quite rich, plain rich, a bit
rich are all living the same lives...

 This is the utilitarian possibility of joy, that which the public
value aspires. to "always perform that act, of those available, that
will bring the most happiness or the least unhappiness"

so, like Epicurus, were hedonists about value.

162. Public Value

Local utilities tick the boxes of Public Value PV. And thrive of their own organic volition,

can't help but survive. It has been a cherished sector for many lifetimes. Right back to the time when

the surname Smith was just that, a Smith who would hoove your horse's shoes & this was *community*.

Now today, we can all reminisce a collective childhood that included this private sector that firmly

 remained as part of the local community & in some cases a second family. The list is remarkable and as

I write, hosts a flood of memories of these people and their part in my family or have a similar story in

anyone's family. The baby sitter from next door, the hairdresser who did our whole family in their

kitchen,

the electrician that told jokes,, the plumber, the mechanic who gave me ball bearings, the cleaner who

came on Saturdays, the fix it guy, the Tupperware party. the half blind woman at the local milk bar. These are the public sector people who bring a character to our lives, nurturing the gap of family to community.

The familial to the stranger.

And it is these bonds that inspire trust and belonging. This is big business of PV.

163. Alcohol

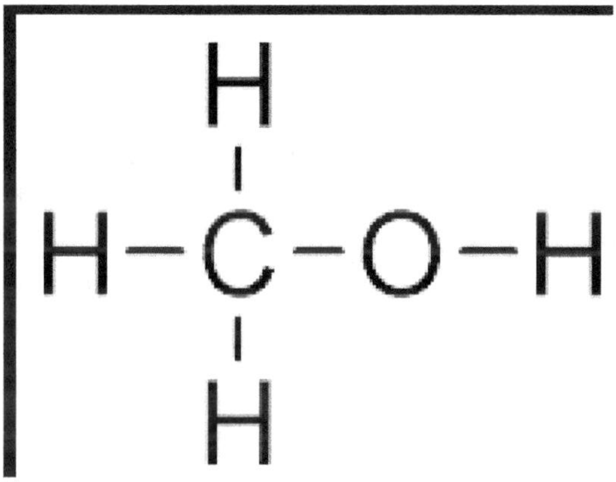

$$\begin{array}{c} H \\ | \\ H-C-O-H \\ | \\ H \end{array}$$

The alcohol masks that other "sortistes" that absurdity or
nonsense of Schopenhauer

"Dans le matin je fais les project dans la soir je fais la sorttise"

In the evening I make absurdities.

& this confused evening can be balance or drowned with alcohol.

This self-developing at this time is vanquished.

What is there and to be reflected upon.

no one knows we terminated it with extreme alcoholic prejudice.

This self is not found.

An alcohol self appears & function.

 I reflected that the soul has been diminished. Alcohol porn. diminishes the soul.

i say with tongue in cheek & without certainty.

164. Prayer for the Long & Dead Day Ahead

Censorship is a good thing and these kinds of obscenity need to be redacted as part of a good society…For example

      "Oh Jesus mother of God fucker .. bless us this day and cast out the sims that have penetrated us the many and the few anal ones   too... Please make the dirt unclean me again and the purity of vanity chase the wars that have gone... Don't leave me in displeasure of the hole and dwell near me in the sense of castration before me without ... let all the mentioned be unmentionable and all the perfect form be mine." ....

The mistakes are "unbewesste une bevue" (Lacan in Zizek 1989, P.62 Sublime Object) .. "the unconscious blunder" is true.

165. The Violence and the Sacred

Whatever I have to say is wrong but I make a start and I am compelled to make a start. "Violence is ridiculous"
S.Zizek

"An oasis of horror in a desert of boredom" (Baudelaire 1992, p.302)

A Program concerning Violence, of Public Value and the Strategic Triangle of Mark H Moore

Violence is a major public health problem, the cause of massive disruptions though communities and a scourge on society. This is a summary, an attempt to solve and/or ameliorate domestic violence, violence against woman, and street violence. Using Mark H Moore's, The Strategic Triangle, of Public Value, Organisational Capacity and Legitimacy /support. This essay will discuss the problematic detail of violence programs with a focus on Public Value.

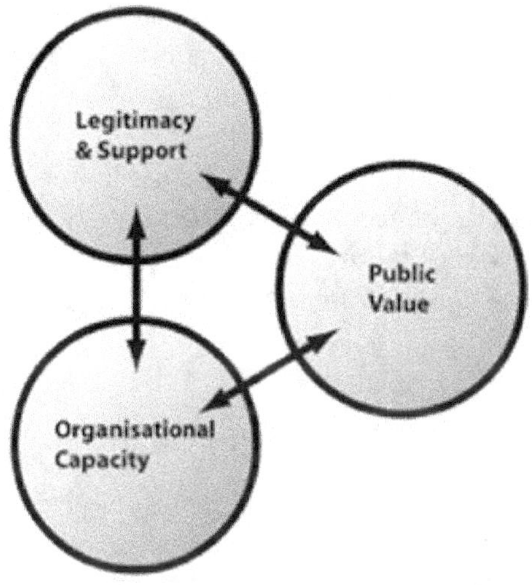

To begin creating Public Value for a domestic violence program, it is first necessary to name the concept of what you trying to create. A story that has a beginning, a middle and an end, in a timeline that expresses the concept and incorporates chronological steps, providing clear evidence of how each stage will be completed and measured. The concept in narrative form is a powerful way of annunciating the program to a political Authorising Environment; in an ability to garner support for the project. The object of the concept is gaining trust of the Authorising Environment, including the trust of the target audience. The Authorising Environment is simply agreeing and acknowledging that the program is feasible and the keepers of the program have the capacity to complete it.

In short, at the concept stage, it is necessary that three questions are answered. "Is it valuable? Is it supportable? And can you, do it?" states Mark H Moore (2019).

Moore recommends not to cite data at the beginning, in concept stage. Asserting that, concepts are doable, statistics are not. "I can show you a hundred failures at government measurement that began with the available statistics" says Moore (2019).

Only after a concept is made, the program is hungry for data, culturally representative and partial to the categories of domestic violence, violence against woman, and street violence.

Mark H Moore uses a three-step process for new ideas in public value.

1. "The Giggle Test. Is the suggestion just laughable?
2. The Getting Real Test. Is there any real chance of the idea being realised and implemented? Do we really think this will be authorised? And is there the operational capacity?
3. Get Off the Dime Test? What are you going to do tomorrow next week etc?"
   (Moore 2019)

The suggestion is for the social scientist to track down the factors at play. Age? Gender? Why? Who are the perpetrators of this violence?

What has gained? Is it self-protection? Is it status? Why is this happening?

These are the questions to be answered that provides data for the political Authorising Environment.

Moreover, in the Covid-19 era of 2020 it has become abundantly clear, Australia's state capacity is remarkable high in comparison to other countries, which makes Australia a place where violence programs are more 'doable.'

If the concept is along the lines of, "Say No to Violence." Then the program is simply making a command. A command that divides the general public into those who follow the command and those who do not. It provides a choice to be told what to do or not. Anti-smoking campaign have fully understood this and therefore have a "Smoke Free Zone, not a "No Smoking Zone." The first axiom gives the subject a chance to make a free choice and become part of a trusted group. The later axiom creates a dialectic and let's face it, nobody likes being told what to do.

Australia is predominately a secular country and under the assertion of the values of the *separation of church and state*, Australia can rely on a philosophical tradition to grant public values. "A moral law within" (Kant 2015, p.118) Immanuel Kant called it. A way of behaving that relies on the individual to take responsibility for themselves, not a transcendent god. Everyone wants to do good, claims Aristotle. "Every act and every investigation, and likewise every practical pursuit or undertaking aims at some good" (Aristotle 1962, p.356). In representing public value as affirmative, the Authorizing Environment can see a positive role model as an option.

Philosopher of social science, Rene Girard asserts that "mimetic desire" (Girard, Rene 1986, p.69) explains violent behaviour. Rene's life-time work revolves around the notion that behaviours are intrinsically "mimetic desire" (Ibid), a copying of conduct and highly intensified between family and friends.

"Everywhere and always, when human beings either cannot or dare not take their anger out on the thing that has caused it, they unconsciously search for substitutes, and more often than not they find them" (Ibid). So, there is a need to be aware that violence in one place and time might then be replicated in another place and time.

Heroic characters from the Hollywood screen are emulated in the community. When this happens, it is taken for granted that people understand the difference between the fantasy of Hollywood and community. Alas when it comes to local movies, the apparent local emulation is too comparable, too close for comfort. It appears the local screen movies are played out as mimetic desire in the community. Here are some examples.

A Northern Territory Warlpiri documentary was released in 2012 named *Conistion,* regarding the murder of a dingo trapper, near Yuendumu Northern Territory. Two years later a pool attendant was murdered at the same Warlpiri community. "An 18-year-old man and a 16-year-old boy have been charged with murdering a swimming coach whose ute was found burnt out in a remote area of the Northern Territory last week" (Murder charges laid over death of Yuendumu pool supervisor Rick Berry 2015).

In the 2009, Northern Territory movie *Samson and Deliah* was released, Deliah, a protagonist in the movie was bashed, on screen, by a gang of youths. In 2010, Rowan McNamara playing the character of Samson, "was sentenced to an eight-week jail sentence for kicking and punching his partner and smashing the window of a vehicle. In 2015 he received a suspended jail sentence for breaching a domestic violence order" (People Pill Rowan McNamarra 2015).

19th December 2020, the ABC reports a violent movie, *Fist of Fury Noongar Daa*

will be translated into Noongar language. "When Lee's character, Chen Zhen, returns to his kung fu school to find his revered teacher dead, he and the school are drawn into conflict with a rival" (Wynne 2020).

You would have to ask the question. What is the public value in making these films?

Is the government promoting violence as "mimetic desire?"

Moore claims that public value is symbiotic of the other two parts of the Strategic Triangle. He asserts, if one part in the triangle falls down the project falls down. So, what is the public value in violent films? Is it not mere entertainment with no public value? So how have these movies managed to get up?

For best practice in providing public value there is now a need to give a call to media, government and stakeholders, to unreservedly discuss issues at stake. Not just in the emulation of direct violence but also under the suggestion from Lacan that "a signifier represents the subject for another signifier" (Lacan 2002, p.304). The idea that, things are connected to violence that are not directly violent; sadomasochism, pornography, intergenerational violence and unrepresented psychology.

Lundy Bancroft in her book *Why Does He Do That? Inside the Minds of Angry and Controlling Men,* believes the mindset is the secret to unravelling the tragedy of violence.

"Abusiveness has surprisingly little to do with how a man feels, my clients actually differ very little from non-abusive men in their emotional experiences and everything to do with how he thinks. The answers are inside his mind" (Bancroft 2003, p.19).

The clients' thinking is a cause for concern and violence, like terrorism, is used as a last resort and deployed in punishment, gaining status, and when an inability to communicate in words has failed. These reasons cited, are all logical understandings, yet the real violence that appears in the book, *Violence and the Sacred,* are said to be illogical. "The fundamental absurdity of its manifestations" says Girard, (Girard 1979, p.13) suggesting violence is ridiculous and irrational.

How do you have a logical program for an irrational behaviour?

Working with Moore's Strategic Triangle, "a guide for you to imagine value creating opportunities in government" (2019) and asking if it is valuable, authorizable and doable. And looking to each of the circles in The Strategic Triangle, 1. organisational capacity, 2. public value and 3. legitimacy /support and using each circle as a question requiring an answer. Then it can be known if the program will work for irrational ridiculous behaviour or not.

If Bancroft is correct and it is about thinking, then let's look to Claude Levi-Strauss' observed theory of conjunctive cultures. Claude understood people of many ceremonial backgrounds and described their cultural topologies as simply conjunctive or disjunctive; practices that brought people together or separated them. Dancing brings people together and individual competitive sport separates people. The first gives a sense togetherness, the later a culture of combative and divisiveness. In conclusion, it must be suggested, a number of community practices that draw upon conjunctive thinking; events, and ceremonies, should be encouraged and/or developed, over combative individual cultures. And of course, it all looks good on paper, until someone from the boxing club tells us how great the boxing is for vulnerable youth. This might look like an exception to the rule but in the boxing ring there is "mimetic desire" (Ibid). Girard points out that when Cain killed Able, it was Cain who was the one who tiled the land and Able who killed the sheep, as a shepherd. So, Cain was mimetic of his brother in his killing, satisfied the jealous competitive nature in "mimetic desire" by killing his brother.

One of the notorious conjunctive cultures is marriage. The coming together of two people in a contract that should include a violence clause. Australian Bureau of Statistics suggests this might part of the solution. "Women who were living in a de-facto relationship were more likely to experience violence from a partner in the last two years (4.9%) than women who were in a registered marriage (1.8%)" (ABS 2020). A technology is already onto this, with an infamous divorce lawyer releasing an app that finds a suitable partner. "If it stops ill-suited couples from tying the knot, it will be good for them" (The happily ever after app from Lady Shackleton, queen of divorce 2020). Hopefully reducing the regular domestic violence between partners.

Winning violent clashes can put the perpetrator in charge and rule the relationship through fear. This movement up the status ladder is easier than the acceptable ways of gaining status. When there is no way of gaining status through social means then particular men turn mean. An examination of status by

411

philosopher and author, Alain De Botton, sees a humanity obsessed with status, manifested in ideals of power, fame and money. Botton suggests an interpretation along the lines of Lacan "a signifier represents the subject for another signifier" (Lacan 2002, p.304) in that money, fame and influence are a sublimation and the real desire is elsewhere. "Alternatively, it might be more accurate to sum up what we are searching for with a seldom used word in political theory: love" states Botton. The violence is built into, not being able to find status through money, fame and influence and possibly ends in a violent reaction. When really all that is required is love.

Violence is the Jungian shadow at work. "The shadow cast by the conscious mind contains the hidden, repressed and unfavourable (or nefarious) aspects of the personality" (Jung 1964, p.118). Recognised as a Darwinian trait of survival, the shadow's dark force needs to be contained, disbursed in a civilised society.

"The shadow is a moral problem that challenges the whole ego-personality, for no one can become conscious of the shadow without considerable moral effort. To become conscious of it involves recognizing the dark aspects of the personality as present and real. The act is the essential condition for any kind of self-knowledge, and it is therefore, as a rule, meets with considerable resistance. Indeed, self-knowledge as a psychotherapeutic measure frequently requires much painstaking work extending over a long period" (Jung1981, p. 8).

The Jungian shadow needs to be ameliorated by recognition and acceptance. Brought to heal under the notion that most men are 33% stronger in upper body strength than females. And this capability needs to be embraced, guarded, cherished and held over in the need for protection.

Criminology experts Walsh and Beaver describe the violent recidivist behaviour as an expensive cohort "Career criminals impose a tremendous toll on society by inflicting injuries on their victims, by tying up the criminal justice system, and by costing taxpayers a substantial amount of money" (Walsh and Beaver 2009, p.206). Extensive criminology literature is another avenue of understanding, and like media, bereft of solutions. Even though solutions are not beyond the purview of media and criminology. Both idioms, could do well to seek experienced professionals in the field and share in their publications the possible solutions suggested by empirical evidence. This is public value proper.

There is a trust in society that any person will not to be beaten. A codified guarantee of safety in families, partners, and between every person unknown. The logical assertion for a functioning community is the cleverest solution becomes the direction in which action is taken for the common good, thus, a well-functioning society. Yet if violence gets its way, it is merely the one with the most brute force, that gets its way. This isn't necessarily the smartest solution. When these things go awry, they are negative, a so called 'public bad.' There is a need to have a peace in community as a part of accepted way of life.

In conclusion, violence needs to be challenged and Mark Moore's Strategic Triangle can play a convincing part in counter violence. Mimetic desire and the reasons why this crime is happening, are rational and irrational. Statistics are not the way to begin a concept and the Authorising Environment has unanswered questions as to how to go about violence programs.

Displaced status can go wrong. This is connected to, as Botton claims, just wanting to be loved.

References

Ames, Johnathon 2020, *The happily ever after app from Lady Shackleton, queen of divorce.*

Viewed 21 December 2020
<https://www.thetimes.co.uk/edition/news/the-happily-ever-after-app-from-lady-shackleton-queen-of-divorce-0xctck8h6>

Aristotle 1962, *Foundations of western thought, six major philosophers*, Cambridge University Press, London, UK.

Australian Bureau of Statistics 2020, *Partner violence in focus partner crime.* Retrieved 12 December 2020, from <https://www.abs.gov.au/statistics/people/crime-and-justice/focus-crime-and-justice-statistics/latest-release>

Bancroft, Lundy 2003, *Why Does He Do That? Inside the Minds of Angry and Controlling Men* Berkeley Books, New York, USA.

Baudelaire, Charles 1995, *Fleur du mal,* Dover Publications Inc, New York, USA.

Girard, Rene 1989, *Violence and the sacred*, The John Hopkins University Press, Baltimore, Maryland, USA.

Girard, Rene 1986, *The scapegoat*, The John Hopkins University Press, Baltimore, Maryland, USA.

Jung 1981, Carl, *Volume Nine Part II Aion researches into phenomenology of the self,* Routledge and Keegan Paul Ltd, Lindon, UK.

Kant, Immanuel 2015, *Critique of practical reason,* Cambridge University Press.

Lacan, Jacques 2002, *Écrits: a selection*, W.W.Norton and Company, Inc, New York, USA.

Moore, Mark 2019, *Mark Moore bij Berenschot (volledig college) - Publieke waarde,* video

recording. Viewed 19 December 2020, <https://youtu.be/UlVBX1UfhBU>

Murder charges laid over death of Yuendumu pool supervisor Rick Berry. Viewed 12 December 2020 < https://www.abc.net.au/news/2015-02-02/two-charged-with-murder-rick-berry-yuendumu-death/6062080>

OECD 2019, Public value in public service transformation: working with change.

Viewed 12 December 2020 <https://www.oecd-ilibrary.org/sites/79a83aa2-en/index.html?itemId=/content/component/79a83aa2-en>

People Pill Rowan McNamarra, *Rowan mcnamarra.* Viewed 12 December 2020, < https://peoplepill.com/people/rowan-mcnamara/>

Walsh, Anthony and Beaver, Kevin 2009, *Biosocial criminology new directions in theory and research.* Routledge, New York, USA.

Wynne, Emma 2020, *How bruce lee classic fist of fury is helping a struggling indigenous language kick on.* Viewed on 12 December 2020, < https://www.abc.net.au/news/2020-12-19/noongar-language-revitalised-with-bruce-lee-film-dub/12987196>

166. Pascal's Wager

Pascal's Wager states "Pascal argues that a rational person should live as though God exists and seek to believe in God. If God does not actually exist, such a person will have only a finite loss (some pleasures, luxury, etc.), whereas if God does exist, he stands to receive infinite gains (as represented by eternity in heaven)"

1623–1662

and so to most this appears ... "mind games for the middle class" (Lydon j 1985)... But in a real way, it is not fitting to do this Girard, When it is pondered that violence is an inevitable outcome of aggression. & so if the wager is on this there is no amelioration possible... a dead end and an observance of the inevitable... Yet put your money on Girard...

" "The principal source of violence between human beings is mimetic rivalry, the rivalry resulting from imitation of a model who becomes a rival or of a rival who becomes a model" (I See Satan, 11)."

Wolfgang Palaver. "René Girard's Mimetic Theory." Well that's a different story... knowing mimetic desire is the problem, rearrangements can be made to obviate , ameliorate , and stop

418

the violence before it happens.... as a wise man once sad... "if we learn anything from history is that nothing is inevitable... "

And then good news from Girard.."Girard rejects any natural aggressive drive and argues that human beings can overcome their violent nature." Wolfgang Palaver. "René Girard's Mimetic Theory."

petit object a (The unobtainable object of desire.)... is our neighbour's ass... "Our neighbour is the model for our desires" Wolfgang Palaver. "René Girard's Mimetic Theory.

167. Psychoanalysis is True, nothing is Permitted.

 If psychoanalysis is true al la Lacan then then unconscious is in control is a given (from Freud) and theorised by Jacques is that this place from which language equates... is the Big Other. inscribed in the Symbolic Order

The big Other designates radical alterity

 "the unconscious is the discourse of the Other." i disagree ... Should be amended to "the subject is the discourse of the Other"

 These all ideas above are Lacan.... then

 When you see yourself in the mirror that is the ego right there.. When you become self-conscious, someone is looking at you ... then the ego right there... When you are in the ebb and flow of psycho geography derive and in a mind of your own.. you are the subject... This is where most language comes from "the subject" ...language can also jump and come from the ego. Talking to the police , officials, people at work...then at time it dips into the comfort of the subject... the person , the unconscious, who is really in control ...

https://soundcloud.com/podcast-co-coopercherry/todd-mcgowan-objet-cherry-a

"desire is what is missing in the symbolic order" TM

Darth Vader is enjoyably evil. & these are the things that are part of self .... & here they are i Star Wars,   They have Othered them ... So the subject doesn't have to confront them in their own unconscious.

Why do you to take sides at a soccer match..

Towards the end of the TM interview he talks of "Das Ding" the Heidegger essay & called The Thing in English but rarely translated... Das Ding is an untrained ego not yet synthesized to robotically respond... The nervousness around young couple not able to correspond TM states is Das Ding.. The ego is gagged in a learnt Othered state of awe.. Not sure what to say..the ego needs to pass through the Symbolic Order before it is announced..

& then as Phenomenology suggests the self is a divided subject ..

168. The Rationale is Founded in Truth.

The rationale is founded in truth.

"The truth is in the whole, the whole is merely the essence completing itself in its own development." - Hegel

Then Hegel goes on to define essence But in an unusual way, he defines it as being in between ontology and notion and tells us ontology is objective and essence and notion is subjective.

To define something in such a fashion is an invention of a understanding .. another 'way of seeing' a truth. As Robert Anton Wilson (RAW) says, there is not one truth, there are many truths. - RAW did really want to slay the *dogmatic beast* as he leant towards a person holding many truths, not the dogmatic righteousness of holding one truth.

169. Rationale

Why? because the artist, the creative, is forever broke and forging ahead with an article that has public value, in creating jobs, thoughts, and quality of life; is a measure of the worthwhile.

"In deinem nichts hoff ich, das All zu finden" (Goethe 1986, p.192).

In nothing you will find the universe. says Goethe.

In these times of a domestic priced cinematic camera it is distinctly possible to make a feature from a domestic budget.. You just need an idea. Irish film Once proved this in 2017. Why? because it is possible, possible in incremental stages. Pilot 3 scenes then 28 scenes shot over 10 days... Why? ,,, Because the answer to "Is it doable ? Is yes.

Of course there are problems. Copyright and finances are the hurdles.. yet presently finishing a

pilot as an incremental stage is immediately doable .. The frame works annotated below. display the obstacles

To define something in such a fashion is an invention of a genre .. another way of seeing the world by playing it between two other things. Two other countries from another perspective.

 So here the film of a remake in Vietnamese, seeks to be wholly Vietnamese, true to a contemporary Vietnam, Here the movie then positions itself into a French cultural life as a post-colonial comment. As a remake it evolves & evolves a a celebration of shared history. on this film is of a shared history. That at one stage for almost hundred years the Vietnam and French lived alongside each other ..

A vision that either side would find cautious. A caution an outsider could dare to take on.

 French Lacanian theory asks for this film to vbe made. As the geography, people and lanhauge are so separtae they would naturally be called 'radical alterity' The definition of Lacan for the big Other. this is the place where language is the discourse. as Lacan says " "the unconscious is the discourse of the Other."

TO Lacan and his reverence to Saussure he maps the unconscious. Here is the first map.

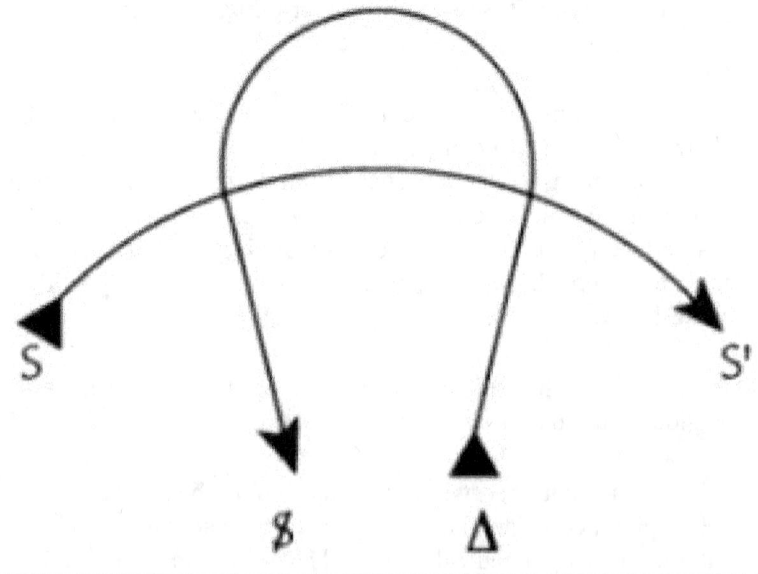

the film is used as a signiyier..the graph has two intersections.
these are the film being made twice.

The first film is the intersection on the right. The second film is
the intersection on the left. Just like a sentence cannot be fully
understood until the sentence is finished. The beginning of the
sentence on the right the end of the sentence on the left. The
meaning is retroactive in the sentence as well as in the movie.
This is the in point to begin the conversation as to what this
colonization means.

This is the start of the conversation concerning the map of the
unconscious

https://youtu.be/67d0aGc9K_I

Filmicly, Lacan has been a draw card for film interpretation &
the library shelves are building in the last decade, replicating a
public sphere all of its own.

Lacan and Contemporary Film Todd McGowan

Film, Lacan and the Subject of Religion: A Psychoanalytic
Approach to Religious Film Analysis
Steve Nolan

The imaginary signifier Christopher Metz

Out of The past Lacan and Film noir Ben Tyrer

Enjoy your symptom! : Jacques Lacan in Hollywood and out

This the beginning of a fascinating story of a French film
otherness, desire, the unconscious that is built into a the identity
of the colonial list. All ideals of the theorist Lacan. Le stade de
mirror for a gaze looking back at you. Played in a french cinema
it is the audience who is being looked at not the film .. a ghostly
short circuit.

"And this is what "Short Circuits" wants to do, again and again.
The underlying

premise of the series is that Lacanian psychoanalysis is a
privileged instrument of such

an approach, whose purpose is to illuminate a standard text or
ideological formation,

making it readable in a totally new way—the long history of
Lacanian interventions in

philosophy, religion, the arts, from the visual arts, to the cinema"

"For *the phallus is a signifier*...it is the *signifier* that is destined
to *designate* meaning effects as a whole"

Our PVM is made for getting things done. The consideration of
the foundations, the future, and keeping close to eye to facets
that need attention

Why ? Why not?

Goethe, Johann Wolfgang von 1986, *Faust: der tragödie erster und zweiter teil, urfaust,* Thomas Munster, Bad Langensalza, Germany.

Not to pique interest. That owuld assume it was known where this is all going and all leading to.

These remain known unknowns.

170. John V Peel

John Peel is an illustration of public and private enterprise working together to great advantage. His stature at the BBC was such that he was the one who would knock out the new music, commonplace in five years time. He was the first to play Bowie, Black Sabbath, Nick Cave, the list is endless… … I met John Peel once, spoke to him on the phone a few times and he read out, on the radio, part of a letter I wrote to him. He had a personal touch that worked in a public institution and appears as a known trusted entity within the system. He became the launch pad for those who had enough money to arrive with their first piece of vinyl and Peel could broadcast to a possible 60 million audience. This enabled the musicians to etch out a living.. or a career.

"The single most important figure in British rock music" Andy Kershaw.

https://youtu.be/jYtCnEf0aY4

"When I hear the word culture, I reach for my gun"

Slavoj Žižek thinks for something to exist it needs an opposition. This is clear in the case of the Australian purchase of Jackson

Pollock's "Blue Poles" and its opposition as a waste of money. Wouldn't the painting just pale into a dark vault if there wasn't such an opposition.

It is here now worthy to remark of the quote regarding culture itself. The Hanns Josht quote "When I hear the word culture, I reach for my gun."

For this is the phrase that keeps culture alive. This is the space where culture is not made for empathy or belonging but because you have no choice, you have to do it.

(the gun is used here as metaphor, a signifier that of mortality, the idea being that we create culture to extend out lives, or even become as long as earth remains. And so with this impending doom, a cessation of earth, why bother to make cultural artefacts, music, film, paint, sculpture)

Declan O'Gallagher

PLATO'S FOUR NECESSARY VIRTUES (WC SDJ)

The pubic value is a question of what is missing and then making changes to fulfil this lack. Even Plato aspired to enquire to what was missing from The Republic. Citizens could assume The Republic would adopt The Four Cardinal Virtues; this was a given.

Here is a dialogue from The Republic, describing the best practice of making a community by adding the necessary changes to provide public value.

"Then it will obviously have the qualities of *wisdom, courage, self-discipline and justice*"

states Socrates.

"Obviously" says Glaucon.

"Then if we can identify some of these qualities in it, the ones that are left will be the ones we are still looking for" (Plato 1987, p.138), remarks Plato.

Plato acknowledges the changes needed in public value by announcing the four virtues "*wisdom, courage, self-discipline and justice,*" and then acting on what is missing.

"Three quarks for Muster Marks!" James Joyce Finegans Wake

Marshall McLuhan, the father of communication theory was a Joyce scholar and much of his poetic style, loose, and prophetic interpretation, can be seen to be influenced by Joyce.

"Three quarks for Muster Marks!" James Joyce Finegans Wake

Knowledge, Information, and data, these are the three quarks that are presented as a communication quest. To interpret comment and edify this triumvirate it is possible to annunciate a discourse of threes.

It is this kind of determinism ie 'where we are up to in science', that can influence the thinking and delivery of communication. How it is understood and acted upon is another question. I say 'another question' yet it should be known that this understanding is a consideration of the delivery of a message. The consideration of how it may be understood and how it may be acted upon considering today's consciousness, precipitated by world debate, science, and media mechanism, to name a few.

It is possible to understand message in a logical fashion, account for the possible interpretations and withdraw any negative interpretations a message may conclude. Then the next stage is to consider the aspect of humanity as an irrational being & that is who is being dealt with as the medium who will be receiving and acting on message, Sean Homer describes this uncovering of unconscious with reference to the work of Jacques Lacan "It is concerned with what is illogical, irrational and unconscious.

Psychoanalysis looks at those aspects of thinking and behaviour
for which we cannot rationally or consciously account."

As presented as triumvirate it is fair to interprets what does the
three universalities mean?

It is not the dialectic adversaries of old, the rich vs the poor, the
good vs evil, the third addition is a passing feature. A fix and
thought-out notion. Notice that 'triage' at the hospital is where
you present to heal your problem.

The triumvirate invokes the Hegelian, thesis-antithesis-
synthesis. The three is an all-encompassing motif, the face of
truth, it appears to be thought through and qualified.

"All men naturally desire knowledge" as Aristotle states at the
beginning of The Metaphysics, 350BC.

171. The Subversion of the Subject and the Dialectic of Desire in the Freudian Unconscious.

The subversion of the subject and the dialectic of desire in the Freudian unconscious.

The graph is "to show where desire is situated in relation to a subject defined on the basis of his articulation by the signifier."

 The button tie (Point de capiton) the signifier stops the otherwise indefinite sliding of the signification.

S to S' sign to signifier.

& the course of the subject.

The graph worked in relation to jokes.

Situating the subject in relation to knowledge. Look at the fish this hooks!

The function of this button tie can be found in a sentence. Suggesting the sentence is topologically split in two. An initial and final understanding.

NB Only two points of symbiotic phenomenology, all the lines alone are an abstraction.

The sentence is understood at the end of the sentence so the subject hook bending from right left indicates the retrospective nature of the subject. As it first signifies at the end giving the beginning of the sentence mean.

From Tony Myers Zizek book. What is subject? "if you take away all the distinctive characteristics, all your particular needs, interests and beliefs, what is left, is the subject.

The DNA, the rom without the ram. The computer without the apps.

Tony Myers "The subject is the form of your consciousness, as opposed to the contents of that form which is individual and specific to you"

This version of the subject allows the theory an *objectivity,* disavowed when including personal influence.

Page 283 Ecrit.

Freud valourises discourse

an aside on the history… "but for Hegel, the story of human history is the discovery of objects, then the discovery of subjects as on the other side of objects, then the discovery of the … subject as that which thinks about objects, and finally as thinking itself... this is Hegel's progressive arc of history.

172. University is the New Bank.

The bank might have extortionate fees but at least they are polite.
When you talk to the University they say "can I start with your
student number?" Not "good morning" or "good afternoon" but
"can I start with your student number?" It appears un human, as
if they are trying to ready students for AI.

University is not the only place with this corporate gaslighting.
Jacana Energy is my local electricity supplier when asked can I
get a transfer of the name on the bill I am told that I want to
connection I tell them that "it is already connected I just need a
transfer of the name" now adamant they insist I want a
connection, even though it is already connected. 'What is isn't' -
is the corporate mantra to the public. According to these
corporate subversives who intend to subject every one equally to
their misanthropy. When you enter a hospital bleeding profusely
from the face, they ask, "why have you come here today?" what
is plain and simple to see and understand why everyone is
questioned by the corporate institutionalise monopoly on
hierarchy by stealth. When asked to describe your pain between
one and zero and you give a number, your pain is not your pain,
it is just a number, your pain is to ride your pain is mathematical
and not human.

University is the new bank.

173. DNA is digital, DNA is analogue, digital is Male and Analogue is Female

Hegel fits together "The truth is the whole and the whole is merely the essence completing itself in its own development" & then taking comparable words he fits them together like a jigsaw. I paraphrase, 'Essence' is placed in-between 'ontology' and 'notion' Then he adds, 'ontology' is objective and 'essence' and notion is subjective .... & so, we place the inner expression between psychogeography, (what the outer expresses to you, ie when the world communicates to you) and the speech

What constitutes me as a subject is my question (jacques lacan)

174. Communism is Good

Badiou's position on Communism is such he believes it to be the ethical position.

174. MORALITY OR CULTURAL, EITHER/ OR

Jean Jacques Rousseau pondered the morality of theatre and died in 1776 never witnessing the French Revolution. He detailed this discourse as the negation by the stage of the streets, home, and government. He posits that the emotional energy expired by an audience has fulfilled a moral obligation. Simply by watching and taking sides in the theatre the impetus to take up the fight for a better world had been satiated. Common in today's practice is the comparison and popularity of A list actors. This too is morally problematic

In the Chicago movie it appears Hollywood can only right the wrongs if they are 50 years old... The issues can appear to have a contemporary place. Yet in the action addressing authority can look the condemnation in the eye and think/say " it was only a movie"

When things fall apart, we get to see how they are put together.

When a Liberal party staffer is allegedly raped, she wants to tell her story publicly & intrinsically she needs a news source that she trusts. Working with media every day, she would have a knowledge of who this would be & who is the best to handle this, perhaps she has some connections. & After her ordeal I would imagine politics would be not front and centre... A news source she trusts is foremost who does she go to..... commercial channel ...Network 10.

Stepping away from the LIB/LAB/ABC machine?

175. Feature Film is So Dead

So dead.

Look at the script and ask when did you ever hear a line you were covetous of?

Nothing new under the sun.

176. An Aphex Twin Poem

There was an ol' twin from Limerick
whose wall was food for popping
His beats were so crass
His dance was alas, you never knew
nothing rhymes with ambient

177. An Egalitarian Society is Spoken to You From You.

 An essay in the tradition of "serious purpose, dignity, logical organization, length," states *A handbook to literature*, based on the original edition by William Flint Thrall and Addison Hibbard

 The Frenchman Michel de Montaigne (1533–1592) was the first author to describe his work as essays; he used the term to characterize these as "attempts," to put his thoughts into writing.

    This essay is on Gender Equality and the notion that it responsible for the increase of violence towards women. This mainstream agenda is willing to be platformed and it can be argued this has bi partisan support. The economic world wants to see women competing with men for two reasons..

1. increase in competition /productivity and

2. The distraction from the main game... The public unrest in the economic divide, that becomes sharp in a time of crisis, everything is subservient to this nature. The companies that pay for the adverting concur with this distraction. And this is no small agenda. I am talking about every media organization that steal our time and thoughts, Facebook, all newspapers, YouTube, a google search.. etc.. all of these are interested in their status quo, security and lean heavily on division that is not rich vs the rest of us. Here we live in simpatico and The Gender Equality

"In the 1930 an intrepid Belgium, Arnold Denis. In Rwanda
helped to create a myth that would have terrifying consequences.
He said the Tutsi were a noble and intelligent race. .... and the
Hutus were a separate race of ignorant peasants. In reality there
was no evidence for this at all, the Tutsi were the ruling elite but
the two groups had always shared the same land" (Curtis, Adam,
All watched over by loving Machines, 2011). Then when the
Belgium colonization left, the Hutus went after the Tutis.
Rwanda was made independent in 1961, estimates of 20,000
Tutsi were slaughtered.

The 1993 mass killings of Tutsis by the majority-Hutu populace
in Burundi are described as genocide in the final report of the
International Commission of Inquiry for Burundi presented to
the United Nations Security Council in 1996

178. The Unconscious

The unconscious of the subject matters.

1. The unconscious is structured like a language

2. the unconscious has no signified only a signifier... (see Sausuure)

So, it begs interpretation, like dreams, it is the coding without the computer.

"The unconscious has no negation" says Freud & you can't stop the entropy either.

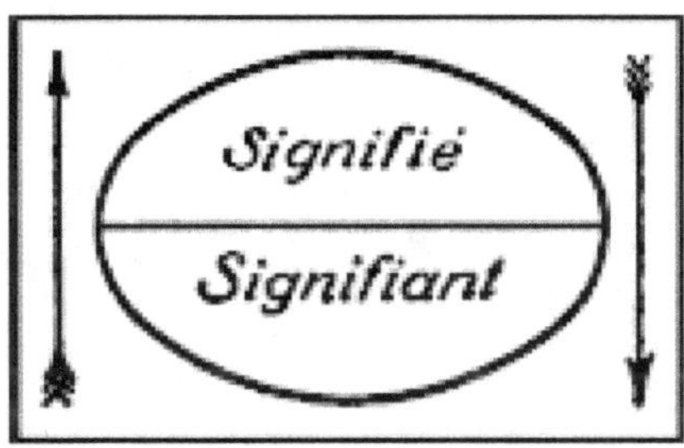

179. The Tree of Life

The tree of life topologically is paths and places. The places are subjective and the paths are objective.

As you might wander from one culture to another... For example, from Western culture to Yolngu culture.

the places are subjective... & the path that you traverse to get from one to the other is objective... The path is the ontological subject...

180. Balance Understood

It was Issiah Berlin who stated that "we want a merciful society" everyone nodded in agreement,

He then says "we want and Justice" and everyone nods. He says" you can't have both"

& in that same method of pointing to the deficiencies in languages and its inability to express a given direction. the journalist is asked for "balance and truth" well i say you try to have both.

181. The Public Value Model for A Vietnamese

**Adaptation of Jean Luc Godard Film Masculine Feminine
1966**

Our MISSION

Keep it simple, make it perfect

Our VISION

To question whether it is the process that is the objective of
the project, or is it the feature film completed is the objective
of the project. The vision is to be open to possibility; good
process makes the possibility happen.

Indicators of Multi Value Framework. Figure B.

Our Values

none

<u>The Remake of a Jean Luc Godard Movie, 1966.</u>

Figure B

Cultural

• Part of the 'New Territory Art,' that of French contemporary culture.
• This unfolding discovery and the many paths that may eventuate are bestowed to the viewer.
• Public value is of a subjective nature therefore cultural benefits can be individualistic.
• A re-invention of New Wave cinema

Social

• An original appeal
• A perspective of history
• Making a new audience
• A reflection on national relations
• The story of colonialism retold as a role reversal
• Another way to make a microbudget filmmaking
• A voice of Vietnamese youth
• Realism as social commentary

Economical

• As a Not-For-Profit any surplus dollars to be given to Peter Singer's *The life you Can Save* https://www.thelifeyoucansave.org.au/
• An alternative way of funding

Environmental

• The film has deliberate scenes of environmental values, displayed in actors' choices and

451

microbudget filmmaking
• Paid writers
• Paid producer
• Paid production crew
• Paid editor
• Paid distributors
• Paid networks
• Paid investors to invest again
• Paid actors

articulated in script.
• The environmental values displayed are subtle but part of the production
• Hanoi has less than 1% take up of electric scooters, therefore, electric scooters are nominated to be used in the movie.
• With the possibility of forthcoming climate events. *The Life You Can Save* charity becomes ever more prevalent

Methodology

The task at hand is to produce a Vietnamese version of the Jean Luc Goddard feature film, Masculine Feminine (1966). The film is thus far translated to Vietnamese and modified for all thirty-one Hanoi scenes. The obstacles to production are funding,

copyright and a plan of action. The creation of a Public Value
Model will provide a roadmap to completion. The Public Value
Model will impart the cohesion needed for this 'start up,'
utilising an array of indicators, purposely selected for this
particular project, such as, Mark H Moore's Strategic Triangle,
The Giggle Test and Meynhardt's Public Value Scale. The
project will move step by step, creating Public Value both in the
process and in completion.

To kick off, Mark H Moore asks. "Is it doable?" (Moore
2019). Can you make a 1966 Godard film in Vietnam?
Moore responds to this by initiating a three-question test to
realise the project.

1. "The Giggle Test. Is the suggestion laughable?
2. The Getting Real Test. Is there any real chance of the idea
    being realised and implemented? Do we really think this
    will be authorised? Is there the Operational Capacity?
3. Get Off the Dime Test? What are you going to do
    tomorrow next week etc?"
    (Moore 2019)

For our purposes this was a reality check, for it indicated our
weakness of funding and copyright; highlighting the attention
needed to overcome this.

Next, The Strategic Triangle (adapted from Moore).

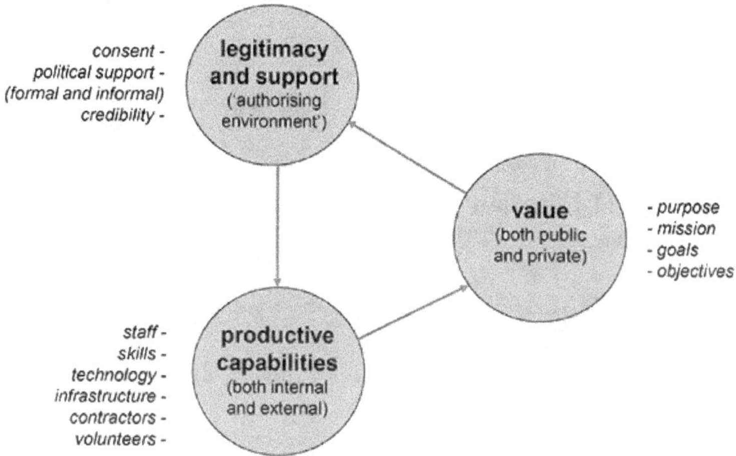

The Strategic Triangle is a heuristic tool to create Public Value and thus momentum for any project. The effectiveness of Mark H Moore's schema is a check list of competencies. Public Value, legitimacy/authority, and organisational capacities, (see above). View the three parts of the triangle and understand, as one part is inflated, so are the other two. View the triangle again and see the three components, as questions to be answered. To this end the project becomes alive, qualifying weaknesses and pointing out missing elements.

What are the steps to completion? The project requires a collection of qualitative and quantitative data, to understand why the film should be funded, a basis for holding copyright, and what is the Authorising Environment thinking. This is where Meynhardt steps in and the use of his "public value scale" (Meynhardt and Jainenko 2020, p.5). Using a 4-dimensional framework of

1. **Moral/ethical**, contributing to "people's self-worth and dignity" (Meynhardt 2020, p.4).

2. **Hedonistic/aesthetic**, "avoid pain and maximize pleasure" (Meynhardt 2020, p.4).

3. **Utilitarian/instrumental**, "a shared value ascribed to utility" (Meynhardt 2020, p.1). and

4. **Political/social**, "a collectively shared value attached to social relationships and what it means to establish positive group relations" (Meynhardt in Meynhardt 2020 p.7).

Meynhardt/ Jainenko concludes in the article, *Measuring public value: scale development and construct validation*, with a collection of quantitative data, not only helping to complete the matrixes of Figure A & B (See attached), but the creation of Public Value. Remember anything that inflates any part of our Strategic Triangle directly aids Public Value. In practical terms, the Meynhardt public value scale, opens the possibility of entrusting funding, copyright and an understanding the public's awareness.

For our purposes, Meynhardt uncovers facets not yet included in the model, Figure A and B (see attached), that is, **2. Hedonistic/aesthetic**. Paul, our protagonist of the movie, is unknowingly somewhat besotted with hedonism, so much so, it becomes a danger. Therefore, it is important to discuss this subject as is a delicate end scene where Paul is missing in a suicide. The Authorising Environment of funding likes this in terms of dramatic effect and therefore economic value, yet ethics would advise to 'err on the side of caution.' Here in the Vietnamese adaptation, Paul doesn't suicide. The script has been edited for 'a public good,' not dramatic effect.

455

The holding of copyright remains a problem for the project and making the Public Value Model provides a well-versed argument to convince Argos Films Paris to share the copyright. From a Hewison point of view, the copyright challenge is, "the ability to marry rhetorical power with practical innovations" (Hewison 2002, p.24). How do you turn the tide on the copyright when confronted with what Hewison "rhetorical power" (Ibid)? Hewison goes on to assert the concerns of the shifting sands of copyright. "Internet art is about the immaterial exchange of ideas and images, rather than the creation of discrete objects, ownership ceases to be significant, and neither public institutions nor private dealers can take possession" (Stallabrass in Hewison 2014, p.391). Considering everything is now digital, it can be expected that some copyright laws may change. It is welcome that Argos Paris Films join our project in partnership to donate to the Peter Singer charity, *The life you can Save*. To view Argos Paris Films as a "rhetorical power" (Ibid) might be true but a view that stands in the way of production. It appears a better approach to work with them in partnership rather than the "rhetorical power" (Ibid).

To find legitimacy will bring support and vice versa. The international film festival can supply funding and be a great way to publicise the movie. Adelaide Festival is one such funding source. It should not be forgotten that Africa has a Francophile population, 350 million French speakers. Africa has its own interest in colonisation stories and a keen international film circuit. I'm already told that our film will be appearing at KIFF, the Kenyan International Film Festival; even though they don't speak French. It is important from the outset to understand the film festival circuit as part of external aspects, providing the film legitimacy/support before the movie is even in production.

To be able to elaborate on the film in terms of its French psychoanalyst is part of the internal Organisational Capacity. In 1966 the French psychanalyst Jacques Lacan had mainstream popularity, (when the original Godard film was made). The Lacanian understanding of film is becoming ever more popular in recent times. Lacanians are using his theories and referencing film, literature and art. Here are a few examples of Lacanian film analysis.

1. Žižek, Slavoj 1992, *Enjoy your symptom! Jacques lacan in hollywood and out*, Routledge, London, UK.

2. McGowan, Todd 2004, *Lacan and contemporary film*, Other Press, New York, USA.

3. Nolan, Steve 2009, *Film, lacan and the subject of religion, a psychoanalytic approach to religious film analysis*, Continuum International Publishing Group, New York, USA.

4. Metz, Christian 1977, *The imaginary signifier, psychoanalysis and cinema*, Indiana University Press, Bloomington, USA.

What would be more applicable than a Lacanian analysis of our film? There are a number of Lacanian theories that can be taken up by an internal/external Operational Capacity.

1.   The Other of a film per se, and the Other of watching a
     foreign film, with differing foreigners.
2.   Lacan's first *Graph of Desire or Point de Caption,* has
     two intersections, the second intersection is our film
     being made; reifying the first time the film is made.
3.   Discuss the protagonist Paul as being the Lacanian Real.
4.   The Lacan theory of *petit object a,* is the unobtainable
     object of desire, yet Paul

is dating Madeline. What could go wrong?

The importance of being able to articulate understanding
to the Authorising Environment cannot be underestimated. This
is providing the movie directly with meaning and depth.

Meanings and interpretations are factors for trust. Voices
of authority that give rise to public trust and business trust. The
project plans, open and transparent dialogue, providing
consultation, collaboration and an open-door policy to internal
/external ideas. This is an adaptation of the article. *Social
Inclusion of the Hard to Reach* by Nicola Brackertz. "We will
keep you informed, listen to and acknowledge concerns and
aspirations, and provide feedback" (Brackertz 2008, p.5). And in
this manner the project builds 'social capital'. These are
promises of a reciprocal nature intended to establish relations
and ease the movie incrementally towards fruition.

In a world of post-covid, environmental disaster and
social unrest. The project takes on a path through external factors
and it is important to read the room. How will any project
proceed in this new consciousness? How do we proceed to make
the quality of life better? If these are questions always at hand
then this is the methodology in which the film is made.

Finally, the project asks itself, would it be able to pass through the gates of Plato's Republic? Does it have the four virtues necessary to enter? Wisdom, courage, self-discipline and justice.

In summary, our process is not easy, nevertheless, the film has already greatly benefited from this Public Value Model. The project has managed, at this pre-production stage, to be orientated with ethical practice through the use of "The Life you Can Save" (Singer 2009). In addition, the film is organised with environmental capacity and the Public Value Model has provided a clear argument for the use of copyright. The giggle test is a tried-and-true method of getting a project off the ground. This then, framed around Moore's Strategic Triangle and Meynardt public scale brushes off shortcomings. There is now growing Public Value for the project.

182. Key Findings from the Research

1. <u>Understanding the Authorising Environment and Task Environment. Figure A</u>

In Figure A, the red colouring refers to the Authorising Environment, that is providing Public Value and procurement of funding. Moore defines the Authorising Environment as "Actors from whom manager formally needs authorization and resources to survive and be effective" (Moore 2012, p.15). The Task Environment is in blue area, where "substantive problems to be solved" (Moore 2012, p.12). The purple colouring is the indication of performance, measuring the output, impact and outcome of the production. This is what the Meynhardt,/Jainenko public value scale of qualitative and quantitative data will measure.

The reflection caused by the Research Tasks enables the project to realise itself.
The project is a film production and a charity donator and in the organisation of this relationship, it has become more aware as to how these things work for professionals and sales that are providing finances to *The Life You Can Save*. This is understood to be a better funding model because bonuses or sharing of surplus value goes to a charity. This Public Value Model is attractive and encouraging, as it gives investors at a given rate of return, 5%, then provides *The Life You Can Save* with donations that it wouldn't have otherwise. It is not a 'not for profit'… It works for all …
From the key finding there are questions to be answered.
1. Why Argos Films Paris would approve of shared? 2. Why

Vietnamese cultural police would approve? 3. Why would a funding body approve?

2.   Indicators of Multi Value Framework. Figure B

It is clear from the matrix, Figure B, that our environmental program is lacking. It can be seen, it is difficult, if not impossible to show leadership, create role models, show good example, when it comes to the environment. The BBC have not one item supporting an environmental ethos. (See here, BBC Public Value Model, https://downloads.bbc.co.uk/aboutthebbc/policies/pdf/bpv.pdf). Our Public Value Model is better. While most productions see themselves, at best, as providing an escape from the worries of the impending catastrophes of climate change. Our film leads by example with two advantages. In production it uses only electric scooters and has environmental actor dialogue. Secondly, our environmental ideas are a market difference, providing possible legitimacy/support.

Rationale

This Public Value Model provides a checklist of possibilities, highlighting unknown aspects; an insurance policy covering the project. It is here, in this knowledge, that the Public Value Model focuses attention on weaknesses to be dealt with in the Task Environment. For these reasons our project includes; Task 1, Task2, The giggle Test, Moore's Strategic Triangle and Meynhardt/ Public Value Scale. Under this guidance the project progresses to completion.

It is important to adopt the Meynhardt, and Jainenko, *Measuring public value: scale development and construct*

461

validation, and particularly useful in its approach to collecting qualitative and quantitative data. Recent work of Joseph Heinrich has established that different nations have different psychology. "Western, educated, industrialised, rich and democratic people are highly individualistic, self-obsessed, control-oriented, nonconformist, and analytical" (Heinrich 2020, p.31). Heinrich goes on to unravel the idea that the world is of differing psychologies. Therein, it is significant for our data to use the Meynhardt method because as noted in the article, *Measuring Public Value: scale development and construct validation,* "The four-dimensional approach allows us to account for an exhaustive perspective, <u>independent of culture</u>" (Meynhardt 2020, p.4).

Copyright was always the issue for our movie and this is more highlighted through our Public Value Model. Leaving no stone unturned, the model has managed to tease out the best way to approach the problem. Currently, with new digital everywhere in the film industry, the copyright world is in a transient state. It is in this era, the question of copyright has moved to a time, where things might change. The Public Value Model has enabled the best argument to present to the copyright holders. There are certain changes afoot, suggests the book *Cultural Capital: The Rise and Fall of Creative Britain,* most likely in law and approach to copyright. This is not with regards the payment of royalties but the actual ability to access and use copyright. Hewison calls this, a human rights issue. He states, "the future of the government ministry that should bear responsibility for access to culture as a human right" (Hewison 2014, p. 405).

It is fair to say that no matter how good our argument is and how grand our film pilot looks, Argos Films Paris, have the "rhetorical power" (Hewison 2002, p.24). My initial conversations on the phone indicated that Argos Films Paris would need a director of some stature to start talking about copyright. This phone call, left us with questions - "What other hurdles do they have?" and "Will they ever share copyright? This is a problem in our Task Environment that needs to be faced.

David Looseley is the professor of Contemporary French Culture at the University of Leeds, UK. He publicises the recently developed notion of retrieving culture. "Departition" (Looseley 2007, p.152), or pastiche of the "quarties" (Looseley 2007, p.152), migrants hankering for their history in a style named "friches" (Looseley 2007, p.152). This all sounds familiar. Is it not the same genre as our film? A coming together of histories, cultures with a fresh way of expression. In an age of "New Territory Arts" (Looseley 2007, p.152), this is significant because, in this light, it is possible for a French cultural authority could lend a hand, enabling a copyright negotiation.

The Vietnamese cultural police or *Phòng An ninh Chính trị nội bộ* are reported to be wanting to go ahead with progressive movies and cut back on gratuitous violence. There are things that have been adapted within the script but it must be clear that recent censorship has included opinions. According to Amnesty International's Asia-Pacific regional director Yamini Mishra. "Human Rights Watch also criticised a crackdown on journalists and bloggers this month, in the lead up to the congress, saying the party was sending people to prison for posting their views and opinions on Facebook" (ABC 2021) states Erin Handley. For this reason, the film must know and obey the Vietnamese rules.

In conclusion, The Public Value Model is not all encompassing. That said, the model provides a practical balanced amenity, sharply indicating weak points and things

overlooked. The Public Value Model can be put to good use, creating a stable work environment and a better quality of life for *The Life You Can Save* recipients.
This is our Public Value Model and the measure of a worthwhile project.

Annotated Bibliography

1. David Looseley 2005 International Journal of Cultural Policy, Vol. 11, No. 2, 2005 2005 Taylor & Francis Group Ltd DOI: *The return of the local, thinking post colonially about French cultural policy.*

In the past, France has espoused a civilising "enlightenment universalism" (Looseley 2005, p.146) and looked to US for its future as a distraction from the colonist past, "retreating intra muros" (Looseley 2005, p.147). Today, France invites cultural identity, aspiring to a post-colonial consciousness; a hybridising of "self/other paradigm" (Looseley 2005, p.147).
This has given rise to a melting pot, the pastiche of the "quartiers" (Looseley 2005, p.151) and a generation of North Africans who wish to "le retour identitaire" (Looseley 2005, p.150). For Loosley, this connotes an idiosyncratic western democracy, a democracy willing to engage in understanding, ideas, and phenomena; particularly concerned in getting it right. In this enthusiastic setting evolves new cultures, where our film fits into a community that ascribes to these public values. Our movie feels at home amongst this genre of "new territory of art" (Looseley 2005, p.153) or "friches" (Looseley 2005, p.152).
Looseley articulates a future French consciousness with the use of a new vernacular shaping the post-colonial future. "Departitioning" (Looseley 2005, p.153), "new publics"

(Looseley 2005, p.148), "everything is culture" (Looseley 2005, p.148), "exclusion agenda" (Looseley 2005, p.149) and "quartiers" (Looseley 2005, p.151). Here, Looseley announces the new words of a new culture.

....

2.   Moore, Mark H 2013, *Recognising public value*, Harvard University Press, London,   England.

Mark Harrison Moore's book, *Recognising Public Value* (2003), is comparable to his seminal work, *Creating Public Value* (1995). The use of case studies for theoretical workings is characteristic of both publications. While the most recent publication *Recognizing Public Value* remains distinct with a focus on external factors of Public Value.

Recognising Public Value adds a new tool to the Public Value Account. Although the tool is heralded with much success, Moore regards the tool as not capable of future improved performance. Moreover, the book recommends an address of The Strategic Triangle with the Kaplan and Norton model of a 'balance scorecard.'

As Moore sorts through the case studies of police, waste management, political organisations, councils and welfare; idiosyncratic needs can be expected. For example, The Oregon Progress board needed an incorporation of "partisan political ideologies" (Moore 2003, p. 313). Moreover, the book Moore draws attention to "public accountability" (Moore 2003, p. 354), "strategic view of performance measurement" (Moore 2003, p.13) and "a hierarchy of values, goals and objectives" (Moore 2003, p.13).

In summary, it can be said that *Recognising Public Value* is in pursuit of a moral compass, similar to John Rawl's, "veil of ignorance" (Rawls 1989, p.136).

………

3.   Meynhardt, Timo and Jainenko, Anna 2020, *Measuring public value: scale development and construct validation*, International Public Management Journal, Routledge, Taylor and Francis Group.

In the study of Public Value, Meyhardt begins by asserting a full explanation of Public Value creation, "situated in relationships between individuals and society, founded in individuals, constituted by subjective evaluations against basic needs, activated by and realised in emotional-motivated states, and produced and reproduced in experience intense practices" (Meynhardt and Jainenko 2020, p.3).

The article presents optimistic and balanced short comings of the ethos of Public Value. Criticisms are made of Moore's case reports, calling them, "context specific" (Meynhardt and Jainenko 2020, p.2).

Meynhardt and Jasinenko requests empirical research and sets out a method and examples of such research. Meynhardt and Jasinenko's Public Value investigation puts an emphasis on four dimensions. 1.Moral/ethical, contributing to "people's self-worth and dignity" (Meynhardt and Jainenko 2020, p.4).   2. Hedonistic/aesthetic, "avoid pain and maximize pleasure" (Meynhardt and Jainenko 2020, p.4). 3. Utilitarian/instrumental, "a shared value ascribed to utility" (Meynhardt and Jainenko 2020, p.1) and 4. Political/social, "basic need for social belonging" (Meynhardt and Jainenko 2020, p.1). These factors are an approach to Public Value satisfying human needs. Meynhardt monitors this approach with three steps.

1.	Collate information with regards each of the four dimensions, according to your organisation/project.
2.	Collect data through survey testing the qualitative data. Include corporate responsibility, reputation, efficacy, and market dominance,
3.	Sample again, refined by a broader larger sample, using conclusion from the previous steps.

This is a unique way to discern Public Value and if true, as claimed, the scale is independent of culture. This means the method has a beneficial factor for our multicultural film.

………..

4. British Broadcasting Corporation 2004, Bbc *building public value. renewing the bbc for a digital world.* Report prepared by Micheal Grade. Viewed 21 January 2021, < https://downloads.bbc.co.uk/aboutthebbc/policies/pdf/bpv.pdf>

The article leads us through governance issues and changes needed in a fractured media environment, while adhering to the royal charter. Notably, The BBC's Public Value document has no mention of Public Value scholars, such as Mark H Moore and no mention of an environmental policy. Coming from principled foundations and attentive to qualitative and quantitative data. Keeping in mind a changing population amongst a change in technology. The seven chapters address both the BBC party faithful and the naysayers. In this knowledge the BBC sees a future, taking the audience along.

The review lists a dozen new digital programs, citing a Public Value or "quality of life" for their audience. And much regard is given to commercial success; $250 million return in 2003, growing 5% over 10 years. The London-centric operations have become less of a focus and the BBC is keen in keeping the annual licence fee, $300 per year. Finally, the report states. "The future…… rests firmly with the owner the British public" (BBC

2006).

References

Beck, Ulrich 2007, World at risk, Polity press, Cambridge UK.

Brackertz, Nicola 2008, *Social Inclusion of the hard to reach,* viewed 23 January 2021, <https://researchbank.swinburne.edu.au/file/1ce31ced-18a0-4867-b797-cc0e3c35707a/1/PDF%20(Published%20version).pdf>

Handley, Erin 2021, *Vietnam's communist party congress meets behind closed doors to map out the next five years post-covid,* viewed 27 January 2021, < https://www.abc.net.au/news/2021-01-27/vietnam-communist-party-congress-five-years-economy-covid-rights/13089984>

Meynhardt, Timo and Jainenko, Anna 2020, *Measuring public value: scale development and construct validation*, International Public Management Journal, Routledge, Taylor and Francis Group.

Moore, Mark 2012, *Creating public value through a strong arts community - powerpoint ppt presentation,* viewed 29 January 2021 <https://www.slideserve.com/abedi/creating-public-value-through-a-strong-arts-community>

Moore, Mark 2013, *Recognising public value*, Harvard University Press, London, England.

Moore, Mark 2019, *Mark Moore bij Berenschot (volledig college) - Publieke waarde,* video Recording, viewed 19 January 2021, <https://youtu.be/UlVBX1UfhBU>

British Broadcasting Corporation 2004, Bbc *building public value. renewing the bbc for a digital world.* Report prepared by Micheal Grade, viewed 21 January 2021, < https://downloads.bbc.co.uk/aboutthebbc/policies/pdf/bpv.pdf>

Heinrich, Joseph 2020, *The weirdest people in the world,* Farrar, Straus and Giroux, New York, USA.

Hewison, Robert 2014, *Cultural capital: the rise and fall of creative Britain*, Verso, London.

Hewison, Robert and Holden, John 2011, *The cultural leadership handbook, how to run a creative organization,* Gower Publishing Ltd, Surrey, UK.

Looseley, David, *The* return of the social, thinking post colonially about French cultural policy, 18:5, pages 579-592. Viewed 21 January 2021, < https://www.tandfonline.com/doi/citedby/10.1080/10286630500 198138?scroll=top&needAccess=true>

Rawls, John 1989, *The theory of justice,* Oxford University Press, Oxford, UK.

Singer, Peter 2008, *Examined Life - Modern Social Philosophy Documentary (2008)*, viewed 21 January 2021, < https://youtu.be/8rEgcLMamZE>
Singer, Peter 2009, *The life you can save, viewed 21 January 2021,* < https://www.thelifeyoucansave.org.au/epub-file-download-and-setup-instructions/>

Bibliography

Billikopf, Gregorio 2006, *Incentive pay (pay for performance), viewed 29 January 2021,* < https://nature.berkeley.edu/ucce50/ag-labor/7labor/08.htm>

Blaug, Ricardo, Horner, Louise and Lekhi, Rohit 2006, *Public value, politics and public management a literature review,* The Work Foundation, London, UK.

Holden, John 2006, *Cultural value and the crisis of legitimacy, why culture needs a democratic mandate,* Demos, London, UK.

Korzybski, Alfred 1995, *Science and sanity,* International Non-Aristotelian Library,
Institute of General Semantics, Brooklyn, New York, USA.

Looseley, David 2003, *Popular music in contemporary france authenticity, politics, debate,* Oxford International Publishers Ltd, Oxford, UK.

Looseley, David 2012, *Democratising the popular: the case of pop music in france and britain*, viewed 23 January 2021, < https://www.tandfonline.com/doi/abs/10.1080/10286632.2012.7 18917?mobileUi=0&journalCode=gcul20>

Metz, Christian 1977, *The imaginary signifier, psychoanalysis and cinema*, Indiana University Press, Bloomington, USA.

McGowan, Todd 2004, *Lacan and contemporary film,* Other Press, New York, USA.

O'Gallagher, Declan 2016, *Blue velvet handout,* viewed 21 January 2021, <https://lacanseminar.files.wordpress.com/2019/02/handout.pdf>

Nolan, Steve 2009, *Film, lacan and the subject of religion, a psychoanalytic approach to religious film analysis*, Continuum International Publishing Group, New York, USA.

Žižek, Slavoj 1992, *Enjoy your symptom! Jacques lacan in hollywood and out*, Routledge, London, UK.

183. No Gravity No God

"The basic DNA mutation rate has been measured to be
0.71% change per million years" (Stillman 2006, p.59), says
Brett Stillman. It now can be shown that the variation from
monkey to human should be concurrent with 6.6 million years.
And yes, in the heart of the Djurab Desert, Chad, Africa, remains
have been found and tested to be six to seven million years old.
Asking if they thought the hominoid was walking upright;
Nature magazine said, "would not be unreasonable" (Brunet
2002, p.150). The monkeys come out of the trees, down into the
savannah and all manner of things started to change; food,
habitat, communication.
- All these were areas of adaption and evolution, a new era in
mankind's history.

In 1974 palaeontologists found skeletal remains in the
Awash Valley, Ethiopia, dating back 3.2 million years. A
foraging and scavenging, 1.1 metre, upright bipedal;
Australopithecus Aferensis. The scientists called her Lucy. This
was a pivotal moment in scientific research because Lucy was
largely intact from head to foot. Did Lucy have language? Did
Lucy believe in God? Did she eat meat? These were questions to
be answered.
 Lucy was now hands-free, able to hunt differently and transition
to a more carnivorous diet. Scavenging meat, Lucy was
becoming a hunter. In her time there was no God to speak of
because no one spoke. A growl or a hand-gesture, but no words.
Lucy was evolving with the 'us and them,' mentality. Within this
awareness of kill or be killed, a sense of friend or foe was
paramount.

With eyes that see and light that reflects, a waterhole
would be a constant reminder of self. In this evolving
consciousness, it is possible that other mirroring was happening.
Noam Chomsky noted in his book, Reflections on Language,

'Language is a mirror of mind in a deep and significant sense' (Chomsky 1976, p.4). The mind was developing gradually and demonstrating a sense of self and other. This mirroring was being imprinted and Chomsky suggests language is a type of mirroring. Was this part of the key that would unwrap language?

The brain of Lucy at 400-500cc progressed to 500-800cc and these hominids, "All had bigger brains than Lucy" (Watson 2005, p.25), says Dr Peter Watson, all were in the realm of toolmakers. They were named Homo Erectus, found in numbers from Kenya, to China and Java. This was the hominoid at the brink of language, tools and higher consciousness. It was the birthplace of the human spirit. At first Homo Erectus was "episodic" (Donald, in Watson 2005, P.30), says Professor Merton Donald, "entirely in the present." In this mind, deity might come and go but never communicated. Then, "1.5 to 2 million years ago, Homo erectus left Africa without language" (Thompson 2009), says Dr Andy Thompson. From this "episodic" era; mind and language was evolving, one aiding the other. It can be said the initial sounds like a bark became a word. As consciousness grew it would be possible to impart more complex information because the imperative to talk was the imperative to survive.

Then the change in eating style provided, "subtle movements in the tongue necessary for the varied range of sounds used in speech" (Watson 2005, p.22), says Dr Watson. The 'upright posture also made possible the descent of the larynx......a much better position to form vowels and consonance' (Watson 2005, p.22) added Dr Watson. This *becoming*, is suggesting a more complex consciousness. Lucy's relations were about to talk. Generations of upright bipedalism had made the voice box descend. Without gravity this was impossible. Without language, God could only exist as a thought in a single person, not as shared phenomena. What is considered God could only be considered and not be today's comprehended God. The logic and the science suggest that without gravity, there would be no God.

References.

Brunet, Michel, 2002, *A new hominid from the Upper Miocene of Chad, Central Africa,* viewed at 10 February 2016, .

Chomsky, Noam 1976, *Reflections on language*, Random House, London, UK.

Stilman, Brett 2006, *Confessions of a moral atheist*, Xlibris Corporation, Indiana, USA.

Watson, Peter 2005, *Ideas: a history from fire to Freud*, Weidenfeld & Nicholson, London, UK.

Why We Believe in Gods - Andy Thomson - American Atheists 09 2009, viewed at 10 February 2016, < https://youtu.be/1iMmvu9eMrg>.

184. Freedom of Speech

The phrase "Nanos gigantium humeris insidentes[1]" was popularised by Issac Newton, paying homage to his great fore bearers. It means "seeing a little further by standing on the shoulders of giants.[1]" This provenance from which we see 'a little further' can be seen as a footnote to the freedom of speech milleu of Aristotle, Plato, Thomas Paine and Mill. However, I will examine the view that all free speech is limited. I will look at the protagonists providing a guide to western freedom of speech. I will inquire into the issues that give freedom of speech a mandate and ask who is this self that necessitates these freedoms. Aristotle begins his "Nichomachean Ethic" book with "Every skill and every inquiry, and similarly every action and rational choice, is thought to aim at some good; and so the good has been aptly described as that at which everything aims.[2]" This would presuppose that all free speech is good and needs no restraint. Not only, does Aristotle say it is good, but affirms it as natural, believing in individual rights that precipitate eudaimonia or full potential. Plato is not so kind. In his The Republic he indicates particular sections of the community are charlatans and should be exempt from the state. "We are quite right not to admit him to a properly run state, because he awakens and encourages the lower elements in the mind to the detriment of reason, which is like giving power and political control to the worst element in the state.[3]" This is the outcome of a sectarian feud within Athens. Poets are well known to refer to the philosophers as "The crowd who know too much3." Plato's republic at first refused their entry then left the door ajar for the poets and painters to show remorse. Analogous to the present day, we have sections of the community in unresolved differences. The contention lies herein. In a modern social life we pursue a sense of truth. A truth that hails a human dignity and eudaimonia. Within this freedom comes a question as to what is reasonably accepted as freedom of speech. Debates arise over what are the limits of free speech. There are considerations over what harm is done and what is practical and attainable as freedom of speech. Christopher Hitchens, author and contemporary champion of freedom of speech contests that a background must start with the three treatises.

1. *Areopagitica* by John Milton
2. *The introduction to The Age of Reason* by Thomas Paine
3. *On Liberty* by J.S.Mill

These are surely the canons of freedom of speech. They resonate and invigorate a sense of freedom. A single-minded affirmation resurrecting a powerful instinct and will that would unite a community against an oppressive government. The cries of limits have little efficacy while a tide of freedom continues to revel. It is a declaration of an existence of authenticity in a modern world. It is a public discord between Lacan's Real and Symbolic, while mass media's freedom of speech plays the ethical role of Le stade du miroir [the mirror stage.] Here is the Lacanian knot. In Areopagitica, Milton continues a tradition of freedom of speech. Poetically, Milton calls upon the Greeks and Romans, even back to Osiris of ancient Egypt to substantiate his claims that censorship is not in anyone's interest. Milton's basis for writing Areopagitica was to fend off the English government's licencing order of 1643. Laws whereby government must give permission to allow printed material. Summarily he states. "He who destroys a good book, kills reason itself, kills the image of God[4]." Crucially, Milton uses the bible as a natural predication of freedom of speech, he quotes St John. "The truth will make you free.[4]" Milton himself has been a victim of this licencing order of 1643, after speaking out against unlawful divorce. This appears often to be the case that it is not until a person is taken to task concerning freedom of speech do they then in turn unravel the laws and implications. Thomas Pain's introduction to *The Age of Reason*, first published in 1784

476

is held in high regard by Hitchen. "When both rights and reason
are under several kinds of open and covert attack, the life and
writing of Thomas Paine will always be part of the arsenal on
which we shall need to depend.[5]" Pain empowers the reader
declaring his deliberation as an accolade to the reader. He
contends that it is slavery unto your own opinions not to listen to
others. His conclusion is that errors of reason may be fought
against by reason alone. In consideration of reason, he states that
"I have never used another, and I trust I never shall[6]" Mill's *On
Liberty* conjures a freedom of speech for the duration of his
entire book. Most notably his thorough examination of harm and
utilitarian are at the core of the Mill's philosophy. Mill's
argument is the "the Greatest Happiness Principle, holds that
actions are right in proportion as they tend to promote happiness,
wrong as they tend to produce the reverse of happiness.[7]" This
has ramifications for those who wish to test the boundaries of
freedom of speech. The implication being that questions should
be asked. Does this freedom of speech tend toward happiness
and whom does it make happy? Still at the centre of Mill values
there is the Harm Principle in which he states. "The only purpose
for which power can be rightfully exercised over any member of
a civilized community against his will is to prevent harm to
others[8]." Does he mean physical harm or just bad advertising?
What exactly constitutes harm? Marion Smiley claims the idea is
closely fixed to what she calls "valuation of personal integrity[9]".
This is a cultural structure. She is saying that different sections
of society or different cultures are going to feel more harm than
others depending on the value system that they subscribe to. As a
generalisation should we not all have a certain amount of
guaranteed freedom of speech? Should a modern sophisticated
respected country have a given amount of freedom of speech?
Mills thinks we should. He suggests that we should be able to
publicly discuss anything "All silencing of discussion is an
assumption of infallibility.[8]" Freedom of speech is the

implication. Later on in his book Mill is not only concerned with immediate physical harm but harm in potentia. Chapter Four. "Whenever, in short, there is a definite damage or definite risk of damage, either to an individual or to the public the case is taken out of the province of liberty and placed in that of the morality of the law.[8]" The limits of freedom of speech are concluded here by the suggestion that our speech has limits as *in potentia* harm, but who decides what is potential harm? To conclude, let us now look at some practical examples of freedom of speech. When it comes to harm it has been argued that violent pornography should be banned. While others contend there is no proven harm. This issue is not helped at all by Mill's harm principle and in fact only adds to the problem by revealing a contradiction. Christopher Hitchens asks, "Who exactly has the right to tell you what you can and cannot view.[10]" This question is brought to bear by those thinkers who view freedom of speech laws as paternalistic. Making a judgment a priori, already deciding what is good for all of us. Mill's suggests that paternalism is never an option. Philosopher H.L.A. Hart disagrees, he claims heuristically uninformed people make bad decisions about themselves causing harm to themselves every day. Again, the implication being to appreciate differing values and understanding. Should a modern society outlaw a neo-Nazi rally calling for Judaic eradication? For Mill this would concur as *in potentia* harmful and therefore demand "the morality of the law.[8]" It is unjustified to outlaw any such address just because it is offensive. Alas, you don't have to go to such a rally. It is easy to avoid such gatherings. So why should it be banned? An embellished speech in a Jewish suburb might not only cause offense but violent unrest. According to Mill if an individual is to be potentially harmed by freedom of speech, then we must prevent the freedom of speech. We must ask who is to decide whether harm is done. The answer here is in the community. Ask the Judaic community what is their opinion on such matters. No

matter how abhorrent, no matter how wild, should we let fly the ignorance of the mouth to be free. Voltaire thinks we should. "I disapprove of what you say, but I will defend to the death your right to say it.[12]" It is a gallant phrase widely attributed to Voltaire but would he defend a racist speech. A well-publicised case in Austria saw the infamous holocaust denier David Irving arrested. He had given speeches stating people had died of natural causes in Auschwitz. He later remarked Jews are "traditional enemies of the truth[13]". Irving was subsequently jailed for three years after being found guilty of "trivialising, grossly playing down and denying the Holocaust.[14]" This Irving controversy caused introspection as he is an historian regarded as an expert on aspects of the second world war. So, should this freedom of speech be tolerated? Slavoj Žižek was full favour of Irving's freedom of speech and calls this incarceration "a secret anti-Semitism". He says that "When anti-racism becomes part of the ego ideal you know you are in trouble.[15]" Here, Žižek claims that anti-racism is an aspiration and the culture of the hegemony is a tolerant multicultural one. In short, the dominant paradigm is racist and it is only the laws that forbid racists to behave that way. It so appears you are dammed if you do and dammed if you don't. Mill's *in potentia* harm would have Irving locked up. Yet Hitchen and Žižek would let the Irving speech run free.
Hitchen's and Žižek's ideals are akin to igniting a terrestrial fire for all to see that would eventually burn out. Mill's option would ignite a subterranean fire. Hidden, appearing infrequently with shocking devastation. The solution I would suggest is on a case-by-case basis. Choose your fire and assess who will be burnt and consider the long term and the short term. In the reality UK TV show Big Brother contestant Jade Goody has publicly enunciated words that have called into question the limits of freedom of speech. The governing body for complaints [Ofcom] received 54,000 against the perceived racism on the show. The applications largely centred on Goody. She was accused of

making derogatory comments with reference to fellow housemate and Indian actress Shilpa Shetty, calling her "Shilpa fuckawalla[16]" and "Shilpa Poppadom[16]". UK Prime Minister Gordon Brown has even commented directly about this show. He says "I want Britain to be seen as a country of fairness and tolerance.[17]" The implication being when using the word "tolerant[17]" that the British are bigots, they just put up with ethnicity so as not to break the law. Therefore, the laws have empowered the normative. The reflexive multicultural society has empowered the "civil racism[15]" of the ego ideal engraining it as the legal side of the law. The law being, the considered outcome of society's institutional consensus. The "civil racism[15]" not only gets away scot-free yet becomes intrinsic to the charter of all modern state institutions. This can be called upon by judges of Goody, Irving et al to hold on to "civil racism," while rejecting the vulgar prejudice from those who have not yet learned to hide it or refuse to hide it. At times those who have learnt to hide it and become protectionist of the minority do so because they believe ethnicity to be weak. This unresolved personal silence. [I think you are weak which makes me strong.] Plays out under a western Christian hegemony, pervasive in establishment modus operandi. How civil? Telling lies about ethnic groups is a common form of prejudice. Here is an example of how lies can work and be presented as freedom of speech. The 1st Amendment of the US Bill of rights introduced to the House of Representatives in 1789 delineates free speech, it states. "Congress shall make no law respecting an establishment of religion, or prohibiting the free exercise thereof; or abridging the freedom of speech, or of the press; or the right of the people peaceably to assemble, and to petition the Government for a redress of grievances.[18]" Americans call it 'the freest country in the world.' This mantra of freedom of speech holds sway for all manner of ridiculous assertions, evens lies. Your freedom of speech is your lies and your freedom of speech is your defence.

Xavier Alvarez 21 never served in the military and never received any medals yet contends his right to lie or freedom of speech as he calls it, under the 1st amendment. He was charged under the "Stolen Valor Act19" and quotes "Congress shall make no law ...Abridging freedom of speech18" to a divided jury in San Francisco. The jury has subsequently thrown out the guilty plea and the case gets heard again early next year [2012]. Certainly, there comes a rallying around when freedom of speech is threatened. Surely the limits are applied when lies are held up as a right. It is here posed by Alvarez that a right to lie is a right to freedom of speech. I wanted here to make a brief but important point about self. When it is said 'an individual has rights' or 'I have a right to my freedom of speech.' It should be questioned what is 'I'. Heidegger explains this as the physicality "Dasein[20]" or 'being-in-the- world.' A consideration away from the physical individual and towards that what exists beyond and including the body, the "Dasein.[20]" Apropos freedom of speech. The self or I, exists as a community and not just a single person's freedom. It is the whole interconnected community's freedom, which is the 'being-in-the- world' freedom of speech of the individual. In conclusion, when human rights are taken for granted and they are subsumed under the prosaic. Mills argues there is an inclination for ground to be lost and a need to be vigilant, he says, "The supposition being that if not continuously reified the freedom of speech will lose its answers.[8]" Mill necessitates a freedom of speech in continuum. We must go back again and again and question what the status quo has to offer, contemplate and discuss its answers, leading us from the wilderness of "dead dogma[22]."

Bibliography
1 John of Salisbury, 1159. Metalogicon. trans. Daniel McGarry. Berkeley: University of California Press, 1955

2 Aristotle, 1953. The Ethics of Aristotle, The Nichomachean Ethics. Trans J.A.K. Thompson Allen and Unwin, London UK.

3 Plato, 1955. The Republic.Trans, Desmond Lee Penguin group UK.

4 Milton, John 1644, January 21, 2006 Areopagitica A Speech For The Liberty Of Unlicensed Printing To The Parliament Of England.
<http://www.gutenberg.org/catalog/world/readfile?fk_files=1442992>

5 Hitchens, Christopher. 2006 Thomas Paines's Rights of Man, Grove Press, New York.

6 Pain, Thomas, 1948, The Age Of Reason [1794], Cidadel Press, New York

7 Mill, John Stuart, 2007, Utilitarianism, [1871], Dover Publications, New York.

8 Mill, John Stuart, 2002, On Liberty, [1859], Dover Publications, New York.

9 Smiley, Marion, 1992, Moral Responsibility and the Boundaries of Community, University of Chicago Press, Chicago USA.

10 Hitchens, Christopher, May 26th 2007. Christopher Hitchens on free speech. < http://youtu.be/ZOck_bDb0JA>

12 Hall, Evelyn Beatrice, 1906, The Friends ff Voltaire, Smith Elder and co. California, USA.

13 Irving, David, 1997, Viewed 16thOctober 2011, David Irving's Action report, < http://www.codoh.com/irving/irvar13.html>

14 Irving, David, 28thOctober 2009, White supremacists stabbed at talk by Holocaust denier David Irving. Mail Online.

15 Žižek, Slavoj, 2010, Living in End Times, Verso, UK.

16 Goody, Jade, 18th Jan 2007, Viewed 16th October 2011, The Guardian, < http://www.guardian.co.uk/commentisfree/2011/feb/11/taming-jade-goody-big-brother-globe>

17 Brown, Gordon, 2007. Viewed 16th October 2011, The Guardian < http://www.guardian.co.uk/media/2007/jan/17/bigbrother.politics andthemedia>

18 CSRA Constitution, 1791, Bill Of Rights, http://www.law.cornell.edu/constitution/billofrights

19 United States Congress, 2005, Stolen Valor Act, < http://www.govtrack.us/congress/billtext.xpd?bill=s109-1998>

20 Heidegger, Martin, 1962, Being and Time, Willet-Blackwell, Hoboken, NJ, USA.

22 Mill, John Stuart, 2007, Utilitarianism, Liberty & Representative Government, Wildside Press, Rockville, USA.

References

10 Hitchens, Christopher, May 26th 2007. Christopher Hitchens on free speech. < http://youtu.be/ZOck_bDb0JA>

11 Lee Plaisance, Patrick, 2009, Media Ethics, Key Principles for Responsible Practice, Sage Publications California USA.

20 Heidegger, Martin, 1962, Being and Time, Willet-Blackwell, Hoboken, NJ, USA. 21 Alvarez, Xavier , Appeals Court Stolen Valor Act,
<http://www.guardian.co.uk/world/feedarticle/9224846>
Media Ethics /Patrick Lee Plasisance Utilitarianism/JS Mill On Liberty/ JS Mill

Living in End Times/Slavoj Žižek Nichomachean Ethics/ Aristotle The Republic/Plato Ethics and Media Culture//David Berry Introduction Lectures to Psychanalysis/ Freud Within Your Grasp/ Kierkegaard 50 Philosophy Ideas/ Ben Dupre Ecrits/ Lacan How to read Lacan /Slavoj Žižek Ethics/ Gordon Marino The Shorter Routledge Encyclopedia of Philosophy/Edward Craig The Really Hard Problem /Owen Flanagan The Oxford Book of Ethical Theory/ David Copp Spinoza's Ethics/ Steven Nadler Being and Time/Heidegger Heidegger and ethics/Joanna Hodge John Stuart Mill on Liberty in Focus/ John Gray Hume On Morality/James Baillie The World and Other Writings/Descartes Friedrich Nietzsche/ Lee Spinks Phenomenology of the Spirit/Hegel Philosophy

Guidebook to Nietzsche on Morality/ Brian Leiter. The Value of
Morality in Kant's Moral Theory/Richard dean Michel Foucault
Critical Thinkers/ Sara Mills Slavoj Žižek Critical Thinkers/
Tony Myers

185. A Government's Convergence Review

[http://www.dbcde.gov.au/digital_economy/convergence_review
] is a considered document hoping to ameliorate the Australian
media sector at a time when outcomes are more about conjecture
than evidence. It appears the government seeks to control the
unknown. Not conscious of where the NBN [National
Broadband Network] will end up, this must surely be a concern
for the government and has led to a template of an a priori
regulation. Fruit or folly, we wait and see but no doubt, the
government will conceive a solution that looks after the
government and Australian citizens. How it manages to
empower citizens and government might be a hard act to follow
but let us not leave it out of the realms of possibility.
Before the Convergence Review, the Internet was assessed as a
non-broadcast media and therefore not under the aegis of the
ACMA [Australian Communications and Media Authority]. The
Convergence Review is intimating at a new institution to
regulate media as a whole, something like the APC and ACMA.
In John Holmes' article "Media regulation must come from
within" he backs the Australian Press Council [APC], giving
countenance to a two-tiered regulator system similar to the
existing institutions of the APC and ACMA. However, this time
they will have powers to levy fines on broadcasters/Internet
publishers/print media. Holmes does not doubt regulation, just
not in the hands of government. He cites a need to "beef up" the
Australian Press Council and talks of "adjudications" for a new

empowered APC. Minister Conroy lambasts the APC as
toothless and calls on the News Ltd's Professional Conduct
Policy to greater scrutiny, referring to regular
breaches by Sydney Telegraph journalists. This declaration by
Senator Conroy only suggests an imminent regulatory body with
teeth.

Convergence Review, Discussion paper Australian and local
Content 2011,
http://www.dbcde.gov.au/digital_economy/convergence_review
Media regulation must come from within 2011, Jonathan Holmes
from the ABC's The
Drum, on the Australian federal government's 2011 media
inquiry,

Mackie, John L,1977, Ethics: Inventing Right and Wrong,
Penguin Books, London

9 798842 387397